More praise for *Reinventing Giants*

"Finally! The best of both worlds—the best case study I've seen describing a Chinese company's global success, integrated with proven managerial frameworks and concepts. The result is practical examples, valuable tools, and useful ideas that you can put to use today to help your firm achieve competitive success."

—**Andy Boynton**, *dean,*
Carroll School of Management, Boston College

"*Reinventing Giants* shows that corporate revival requires both hunting for new ideas as well as implementing the right ones, and renewing your company, even transforming it in an ever-changing world. These key elements are all addressed in this book and essential for all companies to remain agile."

—**Feike Sijbesma**, *CEO, Royal DSM*

"*Reinventing Giants* not only provides a great illustration of how a leading Chinese company has actively developed and renewed itself over the past several decades and as a result has become the global leader in its industry but it also gives valuable and inspiring new insights to all of us who compete in global markets."

—**Matti Alahuhta**, *president and CEO, Kone Corporation*

"As we assess the potential impact of Chinese companies on the future thrust of international competition, the authors have provided us with a series of rich insights into the evolving trajectory of one key firm, Haier. Their provocative research regarding Haier's organizational transformation strongly suggests that we may be witnessing one of the most innovative adaptations of a once primarily domestic player into a truly distinctive new global competitor."

—**Denis Simon**, *vice-provost for international strategic initiatives,*
Arizona State University; member of the Experts Group,
US-China Innovation Dialogue

"For all of us who want to understand Chinese competition, *Reinventing Giants* makes an invaluable contribution: explaining success by focusing on the ability of one of the great Chinese companies to create and re-create an innovative corporate culture. It's all right here, spelled out in Haier's own language: ZZJYTs, strategic income statements, zero distance from the customer and . . . catfish! Read it now. Or else you'll be left behind!"

—**Dan Denison,** professor at IMD; author of *Leading Culture Change in Global Organizations: Aligning Culture and Strategy*

Reinventing Giants

How Chinese Global Competitor Haier Has Changed the Way Big Companies Transform

Bill Fischer, Umberto Lago,
and Fang Liu

Foreword by Alexander Osterwalder

JB JOSSEY-BASS™
A Wiley Brand

Cover design by Adrian Morgan
Cover photograph: Copyright © Dominik Pabis | Vetta | Getty
Published by Jossey-Bass
A Wiley Imprint
One Montgomery Street, Suite 1200, San Francisco, CA 94104-4594—www.josseybass.com

Library of Congress Cataloging-in-Publication Data

Fischer, Bill.
Reinventing giants: how Chinese global competitor Haier has changed the way big companies transform / Bill Fischer, Umberto Lago, and Fang Liu; foreword by Alexander Osterwalder.—First edition.
pages cm
Includes bibliographical references and index.
ISBN 978-1-118-60223-2 (cloth); ISBN 978-1-118-60224-9 (ebk.);
ISBN 978-1-118-60228-7 (ebk.); ISBN 978-1-118-60229-4 (ebk.)
1. Haier (Corporation) 2. Household appliances industry—China—Management—Case studies. 3. International business enterprises—China—Management. I. Lago, Umberto, 1964– II. Liu, Fang, 1984– III. Title.
HD9971.5.E544H3594 2013
338.7'68380951—dc23

2012048779

Printed in the United States of America
FIRST EDITION
HB Printing 10 9 8 7 6 5 4 3 2 1

Contents

Bill:

To that intrepid band of adventurers who moved to Dalian in 1980 to begin the National Institute for Industrial Science and Technology Development, on behalf of the Chinese and American governments; and to my best friend and partner in everything I've ever done, Marie Annette, who not only encouraged me to be a part of the Dalian adventure but brought along Kimberly, Amy, and Billy and changed all our lives. Without her, my life would have been so much poorer!

To Jack N. Behrman, who took me under his wing and taught me to think beyond traditional borders when I was a young neophyte at the University of North Carolina, Chapel Hill.

Umberto:

To Roberta, Giovanni, Francesco: my very special ZZJYT!

Fang:

To Thierry, my partner and best friend, who changed my life, allowing me to look at China from a new and deeper perspective.

To Willem, who brought me to IMD and sparked my passion for research, and whose support and encouragement have been invaluable in every initiative I have undertaken.

To Bill, who offered me the opportunity to work on this project, and always showed enormous trust in me.

And, to my beloved family and my homeland.

Foreword

Competitive analysis is dead. I have believed this to be true for quite a while, but my very last doubts disappeared when I listened to Zhang Ruimin, chairman and CEO of Haier, give a talk at IMD business school. In his presentation, Zhang stressed that the failure of a company typically comes not from its competitors but from itself. He went on to outline the organizational culture that Haier has put in place to resist such failure by challenging itself—all the time.

It is no coincidence that many of today's leading companies, including Haier, share two characteristics. First, they have built value propositions that customers love, combined with business models that offer superior returns. Second, they have demonstrated the ability to do this through continuous reinvention. It is this second characteristic that truly separates the great from the merely good. Haier is such a great company, right up there with organizations like Apple and Amazon.

To achieve such greatness, these companies are not content to rely on executing and improving the known and proven business models that have led them to past success. Instead, they increasingly are investigating new organizational forms that allow them to experiment with bold, daring, and imaginative business models for the future while simultaneously excelling at executing and improving their own successful models. What makes Haier a particularly interesting case is that by choosing to follow the same sort of experimental approach to reinvention, it has come to illustrate the ascent of a new breed of Chinese corporation characterized more by organizational innovation and business model renewal than by a reliance on cheap manufacturing and economies of scale.

Zhang has led Haier from a bankrupt refrigerator factory in Qingdao to become a global home appliance brand. He has been extremely thoughtful in the path he has chosen for the firm, first applying Western and Japanese business practices and management techniques and then later extending these approaches with his own Chinese-based vision of how a twenty-first-century corporation should be organized.

Haier offers interesting insights into three skills that I believe will distinguish future leading organizations that master them from all others that don't. The first skill is the ability to design and build great value propositions that customers really want. This sounds trivial, but it isn't. Great value propositions require a thorough understanding of the lives and dreams of customers. Rare are the companies that are organized in a manner that allows them to deeply investigate customer motivations and then act on the knowledge they have gained. Only the best among them truly understand the "jobs" that customers are trying to get done using the goods and services that they purchase, and rarer still are organizations sufficiently sensitive to the pains and gains that their customers encounter related to such searches. These organizations understand what legendary Harvard professor Theodore Levitt meant when he taught us that people don't want to buy a quarter-inch drill; what they want is a quarter-inch hole. Haier has demonstrated the desire to achieve such a deep customer understanding by relentlessly reorganizing itself to focus on the jobs that its customers need to get done in their lives and then acting on that knowledge by decentralizing its decision making.

The second skill characterizing great organizations is the ability to design superior business models. Whereas it is a great customer value proposition that attracts customers, it is a great business model that brings in the profits to sustain an ongoing business. Nespresso, a daughter company of Nestlé, built a thriving business by introducing an innovative business model for the direct sales of espresso pods in the 1990s. It turned the transactional business of selling coffee through retail into a business that locks in customers with proprietary delivery systems that allow the customer to enjoy a great coffee at home and still produces recurring revenues through high-margin pod sales. This is a great example of how superior business model mechanics can mean both wildly delighted customers and substantially higher profits. In the same way, Haier has substantially reinvented its business model and adjusted its resources and activities in order to produce better-quality products that have led to a better brand associated with that quality and improved its profitability in the process.

The third skill differentiating outstanding organizations from others is their ability to reinvent themselves while they are successful and to do so over and over again. Success so often leads to complacency, and that usually leads organizations to live off a successful business model way past its expiration date. Even Nespresso failed to easily reinvent its business model when its patents on its machines and pods expired. Business models are like yogurt: they inevitably run out of shelf life and expire. Unfortunately, the expiration date of business models seems to be getting shorter by the decade. It is unthinkable today that a CEO can manage his or her company based on the same unchanged business model for an entire career. Companies that fail to continuously renew themselves or even self-disrupt are prone to disruption by others and risk decline and irrelevancy.

Few companies have succeeded in building organizational structures that enable the simultaneous execution of existing successful business models while also inventing new ones for tomorrow. This is where Haier has shown its most impressive performance. Through a culture of continuous organizational innovation, Haier seems to be well prepared for the challenges of the future.

February 2013 Alexander Osterwalder

Reinventing Giants

1

MOVING A COMPANY WITH THE TIMES

What Makes Haier Unique?

Change is the only constant in the brave new world of global competition. Organizations that do it well flourish; those that do not can find themselves looking at their possible demise. Either way, change is inevitable: change in offerings, change in locations, change in strategy, and ultimately change in the organization itself. None of this is easy or natural. Jack Welch of GE was famous for saying, "When the rate of change outside [an organization] exceeds the rate of change inside, the end is in sight," and IBM's former CEO, Sam Palmisano, observed, "Organizational culture thrives only to the extent that it is open to being re-created."[1] But change, especially big change, is difficult, and frequently it is something that all too many organizational actors hope can be avoided, or at least minimized, at all costs. Not surprisingly, those who succeed in orchestrating big change are regarded with admiration by students of business; those who do it more than once are considered exceptional.

This book is about transformational change—the reinvention of a corporate business model and culture not once but at least three times within thirty years. Since change for change's sake is never a good idea, and certainly not noteworthy enough to merit book-length attention, this book is also about the context in which big strategic change takes place: the whys and wherefores that mandate and shape change. And it is about change leadership as well—the hows—because big change is never easy to accomplish, and when it is successful, it is inevitably the result of leaders' ability to create a vision and mobilize the workforce to take this vision seriously and move determinedly toward the desired objectives.

Haier Group

This is a book about transformational change in an old-economy, mature industry. This is not about change in high-tech razzmatazz but about change in household appliances, where margins are thin and innovations few. It's about management fundamentals, such as quality, brand, and supply chains. And the overriding message is that you can't discount the potential for transformational change in any industry or any geographical location. The leadership of any organization must be prepared for the challenge of creating such change, no matter what the industry or location.

Household appliances have been produced in the port city of Qingdao, on China's northeast coast, for quite some time. In the 1920s, a refrigerator factory was built in the city, and over time, after the founding of the People's Republic in 1949, this evolved into a collective factory administrated by the municipal authorities of Qingdao. In 1984, this same factory, which at that point was possibly best known for its poor quality and indifferent work ethic, was placed under the leadership of a young municipal official, Zhang Ruimin, and allowed to experiment with a variety of managerial initiatives that form the basis for much of the story that follows. By 2012, Haier, as it had come to be known, was one of the world's largest producers of refrigerators. It had broadened its product line to include air conditioners, mobile phones, computers, microwave ovens, washing machines, and televisions, and it had the world's largest brand share in major *home appliances*, 8.6 percent,[2] creating what was likely China's most recognized global brand. Haier is also one of the world's biggest refrigerator producers in terms of both brand and market share.

How Haier achieved all of this, and how it did it in such a relatively short period of time despite fierce competition from incumbent global heavyweights, is the central story of this book and one that speaks to the power of business model innovation undertaken at Haier. Despite the company's reputation for innovation that has resulted in the creation of one new product after another, we believe that the real innovative power at Haier speaks to a competency that is far more powerful than just products. It is instead the ability to innovate, and continue to innovate, the business model and the corporate culture that supports it. This is the key to understanding Haier's unparalleled success over more than three decades and potential for the future.

Transformational Change in an Emerging Market

This is also a book about innovation in emerging markets. It is not about IBM or GE, or any of the other familiar, big-name, well-established multinational corporations. This is a book about Haier, a domestic Chinese player that has succeeded not only in defending its home market against stronger, better-endowed foreign competition, but also in opening up new markets on a global stage, something that very few other BRIC (Brazil, Russia, India, and China) firms have accomplished.

Globalization could well be the biggest story of the twenty-first century, yet it has been almost entirely depicted from the perspective of Western multinationals. Obvious as it might be, the challenges and strategies of the emerging markets' champions are virtually invisible. It is as if globalization was a one-way street. But the truth is that globalization is increasingly a two-way story, with BRIC-based enterprises arising to both protect their domestic markets and enter global markets as bona-fide contenders. This book offers an unusual opportunity to get into the details of one such BRIC-based competitor to see how these organizations do it. The lessons here, however, are universal in their applicability. This is particularly important because we have been waiting for several decades for managerial lessons to emerge from the Chinese competitive space, and we believe that there are some to be found in Haier's experiences.

Peter Drucker, the twentieth-century management gurus' guru, predicted as long ago as 1997 that China would be a source of fresh, new managerial insights in much the same way that Japan's industry revolutionized the way we all thought about organizations in the early 1980s.[3] Interestingly, but not surprisingly, Japan's contributions were largely from the operations world, where Japanese companies had built their competitive strengths for succeeding in the global marketplace. The fact that Toyota, for example, is so strong today as a global player is largely dependent on its ability to build reliable, affordable cars, and the reason that it can do this is directly traceable to the management thinkers—both academics and practitioners—who created new approaches to considering operations and supply chains.

What about China, then? Where should we look for a rich source of Chinese managerial secrets? The shelves of international bookstores are already loaded with Sun Tzu's *Art of War* and other similar works of classical thought, but these, in and of themselves, are not a practical source of business insight. Interesting as they may be, they have not had a profound impact outside China (or, we suspect, even inside). Similarly, we are told by China scholars that China excels in building effective interpersonal relationship networks (*guanxi*) within the cultural context of hardworking, face-conscious, bureaucratic, bargaining-oriented, and harmonious approaches to business. Insightful as such learnings might be, once again they are too vague and too culturally specific to gain our attention in the way that Drucker likely imagined.

Where China truly does have something to offer the rest of the world in terms of managerial insight is in the organizing and leading of faster-paced operations and customer relations by some of its most interesting enterprises, and it is here that Haier has some experiences that the rest of us might benefit from. Speed matters today as perhaps it has never mattered before, and the Chinese economy is, arguably, the fastest in the world at both the macro- and microlevels. Repeatedly we hear of instances where the Chinese elements of a multinational corporation are easily outpacing their foreign colleagues in taking on new projects and moving them to successful completion, often through the coordination of multiple partners in pursuit of the same goal. It is in such examples of organizational redesign, such as fast-moving project management, that we believe we should be looking for the Chinese Drucker. The story you are about to enter is very much about how one successful organization is outperforming all sorts of worthy competitors, foreign and domestic, on the basis of being smarter about its customers and faster in its activities, and building an organizational culture that strives to achieve these objectives in a consistent and reliable fashion by getting more contributions out of the talent it employs.

Strategy Is Choice and Execution

This is also a book about how managerial choices come together to produce the strategic outcomes—speed, customer-centricity, the leveraging of talent—that an organization desires. Strategy can be many things to many people, but if we reduce it to its essentials, strategy is about choice—the choices you make, and the choices not made—and about execution, for without execution, choices are only dreams.

Faced with competitive uncertainty, firms make choices, or they don't. Either way, their behavior in a marketplace is the outcome of such decisions. Successful firms either make better choices than their rivals or make the same choices and execute better and as a result outperform the others. A great strategy is marked by two characteristics:

- The choices made are appropriate for the competitive situation that the firm is in.
- The choices that are made can be executed.

This is at the heart of everything we look at from this point on: What choices were made? Were they appropriate to the world around the enterprise? What were the competitors doing? And how well did the firm in question execute?

Choosing the Purpose of the Business

Probably the first and foremost choice to be made by any commercial organization reflects the purpose of the business. This sets the stage for everything that comes next; it speaks to the philosophical soul of the enterprise. Ironically, however, despite the importance of such philosophical foundations, it is more typical that whenever change (and culture) are discussed in organizational settings, it is structural change that receives all the attention, probably because of the tangibility of the changes being instituted and their visibility. In discussions of grand strategy, frequently the implicit view accepted is, "Traditional companies are ends in themselves, and the individuals joining them are means for their growth and perpetuation."[4] Only after structure is determined do we turn our attention to the organization's *physiology*—the roles, decision-making processes, information flows, and so forth that determine how the organization moves. After this, finally, and only if there is any energy left, does the conversation get around to the matter of organizational purpose (probably because frequently it is so vague and ambiguous as to be meaningless). We think that this is a mistake. We believe, in fact, that the emphasis should be perfectly reversed: purpose first.[5] Then, and only after all of this is said and done and agreed on, should we examine physiology and, finally, structure.

The focus should always be on real managers making real choices, and this requires a fundamental understanding of the purpose that drives an enterprise. Despite this, in so many of the firms that we observe, too little attention is given to reflection regarding the purposes that the business serves and what it hopes to accomplish as a result. Consequently, too many managers we see find themselves unable to escape the tyranny of strategic inertia: they keep doing what they've always done, only now they do it bigger, faster, or cheaper. Frequently in such instances, choice gives way to extrapolating legacy. Yet as one consulting firm has observed, this is not the only way to work and choose; it is only the most familiar:

> The most common template for large-scale modern business design, the multidivisional corporation, is not the only way to do it. The multidivisional form, first realized by General Motors in 1920, has become the standard form today. While phenomenally effective in some ways, the multidivisional form also has significant weaknesses when it comes to innovation.
>
> There are things that seem "obvious" about organization design that are in fact not so obvious at all. Some things that we take for granted as fundamental are in fact only optional.[6]

We believe that the difference between "obvious" and "optional" is best discerned by starting with a reexamination of the purpose of the business.

At this point in our conversation, Peter Drucker reappears, as it was he who asked more than a half-century ago: What is our business? And what should it be? The question, now so familiar as to appear trite, is in fact of fundamental importance. What the firm believes about its purpose, or its mission, and how clearly it is able to articulate those aspirations, is a necessary starting point for addressing the next question: How will we go about achieving this? Our task, then, in analyzing any company's approach to strategic change is not only to keep all three of these choices—purpose, physiology, and structure—in mind but also to be equally attentive to the sequence in which these choices are being made.

Choosing How to Grow

To grow or not to grow? The choice, in practice, is not such a big one because most firms instinctively vote for growth. How to go about growing, however, is a much more important choice because there are many ways to attempt it. Here, capabilities and resources are critical. There is no reason to believe that all firms in the same industry will make the same choices because they are all starting out from different places in terms of capabilities or resources, or both, but in some way their choices have to reflect the common market that they are all competing in, and they have to be executable in a way that fulfills the dream that the choices were based on. An MIT study of globalization conducted only a few years ago acknowledged the variety of possible paths to competitive success: "There were winners (and losers) in every sector in every country but in none of them did *a single best model* [italics added] emerge" which led the authors to conclude, "It's not an industry that's important, it's a firm's *capabilities*."[7]

Colleagues of ours have in fact portrayed the enterprise growth model as being one of either defending and, possibly, extending the existing market (traditional growth) or moving out in pursuit of new competencies or new markets (figure 1.1).

We should acknowledge that the choice of protecting and extending versus growth is a nontrivial one. It is perfectly fine in many instances to remain within the protect-and-extend quadrant and to grow, organically or not, along with the market you are part of. All too frequently, however, such a choice is complicated by outsiders who are penetrating your domestic market because they see it as a means for their growth. This in fact happened in many domestic Chinese markets in the late 1980s and early 1990s, which created a strategic decision point for the Chinese incumbents about whether to settle for sharing their domestic market or instead to aspire to a larger role on the global stage. One of the most important lessons of the work by Chakravarthy and Lorange, however, is that any movement out

Figure 1.1 Enterprise Growth Model

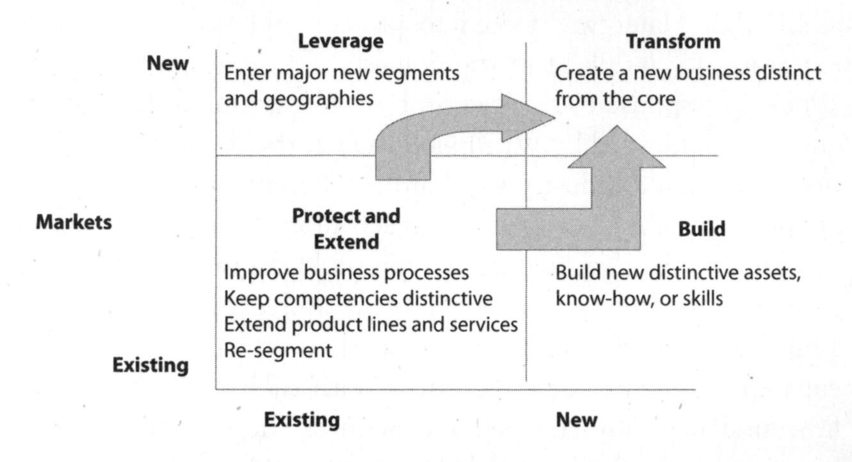

Source: Adapted from Bala Chakravarthy and Peter Lorange, *Profit or Growth?* (Upper Saddle River, NJ: Pearson, 2008). ©2008 by Pearson Education Inc. Used by permission.

of the protect-and-extend quadrant should be done thoughtfully and carefully and never in a diagonal path requiring, simultaneously, both new market and new capability development.[8] Growth becomes clearly an either-or choice regarding new markets or new capabilities so as not to overwhelm the limited attention budget of any managerial team.

As a result of Chakravarthy and Lorange's work, it seems clear that some firms choose to enter new markets with existing competencies, while others apply new competencies in existing markets. Neither path is necessarily superior to the other, provided the choices are both appropriate with respect to opportunities and realistic relative to the firm's execution capabilities. What is interesting for our purposes is to see how such choices are made, what their implications are for execution requirements, and what eventual alterations are necessitated within the organizational cultures involved.

In the story that you are about to embark on, what you will see is that Haier was forced to protect and hope for market extension for its place in the domestic Chinese market in the 1980s, in response to the incursion of Western household appliance companies led by Whirlpool. In fact, the domestic Chinese home appliance industry was hardly coherent and well defined at the time, and Haier was not much more than a local player in Qingdao. So Haier's story is a multifold decision story, where choices ultimately go beyond protect and extend to consider strategic moves based on which markets to enter and which capabilities need to be established. With each such choice, the firm fundamentally changed and, with it, the established organizational culture also needed to change. As a result, as we survey Haier's past three decades, we will repeatedly revisit its articulation of its purpose, the business model that it created in response, the culture that it believed it needed to reinvent in order to achieve its mission within a changing competitive context, and ultimately the structure it had to construct in order to do this effectively.

Anticipating What We Will Learn from Haier

Haier has been an amazing success story in home appliances, particularly white goods (household appliances such as refrigerators and washing machines were initially white in color and so the term *white goods* has come to be associated with that specific part of the broader household appliance industry). The company enjoyed success first in the Chinese market and then in the global marketplace, and it has maintained this reputation for three decades. If we look at the reasons for this success, at least five big headlines must be acknowledged:

- *Innovation:* Haier has consistently led the white goods industry in product, business model, and corporate culture innovation.

- *Fast:* Haier has consistently moved faster than any other competitor, foreign or domestic, in its industry.
- *Customer-centric:* A major part of its claim to being an innovation leader and a fast mover has been its ability to connect with its customers, listen to them, and respond appropriately.
- *Talent engine:* Throughout its thirty-year history, Haier has been a magnet for Chinese talent and has worked to liberate that talent so that it can contribute more to the achievement of Haier's aspirations.
- *Leadership:* Without the exceptional leadership that Haier has had, none of this would have been conceivably possible.

These are all outcomes, however. Everyone wants to be "innovative" or "fast" or "customer-centric," yet most fall short of their aspirations. What Haier has done is to make the right managerial choices to raise the likelihood of actually achieving these aspirations. What is instructive as well is that all of these outcomes are interconnected in a way that ensures mutual reinforcement and amplification. In the chapters that follow, we map the managerial choices that have shaped Haier's culture and will argue that part of Haier's genius has been that the choices it has made, even at the most granular level, are focused directly on the vision that is driving its strategy and that each choice is in concert with each of the others, mutually reinforcing them all.

One thread in particular that runs through all three decades of Haier's choice making is a consistent desire to unleash the talent employed as a means of differentiation in a competitive market that is flirting with commoditization, so that Haier truly does become, in fact as well as in aspiration, faster, more innovative and, as a result, more customer oriented. The bottom line is greater value for the customer, which drives shareholder value as well. The motor that drives this is the creation of unique autonomous, self-organizing microbusinesses, which Haier refers to as

ZZJYTs (*Zi Zhu Jing Ying Ti*, which can be translated as "independent operating unit"). They are run as small profit-and-loss centers that foster both a greater expression of individual talent, through the release of entrepreneurial energies, and a more precise distribution of incentives and rewards for those who contribute. Although such initiatives are not new to the business world, it is both the scale of this effort (Haier had eighty thousand employees in 2012) and the tightly integrated and mutually reinforcing architecture of the approach that attracted our attention.

This is not pursuing being faster or more customer-centric for its own sake. Quite the contrary: Haier desires to be fast, innovative, and customer-centric in order to achieve its vision and mission of "becoming the industry leader and providing competitive beautiful residence life solutions to customers." Perhaps even more interesting is that as challenging as these aspirations may be by themselves, to desire to achieve all of them within the organizational culture of a large, traditional Chinese firm in a mature industry is hard to imagine. It is truly something that Jim Collins, author of *Good to Great*, might refer to as a "Big Hairy Audacious Goal."[9] When you add in the more than two thousand years of China's Confucian tradition, as well as the legacy of China's Maoist dogma, it seems impossible to even conceive of such an achievement. Then, in defiance of all of this, add as well the belief that China's abundant talent should be the idea engine that achieves all, and you have what seems to be a mission impossible. However, we will see throughout this book that what Haier has achieved is not impossible. It is the result of well-thought-out and well-designed change leadership interventions.

What You Will Learn in Each Chapter

Strategic initiatives must be appropriate to the world around the organization, and in this instance the world that we will look at is that of the white goods sector of home appliances. This is an increasingly concentrated, old-economy, mature industry in Western markets, where product offerings have flirted with being close to having undifferentiated commodity status and price competition has been severe. The opening of China promised some new opportunities to this industry, but over the thirty-year span of our review, Chinese competitors have evolved, resulting in an increasingly competitive environment in the domestic market, and the global one as well, which has become much more highly contested and complicated. Chapter 2 explains this world in detail in order to establish the industry context in which Haier's strategic reinvention of its business model and corporate culture has taken place.

Beginning as the Qingdao Refrigerator Factory, a collectively owned enterprise in a coastal town in northeast China, today's globally recognized Haier Corporation has reinvented its business model and corporate culture at least three times in as many decades. One way to think of this is that we've seen at least three different Haiers during that period. In chapter 3, we add flesh to the skeleton by describing the nature of Haier over this span of time and why and how these changes occurred. The chapter provides a rich narrative of the business model reinvention path that Haier has been on for three decades.

Haier's story of continuing reinvention has also been one of persistent pursuit of talent liberation. As we approach the latest reincarnation of Haier's corporate culture, there are six key themes that run through every aspect of the experiment:

- The unleashing of talent through the creation of self-organizing, autonomous work units that essentially run the business
- The coupling of freedom and control through the use of strategic income statements for each autonomous work unit
- The self-governing of the autonomous work units
- The linking of individual value creation to the total corporate value added

- Creating a capacity for responsiveness and improvisation (spontaneity) based on preestablished and contractually binding expectations
- The establishment of a self-correcting governance system

In chapter 4, we go through each of these principles in careful detail as we set out the logic underpinning the entire cultural reinvention effort. These are the first-order aspirations that management has chosen to drive the overall objective of unleashing talent in order to be more innovative and to move faster.

Many organizations contend that they are becoming more customer-centric, more innovative, or faster (or all of these), but all too often, careful investigation reveals business as usual. In such cases, the aspirations of leadership will not be realized. What we find worthy of note with respect to Haier is that its leaders really are trying to execute on their aspirations. Chapter 5 represents an attempt to provide sufficient granularity in understanding Haier's approach to organizational design and governance so that readers can appreciate the managerial choices that Haier has made to compete in demanding markets. We believe that this chapter provides unique insight into how a major, innovative Chinese global player conducts its business at a level of detail that has not been seen elsewhere. The chapter includes numerous illustrations and examples of how Haier's goal of "zero distance with the customer" is being achieved, as well as notes from the field in the form of coauthor Fang Liu's firsthand experiences within one of Haier's self-organizing, autonomous work units.

We believe that Haier's activities should be seen with reference to some thoughts on what benchmark high-performing organizations are doing and have done. Much of this literature comes out of the popular business press and offers a mythology of successful corporate performance. We summarize this mythology in chapter 6 and use it to consider how well Haier's business model development agrees with what might well be considered best practices of high-performing organizations. In addition, this chapter looks at four other reference organizations that have also attempted to unleash the talent they employ through large-scale cultural reinvention: ABB, Nash, Oticon, and the Morning Star Company. We tell their stories and compare them with Haier's experiences. Our conclusion is that not only are Haier's reinvention experiences at the cutting-edge of what the management profession currently regards as "thought leadership with respect to change management," but they also reflect a coherent and well-thought-out approach to cultural architecture for increasing the probability of achieving its strategic aspirations.

Underlying much of what Haier is trying to achieve with the strategic initiatives chronicled in this book is an attempt to fashion a truly strategically agile organization. Any such effort inevitably invites a comparison of the efforts taken and the admonitions of the Nobel Prize laureate economist Ronald J. Coase regarding the relationship between increased organizational complexity and increased transaction costs. In chapter 7, we conclude that Haier has crafted a new form of hybrid organization that emphasizes benefits from organization over Coasean transaction costs and mixes market incentives with controls in a novel fashion. Most firms will likely choose not to go down the path that Haier is exploring, or at least not to go down this route as far as Haier has chosen; nonetheless, the Haier experience provides a valuable reference point for adaptation in the never-ending search for a superior organizational approach.

There is much to be learned about business model innovation, what it takes to really invent and reinvent a new corporate culture, and what it's like to work within a Chinese global organization. In chapter 8, we review all that we have learned from the Haier experience and summarize it in an easy-to-recall format.

2

THE BATTLEFIELD

The Home Appliance Industry in the West and China

The past three decades of competition within the global major home appliance industry tell a story that is representative of many traditional manufacturing industries: rapid growth of domestic champions in developed markets after the conclusion of World War II, when war-repressed demand could finally be fulfilled; followed a few decades later by a softening of growth as these markets matured and became saturated; leading in turn to a search for emerging markets in the developing world order to sustain growth; fierce international competition and severe consolidation of market players in the foreign markets that were "invaded," as too many competitors arrived to serve relatively less demand; and, finally, the ramping up of competition onto a global stage as emerging market companies grew into global challengers.[1] All of this was accompanied by increasing standardization of product offerings across all markets and, subsequently, competitive price pressure among the small set of surviving strong brands that were offering what was fast becoming an undifferentiated product.

China was one of the most attractive emerging markets that Western firms looked to for growth in the last decade of the twentieth century, and today, ironically, many of these same market dynamics have come to represent China's story as well. What we will see in this chapter is the experiences of Western home appliance companies as they entered and failed (for the most part) in the Chinese market, as well as the surprising and successful defense and ultimate dominance of that market by Chinese local companies. Along the way, we'll see how the global home appliance industry has changed over time and the role that China has played in this saga. The principal purpose of the chapter, however, is to establish the competitive context in which Haier's strategic choices were forged so as to be able to appreciate the appropriateness of those choices.

The Global Battlefield Emerges in the 1980s

The major home appliance industry consists of washing machines, refrigerators, dishwashers, microwaves, cooking appliances, and other big appliances. Because these appliances were all traditionally white in the early days of the industry, the business itself came to be known as "white goods," which separated them from such "nonwhite" goods as television sets, radios, video equipment, and other digital appliances.

In the late 1970s and early 1980s, Whirlpool, GE, and Maytag were the leading brands in the United States. The European markets were much more fragmented. Sweden's Electrolux was the market leader across Europe, followed by a large number of small local players. In Japan, brands such as Mitsubishi, Panasonic, and Sanyo were well established as the domestic leaders. Despite the fact that the triad of the United States, Europe, and Japan made up 60 percent of the world's major home appliance demand, machine design and consumer preferences shared few common traits across these three regions.[2] In terms of global market share, however, European styles dominated all product lines: refrigerators, washing machines, and cooking ranges.[3]

By the mid-1980s, after the boom decades of the postwar period, most Western markets had reached a high saturation level for refrigerators (over 95 percent), ranges (98 percent), and washing machines (70 to 95 percent). The main players in these segments saw a shrinkage of demand, declining profit margins, and excess manufacturing capacity. Whirlpool's net margin remained around 5 percent from 1980 to 1985; over the same period, Philips's net margin was even lower, ranging from barely 1 percent to 2 percent.

In such a competitive landscape, the challenges that every company faced were growth and profit. *Protect and extend* was an obvious strategic choice regarding well-established domestic markets, but most of the major players also considered expansion as a possible path for organic growth. These expansion options included both new geographical markets and horizontal product lines or consumer segment expansion. Many also considered vertical integration as a growth strategy. Choosing between global expansion and domestic consolidation typically reflected a company's appraisal of its resources, competencies, and aspirations.

A wave of American brands expanded to Europe, while some European brands, mainly Electrolux, moved into the U.S. market, marking the first globalization phase of the home appliance industry, although it was truly more transatlantic than global. Geographical expansion was preferred over exploring new consumer segments as premium, midlevel, and lower-end segments were already firmly occupied by well-established brand names. The possibility of increased vertical integration, particularly with distribution channels, never emerged as a serious consideration for most of the manufacturers, possibly because of the absence of local knowledge that would be required to make this successful. The ignorance and lack of experience of this vital part of value chain knowledge for countries other than those in the developed world would later be seen to explain part of the failure of Western brands in the Chinese market, where distribution channels were not yet well built. As a result, foreign entrants had great difficulty delivering their products into the hands of end consumers.

Not surprisingly, in times of such slow growth, cost reductions were looked to as a key weapon for increased profit margins, emphasizing process improvement over product innovation for competitive success. However, diverse consumer preferences across the fragmented market regions of the West raised challenges for achieving economies of scale. Firms struggled between the choices of establishing a standard product to achieve lower costs and of adapting product offerings for local needs at the expense of economies of scale. As geographical expansion became more attractive, many firms also faced the choice of setting up numerous manufacturing sites to get closer to local markets, which also resulted in a loss of economies of scale.

The U.S. Market in the 1980s and 1990s

Leading American appliance manufacturers (Whirlpool, GE, and Maytag) all originally began as producers of a single major type of home appliance, but eventually each acquired a full range of smaller companies to complete its product lines across all major home appliances. By the mid-1980s, almost all of the small North American players were gone, assimilated into the major competitors, and the five biggest major home appliance companies dominated the market, accounting for 93 percent of the U.S. market share, with well-established brand recognition and good quality products.[4]

Following consolidation, the main competitors started looking at geographical expansion as the next basis for growth. Whirlpool was the most aggressive of these in forming ambitious plans for Europe, Latin America, and Asia. Maytag had a more focused strategy for Canada and Mexico, as well as Asia. GE was the outlier, with a much more conservative approach to geographical expansion.

By 1985, the home appliance markets in both Europe and the United States were around 40 million units. By 1998, the European market had grown to 71 million units, while the U.S. market was only 50 million. The market size of China was only 12 million units in 1985 but had more than doubled by 1998 to 30 million, and has continued to grow, reaching 130 million by 2011. China is now the biggest home appliance market in the

Figure 2.1 Major Home Appliance Market Sizes in China, the United States, and Western Europe, 1998–2011

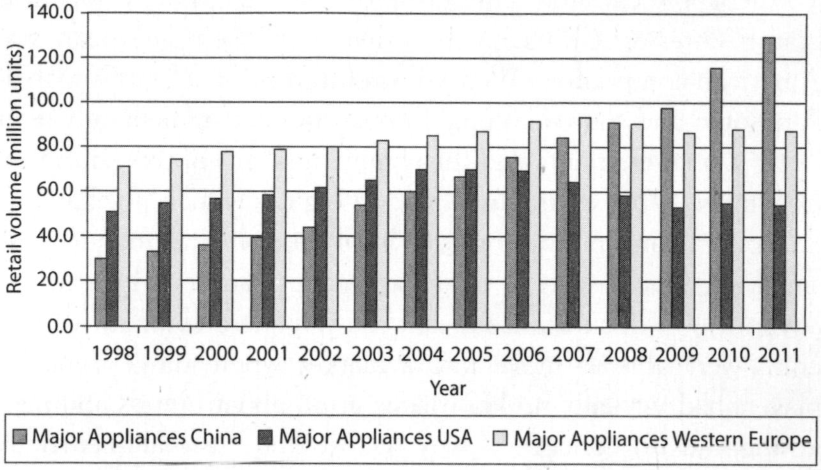

Source: Euromonitor.

world (figure 2.1). The home appliance market in the United States was essentially saturated by the late 1990s.

Although we speak of a single European market for home appliances, the fact is that competition in Europe has remained quite local—so much so that across the continent, consumer preferences and product design have not been able to converge, which probably explains why European manufacturers were not investing in radical new product development similar to their American counterparts.

The Chinese Market

The major home appliance market in China is one of the many markets that started under government planning and evolved into a full-fledged market-governed industry in a fairly short time.[5] Foreign firms wanting to enter China's home appliance market experienced four phases over a twenty-plus-year period. First the government required technology transfer then it allowed joint ventures, followed by wholly owned foreign subsidiaries, and finally vertical integration along the value chain.

Geographical and cultural proximity facilitated Japanese brands entering China much earlier than their European and American competitors. Well-known international brands such as Panasonic and Sanyo entered China's market immediately after Deng Xiaoping announced the commencement of the reforms in December 1978, setting up offices in big cities such as Shanghai and Beijing and partnering with local producers to manufacture small appliances such as radios and tape recorders. First-mover advantage in this instance meant that Japanese competitive veterans were able to move into a market where naive domestic players had virtually no knowledge at all about brands and marketing and no concept of why quality and customer-centricity might be important and were able to rely on their existing competencies in these regards to dominate local competitors in the new space. Massive advertising on radio, newspapers, and posters earned Japanese brands such high brand recognition that they continue to benefit from this more than thirty years later.

China's domestic market for household appliances was virtually nonexistent in the 1970s. By the late 1970s, only twenty-eight thousand refrigerators were made in China by local firms. Attracted by a growing demand, many local governments began to sponsor their own firms, and by 1985, the number of Chinese domestic manufacturers had risen to 115 from the 20 that had existed in 1978.[6] Although the number of firms had increased, ungrammatical so changed their products remained of very poor quality and were so expensive that such luxuries were imaginable only to serve as a dowry.[7] Imported Japanese machines soon occupied the higher-end market niche. With little production experience and no tradition of respecting the customer, Chinese domestic factories had difficulty producing good-quality machines. Ironically, despite these quality problems, the price of their machines skyrocketed because of scarcity: customers were willing to spend a year's savings to buy a damaged machine and felt proud of owning it.

To acquire sound manufacturing technology, some of the Chinese companies turned to Western producers. It was at this time that the Qingdao Refrigerator Company, now Haier, partnered with the German company Liebherr. This was the first time that Western brands became acquainted with their Chinese counterparts. In Haier's case, the technology transfer was successful, and its reputation for good-quality products spread quickly by word-of-mouth. Potential customers lined up in front of department stores and the Qingdao Refrigerator Company's offices to buy their refrigerators. The high brand value and the short supply allowed many companies to make as much as a 30 percent profit margin. In the 1980s, the average monthly salary of a middle-class Chinese family was 100 renminbi (RMB), and the price of a Qingdao-Liebherr refrigerator was RMB 1,700, seventeen times the average monthly salary. Today the lowest salary allowed by the government is around RMB 2,000 in eastern China, while the price of a refrigerator remains essentially unchanged despite inflation.

China's home appliance industry was opened to private investors in the mid-1990s. Attracted by the high profit margins, many private companies entered the industry, and the number of Chinese home appliance brands rapidly increased to over four hundred, further fragmenting the market. At around the same time, foreign companies were allowed to form joint ventures with local manufacturers and to have more than 50 percent ownership. This incentive attracted many foreign brands whose leaders foresaw that China would become the world's biggest major home appliance market. They also recognized China's potential as the world's factory and planned to exploit the cheap labor in China to produce their own products as part of their globalization strategy. The leading American brands, Whirlpool and Maytag, as well as Europe's leader, Electrolux, and Korean brands Samsung and LG all entered China at that time.

The liberalization of firm formation and the entry of foreign investors inevitably led to greater competition, which quickly drove profits down. In the late 1990s, despite the growing market, the profit margins of the major home appliance players slumped, which accelerated industry consolidation. Smaller players lacking economies of scale were either wiped out or acquired by bigger firms. By 1997, the four biggest Chinese refrigerator brands—Haier, Rongsheng, Meiling, and Xinfei—counted for 71 percent of the total Chinese refrigerator market share. The price war continued, and by 2011, the average profit margin of the industry was around only 3 percent.

It did not take long for Western brands to realize that ambition alone was not sufficient to succeed in the Chinese market. Almost all of them paid an expensive lesson to understand how to do business in China and to understand Chinese partners, consumers, and competitors. American brands such as Whirlpool, which were used to producing large, bulky, energy-consuming products in the West, faced huge problems with their existing product lines, which fit poorly into the small living space and energy-conscious homes of Chinese consumers. Japanese competitors, which came from a market with similar-sized living spaces, had more experience in producing space- and energy-efficient machines and therefore had a natural advantage. Foreign brands also had a hard time delivering products to the end consumers because of policy constraints and a lack of established distribution networks at the time, that is, large national electronic distribution chains were nonexistent. In this sense, local producers had the host advantage and distributed products through state-owned department stores and scattered private electronic stores.

Despite the growing foreign presence, the Chinese domestic producers' attention was focused mainly on their domestic market and did not feel threatened by the foreigners until China entered the World Trade Organization (WTO) in December 2001, because they had been partially protected by the government and the local knowledge mentioned previously. Prior to membership in the WTO, when foreign companies were subject to sales quotas and had no right to engage in activities other than manufacturing, Chinese firms were free of such constraints. As part of the agreements to enter the WTO, however, China promised to open up the major home appliance industry, which meant foreign brands would have the right to carry out all the same activities, including distribution and service in China, as their Chinese counterparts. In short, foreign companies would be able to compete openly and equally with local players. No longer would they be the victims of sales quotas; in fact, they would also now have incentives to invest in production, design, and development to produce locally adapted products and achieve economies of scale. Soon after China entered the WTO, all of the major Western home appliance brands (with the exception of GE) set up their own manufacturing sites and research and development centers in China.

Facing overcapacity for the first time in their short history and worried about losing their home market, the Chinese major home appliance players began to establish their own agenda for globalization. Haier was the first and most ambitious of the pack; its leaders believed that globalization meant not only exporting to other countries the products that were produced in China but also manufacturing in other countries. Haier's vision was clear: to build a global brand. Following this dream, Haier established a U.S. factory in South Carolina in 2002. Some other leading companies adopted different strategies, keeping production in China.

The first decade of the twenty-first century witnessed considerable success by Chinese brands in defending their home market; several have gradually become among the world's largest home appliance manufacturers. Although their brand recognition is still low in overseas markets, particularly in developed countries, their worst scenario—the one that Western brands would dominate China's domestic market—did not happen. In fact, except for the Japanese brand Panasonic and the German brand Bosch-Siemens, no foreign brand has been able to enter the top ten list of Chinese market share for major home appliances.

By 2011, the four biggest companies in the Chinese domestic market were Haier, GD Midea, Galanz, and Hisense, accounting for 52.8 percent of the total market, estimated at 130 million units in total. This was a long way from 2002, when the top four brands accounted for only 28.7 percent of the total market share. The market has been slowly consolidating but remains fragmented.

The Challenge of Globalization: Key Lessons of Western Brands in China

There are many ways to internationalize, and being multidomestic is not the same as aspiring to become global. The home appliance industry, because of different cultural preferences, has largely been perceived as a multidomestic industry rather than a global industry. In his book *Selling China*, Yasheng Huang argues that theoretically a local firm has a better chance of succeeding in the home appliance industry than in other industries competing against foreign firms because of the need for local knowledge and local adaptations.[8] One senior vice president of GE's household appliance division observed, "The only worldwide appliances to me are small refrigerators, room air conditioners and microwave ovens."[9] The economic significance of such a perspective was expressed in the late 1980s by Whirlpool's CEO, David Whitwam:

> Don't get carried away with the pieces on the board. It's easy to conquer geography—to buy companies outside your home base, to build factories in Asia or Latin America, to plant flags. We are not planting flags. We are building a global enterprise. . . . The difference is leverage and integration. Unless we leverage our assets and integrate the organization on a global scale—unless we are stronger in Brazil because of what we do in Italy, unless we are smarter in Hong Kong because of what we've learned in Mexico, unless we can apply our core technologies all around the world—the strategy is not going to work.[10]

Whitwam forecast a "world washer," which would be sold everywhere as consumer preferences converged.[11] Yet despite this vision, the existing empirical evidence seems to support the multidomestic option. GE and Whirlpool were the dominant brands in the U.S. market, and Electrolux dominated the European market in the 1990s. By 2011, Whirlpool remained number one in the United States and GE number two. In Europe, however, Bosch-Siemens had achieved the top position, with Electrolux falling to second place.[12] Today in China, local brands Haier and GD Midea remain the leading mainstream brands. Clearly this is not a strong vote in favor of one global offering.

Brand Positioning and Brand Building

The global players that entered the China home appliances market had to choose whether to maintain the same brand positioning in China as in their home markets. A mid- or low-end Western brand could find itself in a challenging situation if it was unable to retain the same cost advantages in an emerging market that it enjoyed in a more mature market and yet also not have the brand cachet to compete at the high end either. Furthermore, there was no way that they would be able to compete on price with the local players, especially with Chinese consumers expecting foreign products to have high-end quality. But if they retained their brand and compromised on their offering, they could be running an even bigger risk: once the high-end brand was diluted into becoming a cheap brand, it could be difficult to rebuild the high-end image. In fact, given the global awareness of sophisticated customers, the diminishing of a brand's positioning in one market might contaminate its reputation in other markets as well.

Forced to form joint ventures with local companies, Western brands had a third option: using the acquired local firm's brand. When Whirlpool formed its joint venture with Snowflake, the best-known Chinese refrigerator brand in the 1980s, it chose to brand its products under the name of Snowflake in an effort to exploit Snowflake's brand name. Whirlpool's intention to leverage the brand equity of Snowflake seemed to be valid at that moment, but it actually lost its best opportunity to build a first-mover Whirlpool-brand advantage against all the other Western home appliance brands. Following the failure of the joint venture, the Snowflake brand vanished at the end of the 1990s, and today Whirlpool still suffers from low brand recognition in China.

Facing the cut-throat price war that was characteristic of low-price, low-quality Chinese domestic brands fighting for their home market, if not their existence, many Western brands were lost in brand positioning. It was indeed a dilemma for Whirlpool, a midrange brand in the U.S. market, to implement the same brand positioning strategy in China as it had elsewhere. Electrolux, in contrast, chose to jump in between premium and midrange, yet it offered a large-scale product discount strategy, which confused its brand positioning; as a result, it lost much of its brand equity in the Chinese market.

Bosch-Siemens had a much clearer positioning from the beginning. Although it took a lot of patience to build a high-end brand, the management team was convinced that it was the right way to go, and that commitment paid off. Today Bosch-Siemens is the biggest Western home appliance brand in the Chinese market, with a 3.1 percent market share and an almost 40 percent share in the high-end sector. Patience and consistency are the keys in its success.

Playing the Value Chain: The Choice of Distribution Channels

How best to go to market is always a challenging choice for newcomers to a market, and in China, where the nascent market was characterized by a poor and fragmented distribution infrastructure, the choices were often new and confusing for everyone, foreign and domestic, hoping to compete. For foreign players used to relying on distribution channels that were highly consolidated and well established, China required a lot of time and resources to figure out how to deliver the products to end consumers efficiently and effectively under such unfamiliar conditions.

Compared to the flat distribution structures common in the West, the distribution system in China was more in the shape of a pyramid in the mid-1990s. Starting from a single national wholesaler at the top, moving to regional wholesalers at both provincial and municipal levels, and ultimately, to the retail outlets, which were mostly traditional, market-averse, collective-owned department stores, this fragmented distribution channel increased the price of the products because each layer needed to make a profit. Moreover, for the Western brands, the price negotiation process and operational collaboration with thousands of independent national wholesalers was time- and resource-consuming. It could also involve unrelated, if not competing, stakeholders such as local or central government agencies that might oversee foreign company activities in China. All of this worked to slow down the successful penetration of Chinese markets by foreign offerings. Therefore, most of the time, the Western brands' local partners were given the responsibility of dealing with the distribution but then the foreign brand partially lost control of its image.

If there was any consumer feedback on the product, distinctly unusual in an economy where people were used to scarcity and were grateful even to receive a product—no matter what its condition—the time delays and distortion resulting from the complexity of the system rendered the feedback virtually useless.

The maturation of the market by the late 1990s saw the birth of large retail stores such as Gome and Suning, which have been expanding rapidly, although the scale remains far below that of the West. In rural China, the most promising segment for the future, distribution difficulties are even more challenging, and no mature retail chains have yet been established.

Achieving Customer-Centricity

Although commonly expressed as a strategic aspiration by most global players, customer-centricity has not received similar attention in the Chinese market. The three decades following the foundation of the People's Republic of China in 1949 saw an economy of scarcity that has resulted in indifference to the customer, reinforced by the administration of a centrally planned economy. Western brands believed that they could exploit this indifference, but they faced the need to educate Chinese consumers to appreciate the benefits of both the technological and service advantages that they were prepared to offer.

Customer-centricity, however, is more than just new products and new services; it also requires being in close touch with local consumers, and it is here that the Chinese competitors had a real advantage if they could capitalize on it. Compared with Western brands, which almost instinctively tended to lead with their technical superiority, some local players were able to listen better to local customers and deliver on what they heard. Haier, for example, based on its ability to hear, listen to, and react to local concerns, introduced and successfully marketed an antielectric-shock water heater. For the most part, Western firms were too far away to pick up such weak signals and not sufficiently flexible to respond to them.

Developing Local Talent and Management

If a company's intention is to get closer to the local market, then attracting, acquiring, developing, and retaining local talent become critical strategic objectives. In the mid-1990s, when Western home appliance companies began to enter the Chinese market, they tended to follow one of two talent paths: relying on experts sent from headquarters, who lacked local knowledge but had rich industry experience somewhere else, or delegating local operations to Chinese management in the hope that local adaptation would be facilitated. Neither strategy was promising in its pure form. When foreign managers were teamed up with local managers with the best intention to achieve synergy, cultural and language differences turned out to be big barriers. Maytag was a victim of vacillating from one approach to the other, and Electrolux, which frequently changed local managers, eventually lost its brand positioning and market share as a result. Bosch-Siemens, a rare successful example, had a single sales director, Wu Jianke, committed to the company for over fifteen years since 1995 and who took it to its present status. (In contrast, Siemens's China chairman changed three times while Wu remained the sales director.)[13]

In an interview in 2006, Wu attributed his success to luck and his former experience as a teacher and hotel manager.[14] His fluent English also facilitated his communication with foreign headquarters. He believed that Bosch-Siemens's success was the result of a long-term focus on high-end brand building and courageously innovating the operating model based on its experience in the West.[15]

As China gradually gains strategic importance in the global market, the talent war in China is getting fierce. Key individuals such as Wu Jianke are becoming much harder to hire. Western companies' talent strategy has significantly changed along the way. For example, young graduates are the target talent pool for many Western companies, which now show expertise in identifying potential future leaders. However, this raises a new problem because these brilliant young people are constantly offered more attractive positions and pay by competing companies. As a result, the employee turnover rate has climbed year by year. Western companies now have to compete not only with their Western peers to attract such talented managers but also with Chinese local companies that are growing quickly. The allure of working for a foreign firm has begun to fade. More and more talented and ambitious young Chinese realize that big domestic companies can offer them better career development than Western companies can. As a result, customer-centricity and a strong local character become even harder to achieve.

Home Appliance Manufacturers' Approaches to the Chinese Market

Among the most interesting lessons to come out of the first three decades of competition in China's household appliance industry has been the overwhelming failure of global brand champions, such as Whirlpool, Maytag, and Electrolux, in this market. Their inability to adjust to the local market context, be it distribution, product adaptation to local needs, or local talent engagement, resulted in their not being able to emulate their success in the West in the Chinese market. Only Bosch-Siemens, with its steadfast commitment to maintaining a consistent global brand image and its ability to define what it would not do to compromise that brand image, has been successful. The remaining lesson, of course, is a tribute to the ability of the domestic Chinese manufacturers, underestimated and ridiculed by the larger global players, to protect and defend their home market, often by ensnaring global players in competitions that they should never have chosen to enter but could not figure out how to avoid.

Whirlpool

According to industry observers, Whirlpool's failures in the Chinese market can be attributed to three factors. First, it underestimated China's market growth. Soon after its entry into the Chinese market in the late 1990s, Whirlpool misread the urban market and determined that it was already saturated because Chinese consumers did not appear to buy new machines as long as the old ones still worked, a habit that did not persist for long. Second, Whirlpool's management team was overly confident that China's market could be managed only by Westerners with Western experience. And third, the inflexible bureaucracy of a large, complex corporation impeded Whirlpool's speed to operate in a fast-moving market such as China. On top of these, the ambiguity and difficulty of repositioning an American mid-end brand in China's market added another layer of complexity besides the operational inflexibility.

Yet despite such disappointments and its eventual withdrawal from the Chinese market, Whirlpool decided to reenter the Chinese market in 2002 with a more cautious strategy: it sought to reestablish brand recognition in refrigerators and air conditioners, yet with less American dominance in its joint ventures and partnerships. One way of attempting to achieve this goal was through strategic partnerships with Gome and Suning, the two leading home appliance retail chains, and concentrating its efforts on first- and second-tier cities. (China employs a multitier designation to characterize the relative importance of its cities. Beijing, Shanghai, and Guangzhou are first-tier cities; below them are twenty to thirty provincial capitals and important second-tier cities; and below them several hundred third-tier and fourth-tier cities.) The second time around, Whirlpool positioned itself as a brand licensor. The results, however, once again did not turn out as hoped for, and from 2002 to 2011, Whirlpool's market share in the China home appliance market remained at 0.4 percent, an ironic contrast with its position as the largest global home appliance company.[16]

General Electric

General Electric's home appliance business held the largest market share in the U.S. market until 2005, when Maytag was acquired by Whirlpool, thus boosting the latter's market share. GE did not have any intention to globalize its home appliance business, however. It chose instead to remain a completely U.S. domestic-market-only brand. Nevertheless, the company started procuring components from China in the early 1980s and eventually outsourced part of its production to Chinese original equipment manufacturers (OEM). GE partnered with Aucma in

2001, a Qingdao-based major home appliance company whose product line spanned refrigerators, washing machines, freezers, kitchen ranges, and other appliances, and with refrigerator producer Xinfei, based in Henan province.

Today China fulfills one-third of GE's global material and product procurement for home appliances. GE's explanation for its choice of not entering the Chinese market as a product seller was reaffirmed in 2005 by CEO Jeffrey Immelt, when he emphasized that GE appliances, as well as GE lighting, had no plans to enter the Chinese market, where the two divisions had no competitive advantages. He added that there were already outstanding Chinese competitors and that GE would not be able to differentiate itself.

GE's choice not to pursue global expansion in the 1980s might appear incomprehensible at a time when every other player was expanding. Its choice not to enter the Chinese market, however, appears in retrospect to be sound. The lesson that GE gives to other companies is that sometimes it is smarter to choose to protect and extend a home market than waste resources in price wars resulting from market expansion elsewhere.

Maytag

By the 1980s, Maytag had become one of the most respected premium brands, with the superior quality and durability of its products attracting high customer loyalty in the United States. The value proposition of the company was to produce the highest-quality products at the lowest cost; as a result, the price premiums that Maytag products enjoyed were between 10 and 15 percent.

Despite its success in the U.S. market, Maytag succumbed to the temptation of attempting to establish a global brand presence that turned out to be a complete failure. Maytag began its internationalization experience by entering the European market in 1989. Having enjoyed success as a premium brand at home, Maytag was not at ease with the price war it faced in European markets. With its profits continuing to decline, it withdrew from the European market in 1995.

In China, Maytag established a joint venture with Rong Shi Da, a Chinese washing machine company based in Anhui province in 1997, holding a 49.5 percent stake. Maytag provided the technology transfer, while its Chinese counterpart was in charge of local management and sales. The joint venture turned out to be a huge success the first year. However, when the company's performance was eventually challenged by strong local competitors, Maytag panicked. Maytag's headquarters chose to replace all senior Chinese managers with Western managers who were relatively unfamiliar with the Chinese competitive landscape. Meanwhile, corporate headquarters also switched its strategic focus away from China and toward the Canadian and Mexican markets. The China joint venture came to a sorry end when Maytag failed to lower its manufacturing costs to compete with the local producers. In 2002, it withdrew from the joint venture. Ultimately Maytag also lost the battle for survival at home. In 2005, it was acquired by Whirlpool, which made Whirlpool the biggest major home appliance company in the U.S. market.

The primary and important lesson from Maytag's experience, which should be taken seriously by everyone embarking on the road to globalization, is that a mismanaged globalization initiative has the capacity to distract corporate attention from larger strategic concerns, sometimes with catastrophic consequences. The reason that such a fabled company with such a rich heritage had such a sorry ending lies in its inability to adapt to changing competitive landscapes and keep its eye on its important priorities.

Electrolux

Before Whirlpool acquired Maytag in 2005, Sweden's Electrolux was the world's largest major home appliance company.[17]

In 1997, Electrolux entered the Chinese market by acquiring the Zhongyi refrigerator company, based in Changsha, and the

Hangzhou Wanbao air-conditioner company. Electrolux originally wanted to build a premium brand in the Chinese market but lacked sufficient local management to achieve this objective. To its credit, Electrolux realized that the marketing and management experiences it had accumulated in Western countries were not perfectly applicable to the Chinese market.

In its first three years in China, Electrolux found itself drawn into the local price wars, and it lost RMB 60 million (about $8 million). It quickly replaced its expatriate management team with a Chinese manager and delegated complete freedom to the new leadership team. Almost immediately, the new team engaged the local market by lowering prices aggressively, which quickly raised Electrolux's revenue to RMB 3 billion but resulted in eroding Electrolux's image as a premium brand. In an effort to rebuild its brand, Electrolux once again changed its Chinese-market management team, again led by a Chinese manager, but such frequent changes in leadership at the top failed to correct its problems. Since 2002, Electrolux has been gradually losing market share—from 0.9 percent to only 0.5 percent by 2011.

Electrolux's problems were more than simply attributable to leadership change, however. A choice to emphasize regional marketing failed to effectively establish it as a high-end Western brand, particularly since it had already been compromised in the shortsighted price war that it had allowed itself to be pulled into.

Bosch-Siemens

Bosch-Siemens is a fifty-fifty joint venture between German manufacturing giants Bosch and Siemens created in 1967 for the express purpose of white goods manufacturing. Bosch-Siemens entered the Chinese market in 1994 by setting up a joint venture, BSW, with Wuxi Littleswan washing machine company, creator of China's first automatic washing machine in 1978, to produce a European-style front-loading washing machine.[18] The company had sound performance through 2011, when Littleswan sold its 40 percent stake in the joint venture to Bosch-Siemens.[19]

By 2011, Bosch-Siemens held 3.1 percent of the market share in China, the largest among Western home appliance brands. It has remained committed to creating a high-end, technology-driven brand image in the Chinese market. It appears that China is clearly a strategic market for the firm and that it is not hesitant to introduce state-of-the-art, global-standard technology on the products that it sells in China. It has invested heavily in local research and development as well.

Bosch-Siemens's success in the Chinese market might well be attributed to patience, consistency, and a long-term view that has frequently been absent in many other multinational entrants. A big part of the early success should also be attributed to its ability to identify talent, show trust, and retain those valued employees. Bosch-Siemens has demonstrated to others that a premium brand is possible even in China's cutthroat market environment. It appears as if choosing what not to do and whom not to serve has been as important for Bosch-Siemens as defining what it will do and for whom.

Japanese and Korean Brands

Japanese brands enjoyed considerable success and brand reputation in the 1980s, when they were able to exploit geographical and cultural proximity and move faster than other foreign household appliance manufacturers in entering the Chinese market. While their brand recognition remains generally high, nearly three decades later, Panasonic is now the only Japanese brand that still appears on the top ten market leaders list, with a 4 percent market share. Korean brands Samsung and LG entered the Chinese market relatively late, in the mid-1990s, at the same time as the Western brands did, and they were positioned as premium brands at the onset of the price wars that erupted in the late

1990s. But they were soon forced to lower their prices in order to meet the local competition and suffered brand erosion as a result.

China's Major Home Appliance Manufacturers

Starting in near obscurity and enjoying a sellers' market for the first decade of the reforms, the market for household appliances in China has grown consistently over the past decade or so and has also experienced two growth spurts during that period—one in 2002 and the other in 2009. The first demand peak was generated by the fierce price war precipitated by local players worried about the incursion of Western brands into their market following China's entry into the WTO. They fell back on low-price offerings as not only their best defense against the technical sophistication of the invaders but also the most appropriate offering for local economic conditions. This strategy seriously wounded many of the foreign competitors, and several of them withdrew. The second peak in market demand was stimulated by a government subsidy program for rural areas as a rescue package in the face of the gloomy economic aftermath of the 2008 global financial crisis. By 2011, China's market size for major household appliances had risen to 130 million units.

Despite a strong effort by nearly all of the big-brand global players to enter the market, China's domestic market has remained dominated by Chinese local players, with Haier the consistent market leader. One trend that has appeared in nearly every major segment of the Chinese home appliance market is increased consolidation within the industry, typically the result of domestic players getting stronger. In washing machines, this has meant that the two top players, both domestic, hold more than a 60 percent market share, and in air conditioners, the two top players in the Chinese market, both Chinese, together hold more than a 50 percent share. Similarly, refrigerators are also highly consolidated and Chinese as well (Haier alone has a 35 percent share).

Haier has strongly defended its home base against both foreign and domestic competitors while developing a globalization strategy. In 2010, it overtook Electrolux to become the world's second largest major home appliance company, with a global market share of 7.2 percent that grew to 9.2 percent in 2011. The company has been growing on average more than 25 percent per year over the past ten years, with an average profit margin of 4.37 percent. In 2010, refrigerators, washing machines, and air conditioners counted for, respectively, 38 percent, 19 percent, and 19 percent of Haier's total revenue, and 90 percent of the revenue is generated in the domestic market.[20]

In early 2009, Haier announced its strategic transformation from being exclusively a manufacturing company to becoming a *service-oriented* company. In the subsequent two years, it also acquired Japanese manufacturer Sanyo's white goods division and Fisher & Paykel Appliances of New Zealand. Carlyle Capital invested $194 million in August 2011 to support Haier's initiative to build a home appliance distribution network in rural China. Besides the service-orientation transformation, Haier has introduced two new brands to meet different consumer segments: a premium brand, Casarte, designed for high-end customers, and a low-end brand, Tongshuai, tailored to young consumers.

China's channels of distribution have also matured, to the point that they have become strategic options to be considered. In 2009, electrical and electronics retailers accounted for 55.2 percent of the Chinese market's total value, followed by department stores with 37.8 percent.[21] How to play in this new downstream environment is fast becoming a differentiator for appliance manufacturers, and such well-known retailers as Gome and Suning have already been rejected by several manufacturers, such as Gree and TCL, which have sought to build their own channels of distribution in order not to be controlled by these strong owners of their own branded retail channels. Gree has chosen to build its own channel, and Haier's transformation toward becoming a service company by building a rural distribution network also takes it in this direction. The one difference between the two is that, at the moment, Haier's choice is not to constrain its channel to selling only Haier products; it will also include the products of competitors.

The Global Major Home Appliance Industry

The home appliance industry is becoming more and more global. Whether it is Western brands or Chinese brands, the objective is the same: protect home markets and expand overseas. The emergence of strong BRIC competitors, especially Chinese, has added an extra level of complexity into the nature of the competition. In 1985, Electrolux, Whirlpool, and GE were the market leaders with 9.6 percent, 8.1 percent, and 4.8 percent global market shares, respectively. By 2012, the top five global companies ranked in terms of brand share by Euromonitor were Haier, LG, Whirlpool, Samsung, and Electrolux, holding, respectively, 8.6 percent, 5.5 percent, 4.2 percent, 3.8 percent, and 3.4 percent world market share. The top five companies' aggregated market share decreased from 30.1 percent in 1985 to 25.5 percent in 2012; among the top players are two Chinese manufacturers: Haier and GD Midea. The possibility that Chinese manufacturers will dominate the world home appliance market in the future is increasingly likely.

In 2010, China exported 85 percent, 45 percent, and 30 percent, respectively, of the world's air conditioners, refrigerators, and washing machines.[22] Although the numbers are big, China does not yet have a global home appliance brand that works across global markets. Haier is by far the leader in building such a brand but still has a way to go, especially in the world's most-developed markets.

The Essence of Success

The household appliances industry is both fast paced and full of surprises. Far from being a sleepy, mature, old-economy industry, what we have seen here is a drama of high suspense where, despite the familiarity of the products, there is still a strong commitment to innovation on the part of many of the competitors, as well as the almost continuous emergence of new competitors from emerging markets that combine their low-wage advantages with customer sensitivity to dominate markets that were once thought of as the future territories of the European and North American incumbents. Haier is one of these emerging challengers, and we can gain a sense of the challenges that it has had to overcome on its path to becoming a global player and that have also prepared it for competition on the global stage.

If we consider what it has taken to succeed in this industry, the lessons for the multinational market entrants that might be found in this chapter are these:

- The severity with which domestic producers, even though far less sophisticated, can resort to price competition to defend their markets
- The importance of understanding local consumers' needs as a means of escaping pure-price competition
- The need for a consistent brand strategy which typically requires good communications and coordination between the foreign headquarters and the local venture
- The desirability of collaborating efficiently with local value-chain partners when entering emerging markets

These conclusions were present in every example related about multinational players entering the Chinese market.

In addition, it is possible to argue that the home appliance industry is one of the least regulated in the Chinese economy and, as a result, has provided an unusual view of competition between several Chinese domestic champions and the multinational incumbents. Over the past thirty years, China has also witnessed the increasing opening up of former state-affiliated enterprises, including several home appliance champions availing themselves of private capital. As a result of such dynamics, the experience of Chinese home appliance companies as they successfully defend their home market may serve as a model for other Chinese players in other industries that aspire to be globally successful.

What we have also seen is support for the wisdom of following a growth trajectory that builds on existing knowledge. Western firms that abandoned existing competencies in the pursuit of a new market almost always met confusion and, ultimately, failure. Only Bosch-Siemens, which remained faithful to its existing business model on entering the new Chinese market, and GE, which spurned international expansion in order to protect its domestic market and build new competencies in the process, were successful.

Haier appears to have recognized the importance of customer-centricity at least two decades earlier than the majority of Chinese companies and has used the knowledge accumulated from understanding customers to become a more efficient innovator and manufacturer. This again supports the wisdom of building a future on the basis of past achievements rather than recklessly entering new markets or acquiring new competencies without being able to rely on a secure base in either familiar competencies or familiar markets, respectively.

The following chapters reveal how Haier has continued to plot its journey of self-transformation to become a consistently more ambitious customer-centric company, building on past achievements and the associated knowledge that it has gained along the way.

3

THE STORY OF HAIER AND THE EVOLUTION OF ITS CORPORATE CULTURE

Although many Chinese domestic appliance manufacturers have enjoyed competitive success in protecting, defending, and extending their domestic market, only a very few have proven themselves worthy of being regarded as global players. Haier is the leading candidate for such recognition, based on its success in competing in a difficult competitive market against some of the world's best firms and also because it has achieved this success by repeatedly rethinking its business model and then reinventing the organizational culture that it needs to deliver that model. In other words, Haier's competitive success is based on a thoughtful, strategic, and ultimately creative way of responding to changing needs within the marketplace. As a result, it provides a good illustration for appreciating what it takes to think about how to go to market and then identifying the managerial choices required to make such offerings successful. Its business model and supporting corporate culture serve as the blueprint for understanding how Haier has achieved all it has.

The function of a business model is to translate a firm's vision into a blueprint for how it will make money if the vision is achieved. Business models reflect the aspirations of the organization in the way the firm's offerings are described. What are we actually offering? Through what channels? To whom? Involving what sorts of resources and activities? At what cost? For what price? In what geographies? With which partners?[1] These elements of a business model are illustrated in figure 3.1 in what has been

Figure 3.1 The Business Model as Depicted in the Business Model Canvas

The Business Model Canvas

Key Partners

Key Activities

Key Resources

Value Propositions

Customer Relationships

Channels

Customer Segments

Cost Structure

Revenue Streams

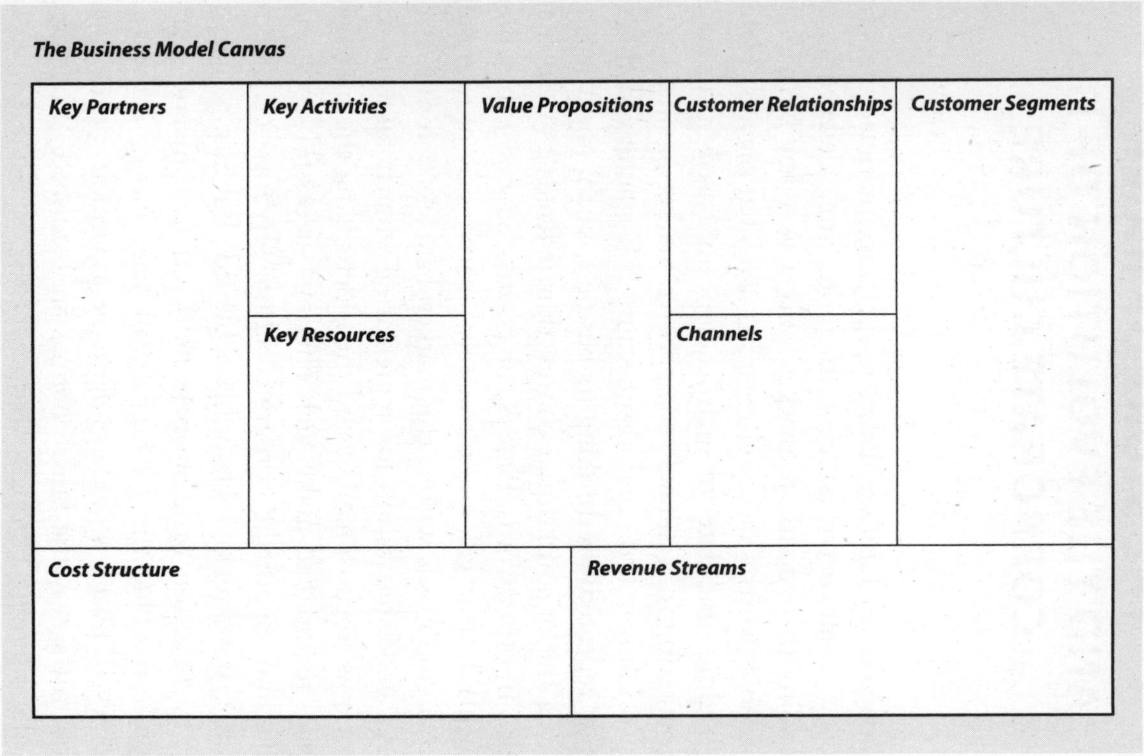

Source: Alexander Osterwalder and Yves Pigneur, *Business Model Generation: A Handbook for Visionaries, Game Changers, and Challengers* (New York: Wiley, 2010).

referred to as a *business model canvas*. Together, they cumulatively add up to the financial results that are to be expected from a particular business model. These specifics invite an awareness of all of the granular details that ultimately will determine the acceptance of the firm's offerings.

The creation of a corporate culture to support a business model is the outcome of the multitude of managerial choices the firm makes to achieve its business model and the relationships among these choices. The opening expectation for corporate culture analysis is that the vision of the firm will be appropriate to its competitive environment. This strategic fit plays an important role in any discussion of corporate strategy. However, it is often in the execution of such a vision that its success or failure is determined. This, then, is all about managerial choices made at the functional level. To the extent that these choices agree and reinforce one another, we speak of alignment, and it is the outcome of all of these choices put together that is the *corporate culture*. For Haier, with its many strategic changes, our approach will be to trace the evolution of its business model and corporate culture over time by examining the strategic vision it articulated and the specific managerial choices it made to support that vision.

The Origins of Haier's Business Model and Corporate Culture

There were virtually no modern household appliances available in China in the early 1980s and no domestic white goods industry to speak of. This is not to suggest that refrigerators, washing machines, and other home appliances were not produced in China at the time; rather, the industry did not behave as one that we would recognize in a market economy: it was fragmented, typically local and backward, owned and overseen by light-industry bureaus located within local governments. Furthermore, there was little *effective* demand for such products at the time; although Chinese consumers desired such appliances, they were scarce, expensive, and often of poor quality. All in all, the Chinese domestic home appliance industry was suspended in time between the state-planning days of the prereform era and complete uncertainty as to what would come next.

By 1984, a few home refrigerators were at last becoming available in major cities, and the demand for them overwhelmed the supply. This was a time when state-owned enterprises ruled the Chinese market and few, if any, foreign white goods were even thought about for the domestic market. At this time, any product sold, no matter what its condition. One of us remembers seeing battered and damaged refrigerators being unloaded on Shanghai's largest shopping street, Nanjing Lu, with customers crowding the sidewalks and being swept up into a buying frenzy, literally holding money up to catch the attention of the truck drivers and trying to buy the appliances before they even made it into the store, no matter what the condition of the machines.

Today it hardly seems possible to imagine that as recently as the 1980s, Chinese people were familiar with scarcity in nearly every area of their lives. Many necessities of life were sufficiently difficult to procure that they could be considered luxury goods, and the aspirations of most people focused on three big objects: a television, a refrigerator, and a washing machine, an indicator of a family's wealth and living standards. Just a decade before, these "big three objects" had been a bicycle, a watch, and a sewing machine.

Without effective competition, lacking a coherent national market, in an economy where scarcity was the norm, products tended to exhibit little differentiation in terms of price, design, or functions, due partly to the limited production and the absence of design capabilities, and partly to the widespread sharing of such information across factories by the ministry responsible for the firms that participated in that industry. Yet despite the apparent homogeneity of product offerings within an industry, there was still a form of brand differentiation based on popular perceptions of product quality, spread mainly through word-of-mouth and occasional media commentary. As a result, Chinese people became experts at relating certain brand names to good quality and were willing to pay a premium for such brands.

Qingdao General Refrigerator Factory

One of the emerging manufacturers of household appliances was the Qingdao General Refrigerator Factory, a relatively small, collectively owned producer of refrigerators. In 1984, a thirty-five-year-old vice manager of the Qingdao municipality's home appliance company, a local government bureau within the municipal government that oversaw home appliance activities for Qingdao, assumed the general manager's position at Qingdao Refrigerator. He was familiar with the company: he had been in charge of importing production line technology from overseas to improve competitiveness; the factory had lost RMB 1.47 million the previous year. This young man, Zhang Ruimin, had managed to buy production lines from the German company Liebherr in 1983, but implementing this new technology had been frustrated by the resignation of Qingdao Refrigerator's previous general manager, who had given up in the face of persistent management difficulties. Zhang was immediately given the assignment to search for a new leader, but was unsuccessful. Without an acceptable replacement, he took up the challenge himself; it was the only way to keep his promise to Liebherr and to ensure that the fruits of his purchasing efforts were actually realized.[2]

Zhang Ruimin was born in 1949. He had started working on the factory floor in a manufacturing plant and was quickly promoted to factory manager. He eventually became the vice manager of the municipality's home appliance company.

Zhang's initial business model for Qingdao Refrigerator was premised on the belief that the enterprise could differentiate itself by building a strong and valued brand based on good product quality, and he recognized that selling damaged refrigerators was not the right way to do this. In 1985, a disappointed customer returned a faulty refrigerator to the factory and showed it to Zhang. Zhang and the customer then went through his entire inventory of four hundred refrigerators looking for a replacement. In the process, he discovered a 20 percent unacceptable quality rate among his merchandise.[3]

Zhang's response to this level of poor quality was to instruct seventy-six incredulous employees to place seventy-six poor-quality refrigerators in the street outside the factory and publicly smash them to bits with large sledgehammers, despite the fact that they could have been sold at prices as high as if they were undamaged. So memorable was this event in popular memory that at least two generations of Haier employees and customers still speak about it, and it indelibly associates Haier's brand with a commitment to quality in the mind of nearly every Chinese consumer.

Zhang's business model idea, to be able to sell otherwise undifferentiated products at premium prices as a result of quality, was not only visionary for the time but also unthinkable to most stakeholders within the Chinese economy. It would be difficult to identify another enterprise leader at the time within the appliance industry who possessed a similar interest in brand building or consumer marketing, particularly based around superior quality. As long as there was supply in China, there was demand. China was a complete push market: what you made, you sold. Yet Zhang had lived through both the Great Leap Forward and the Cultural Revolution and was now facing an economic revolution that he believed was no less of an upheaval than these previous ones had been.

Despite having spent the entirety of his prior life in a planned economy, Zhang already recognized the importance of quality and brand and their interrelationship. In fact, in many other sectors there had long been well-known, high-quality brands, such as Feng Huang and Flying Pigeon bicycles, Hongqi cars, Hero writing instruments, Seagull cameras, and Shanghai brand watches. Each of these brands enjoyed a high reputation that was built solidly on good quality. But no Chinese person at the time could name a famous brand of refrigerators. Zhang was the visionary who wanted to build a strong brand of refrigerators.

The public smashing of the refrigerators was audacious and well publicized, and the action received considerable attention across China. It captured the interest of a public amazed at images of the smashed refrigerators, and it provoked controversy as well; many citizens wondered whether it was the right thing to do when refrigerators of any quality were so hard to find. But they all remembered the name of the factory: Qingdao. (The brand name Haier was created following the dissolution of the joint venture between Qingdao General Refrigerator Factory and German appliance maker Liebherr Group.)

Outsiders could hardly appreciate the long-term implications of the smashed refrigerators for Haier's brand. The picture of a worker with hammer in hand, about to smash the refrigerators, was prominently displayed in the Haier's headquarters museum in Qingdao, along with the hammer that was used, and it remains among the first things that employees proudly present to visitors even today. To some extent, it has become the physical manifestation of the spirit of Haier—a durable symbol that says, "This enterprise is different!"

Stage 1, 1984–1991: Brand Building Through Focusing on Quality and Manufacturing Excellence

While the smashing of the poor-quality refrigerators marked a highly symbolic beginning to the first phase of cultural transformation that Zhang had in mind for Qingdao Refrigerator Factory, it was not a business model. The business model that Zhang envisioned was Qingdao Refrigerator's growth being built on quality with the aim of establishing a well-known brand, and this required major cultural changes within the organization.

A Focus on Quality and Manufacturing Excellence

Early in his tenure as the managing director of Qingdao Refrigerator Factory, Zhang had placed quality improvement at the top of his agenda. Alarmed by the magnitude of the quality problem, he realized that something had to be done to change the mind-set of his workers. Ten years of Cultural Revolution mentality had left China with not only low productivity but also low worker motivation. Workers knew that harder work or better quality did not lead to more money for them, yet Zhang believed that good quality would be at the heart of his new business model, and in order to achieve it, he had to convince his employees that it was the responsibility of every worker. He proceeded to make quality a personal matter by his symbolic destruction of the faulty refrigerators, establishing a vivid and inspiring vision for the firm. He also established unambiguous rules of the cultural changes he expected, such as, "It is forbidden to steal materials from the factory," and he punished those who violated these rules in order to instill the necessary discipline among the workforce. This was all in the pursuit of a new quality mind-set at Qingdao Refrigerator and a new vision: build a strong brand through quality products.

Articulating the new vision was only the beginning. Aware of his lack of management knowledge, Zhang started reading the management theory literature extensively. By 1989, inspired by his reading of Japanese management successes, he introduced the practice of "overall, every, control, and clear" (OEC) at Haier. The goal of this process is to control "everything, everyone, and every day," so as to encourage employees to constantly challenge their previous performance and take accountability for their work. This approach requires that all working requirements be written down, and then employees' performance and the establishment of a relevant payroll base are made and evaluated with respect to these requirements. In order to establish such detailed evaluation on a daily basis, managers ensured that each task was attributed to a specific person, and if a mistake happened, that the responsible person could be identified.

OEC was applied to activities at the individual, division, and corporate levels. It consisted of monitoring two paper-based forms:

- The OEC form, which contained the detailed working requirements for a task, consisting of seven basic requirements: quality, technology, equipment, material, production plan, production property, and labor discipline
- The 3E (everyone, everything, and every day) card, which recorded employees' daily performance in a quantitative manner against the seven basic requirements on the OEC form

Not only were work processes changed; so were the associated measures and rewards. Workers filled out the 3E card at the end of each day under the supervision of their managers. The card was then given to the supervisor and the manager, and at the end of the month, wages were determined by the following formula:

Wages = Number of points [which consists of point value × quantity] + awards − penalties[4]

Different point values were attributed to different types of manual work and different products. Awards referred to recognition of exceptional contributions to the manufacturing process (e.g., an innovative way to save costs or a new idea for producing a component might earn a monetary award). If a mistake was made, a quantitative loss would be attributed as a penalty, and the worker would receive less payment as a result. This was done in a transparent way that provided workers with clarity and incentives. However, Haier's information system was inadequate, and the calculations had to be done manually, frustrating the timely delivery of results and rewards.

Despite such limitations, OEC was seen as an effective tool to promote higher quality. It improved Qingdao Refrigerator's precision management, control processes, incentive mechanisms, and employee performance. It also contributed to building its distinctive corporate culture, which was now seen as rewarding excellent work and eliminating nepotism and favoritism. The idea of self-management began with encouragement to challenge anything that reduced a worker's OEC scores and has continued to weave its way through Haier's evolution; it remains at the core of everything that Haier has developed in the effort to build a faster, better, more competitive organization. This is yet another example of how Haier has grown by building on the accretion of successful competencies as it moves into new initiatives and markets.

Not surprisingly, there were problems along the way. The frequent checking of performance on so many levels of hierarchy, for example, had high administrative costs. Zhang felt that such checking was necessary because Chinese workers needed to learn once again about discipline and rules that had been lost during the Cultural Revolution. In an effort to encourage innovation without incurring high costs, Qingdao Refrigerator adopted the custom of naming technical innovations after their innovators. In this way, even though OEC seemed to be harsh and workers knew that they could be punished for even minor errors, they also understood that they could be recognized for good ideas as well.

At about the same time, Qingdao Refrigerator also adopted the so-called 6S footprints. At the end of each day, underperforming workers were asked to stand on a pair of big footprints in front of a poster of six words starting with S—*seiri* (sort), *seiton* (organize), *seiso* (neat), *seiketsu* (clean), *shitsuke* (habits), and security—and to self-criticize their performance. 6S was an extension of a Japanese management practice that contained five S's to which Zhang added the sixth. It became an important part of the "daily work, daily clear" approach to management. Complementary to the positive incentives, standing on the 6S footprint and offering self-criticism was a negative incentive. This military-like practice has been quite controversial, especially when Haier later attempted to implement it in its South Carolina factory, but it served to symbolically emphasize Zhang's philosophy regarding personal responsibility for work performed.

In spite of this seemingly draconian approach to the reorganization of work, Zhang wanted to build his organization like a big family. The Qingdao Refrigerator culture was such that when an employee was sick, his colleagues visited him in the hospital. Illustrations like this were abundant and were promoted by Qingdao Refrigerator's corporate culture department, the corporate newspaper, and, ultimately, what would become Haier University, in order to create a family-like culture. Haier's culture department, in charge of both external and internal communication, has continued to play an important role in disseminating Haier's values about work and personal life. The corporate newspaper, *Haier Ren*, is a major tool for internal communication. It not only shares information about recent visits of important guests but also updates employees about the newest corporate strategy, and includes some poems, articles, and photos by employees on whatever topic they are interested in.

The New Business Model

We can portray Haier's first reinvention of its business model, (when it was still the Qingdao Refrigerator Company) by using the business model canvas in figure 3.2.

What we see there are the choices that Haier decided on to move beyond its prior business model toward a new model based on the value proposition of producing quality products in a marketplace where no one else was doing that. Not only did it change its value proposition to emphasize better quality but it also bet that improved quality would create a brand differentiation that would become an important competitive resource for the future. It believed this would allow it to appeal to a previously unrecognized segment of potential customers who were not only looking for quality but were willing to pay a premium for such quality. Customer loyalty would be about great product quality and a great brand, but this would likely result in additional administrative costs as new quality control factors were introduced into the factory and monitored and a new wage scale was applied. All in all, if the model were truly appropriate to the world that Haier was competing in, Zhang believed that the business model would result not only in Haier's competitive success but would also lead to satisfactory profits.

This new business model was challenging. It required identifying and satisfying a new customer segment with a new value proposition, and doing this through major internal managerial changes. The essential internal nature of Haier's stage 1 changes in figure 3.2 are not surprising because according to Zhang the mind-set of the organization's employees needed to be changed internally. It was also not surprising, given the fairly primitive state of the Chinese economy at the time, that aside from the preexisting technology transfer relationship with the German Liebherr Group, there were virtually no major changes to be made regarding other external partners, either upstream with suppliers or downstream with distributors.

Mapping the Cultural Changes

The choices identified in the preceding section represented the first steps in Qingdao Refrigerator's efforts to create a new business model of producing high-quality products that could be sold to discriminating customers at a premium price. It then became necessary to break out of a traditional, premarket Chinese enterprise functional structure, create competitive differentiation around great product quality, and build an organizational culture that would support and sustain that aspiration.

One of the attributes of a great business model strategy is that the choice of vision, as expressed by the value proposition,

Figure 3.2 Stage 1, 1984–1991: Brand Building Through Focusing on Quality and Manufacturing Excellence

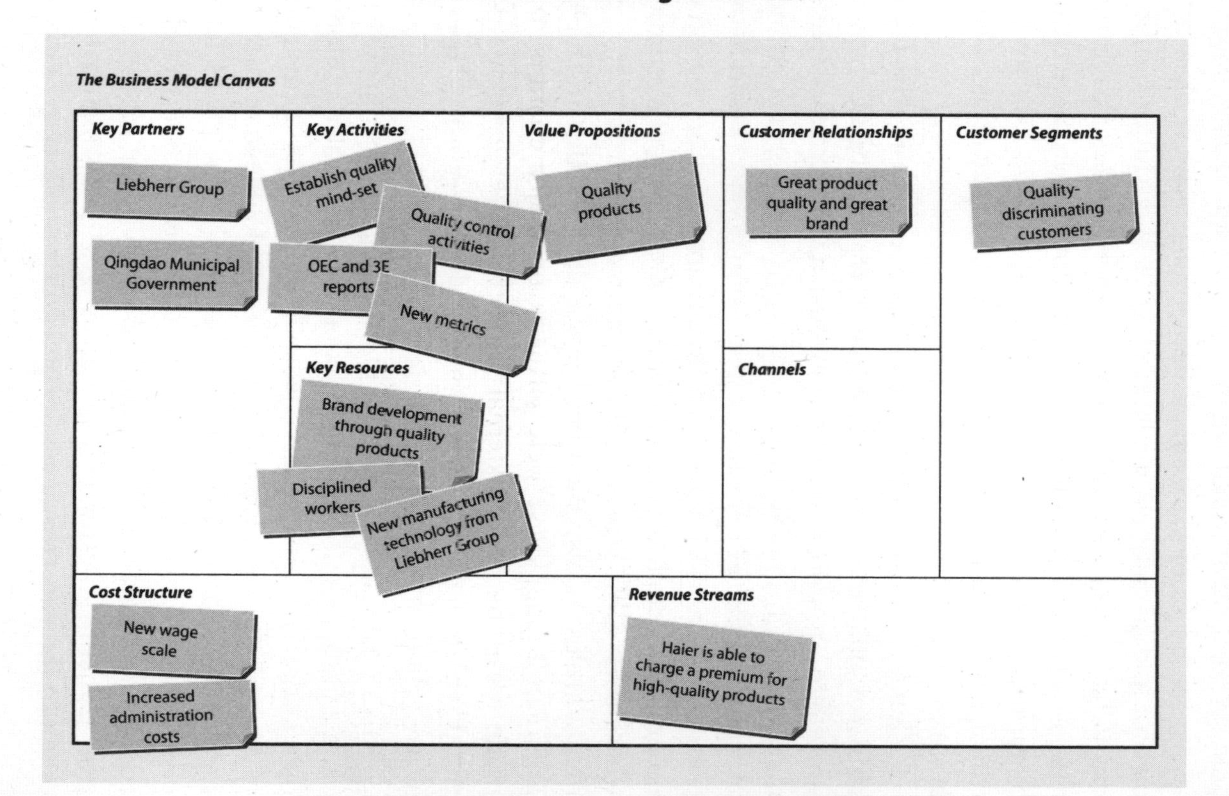

Note: The canvas is for illustration purposes. It is not meant to be comprehensive or exhaustive.

is appropriate to the competitive environment. We think this is true of the choice of employing great quality to build a brand reputation at a time when, industrywide, quality was poor and regarded as of no strategic importance. The second attribute of a great business model strategy is that the organization can actually execute on the choices made. In order to achieve this, Qingdao Refrigerator had to reinvent its corporate culture by making choices that supported the vision across all key functional domains and reinforced each of the other choices being made as well.

Zhang not only chose to symbolically emphasize the importance of quality as the differentiator for the brand but also started to introduce ideas for evaluating professional performance through improvements to the performance management process, linking individual compensation to performance, and creating the basis of a meritocratic culture based on the expectation that employees would fully enter into conversations where their OEC scores (and pay) were affected. Not only was he ambitious in his vision but he was also detailed in the way in which he employed both strong leadership and strong discipline, which he felt were necessary to ease the company into a world where market reactions would ultimately rule. This was all well thought out and well designed.

If an organization's culture can be thought of as the outcome of an ambitious and inspiring vision and the mutually reinforcing managerial choices that are made to support the achievement of that vision, then we can map the development of such cultural change using the five-factor star model that Jay Galbraith created to describe the choices available to managers to shape corporate culture. Galbraith has argued that any organization's management has essentially five areas that it can manipulate to establish the effective capability of the organization:[5]

- *Vision:* The more ambitious, vivid, precise, and inspiring the vision, the greater the probability of success (assuming that the vision is appropriate for the competitive situation of the firm in question)

- *Skills and talent:* The set of human talent necessary to achieve the vision (either chosen or inherited)
- *Organization:* The structure in which the talent is organized and the power relationships that characterize that structure
- *Processes:* The ways in which the organization works together
- *Measures, rewards, and values:* The belief system of the organization that not only defines what is of value but also measures and rewards it

According to Galbraith, the extent to which each of these choices supports the vision and to which they mutually reinforce one another determines the probability of whether the firm will achieve its vision.

In figure 3.3, which uses Galbraith's star, we see that Zhang began his quest to achieve his vision to build a strong brand through quality products by relying on the OEC process for improving quality. This required that employees be encouraged to challenge anything that resulted in a lower OEC score, and he supported this by tying OEC performance directly to pay using the 3E reports. By insisting that everyone in the organization take part in the OEC process, he tried to remove some of the hierarchical impediments to getting full employee engagement in the process improvement conversations. Nonetheless, Qingdao Refrigerator had inherited a top-down, hierarchical structure, and Zhang took advantage of this to convey a forceful, visionary leadership style that he felt was necessary to drive the sorts of momentous changes that he envisioned. He also desired to create a big-family environment, and so he established a department of corporate culture and gave awards for manufacturing innovation, including naming innovations after their

Figure 3.3 Stage 1: Brand Building Through Quality

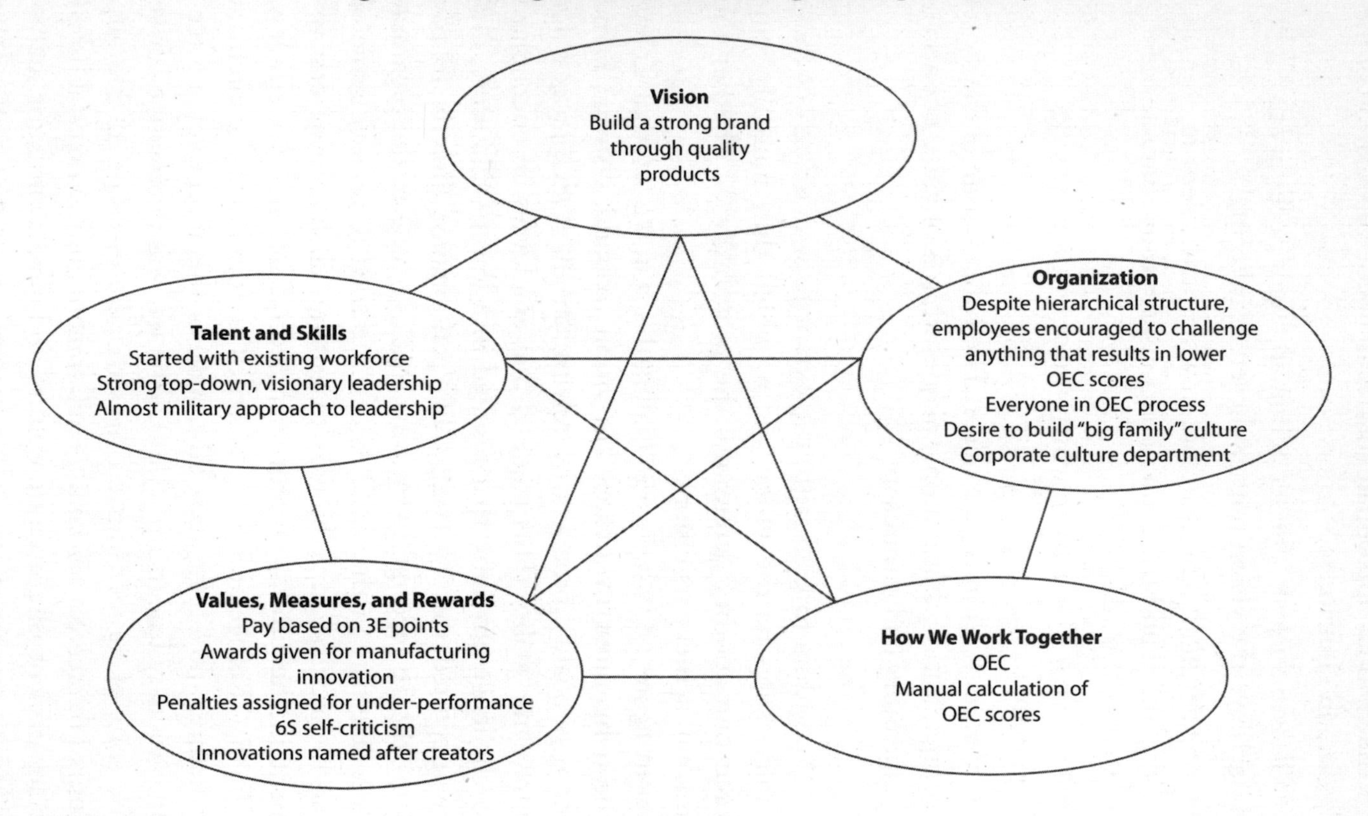

originators. All of this had effect seriously changing the culture at Qingdao Refrigerator into something in which a new business model that relied on higher product quality to build a strong customer brand actually had a chance of succeeding.

The model was not perfect. The Qingdao Refrigerator brand was relatively unknown outside of its refrigerator smashing notoriety, and it was provincial as well. In addition, the scale of the OEC and 3E processes overwhelmed the ability of the organization, which lacked computational capability to process such large amounts of data by hand. The organization was also starting with an inherited workforce, and many of the employees were not the types of workers Zhang dreamed of building the future around. Still, it was a start.

Zhang recognized that OEC and quality campaigns might be a start toward building a strong brand through quality products, but they could not be the end. Thanks to Zhang's prior efforts on behalf of the municipal government, Qingdao Refrigerator Factory had already begun importing production technology from the German household appliance maker Liebherr Group through a joint venture. This joint venture brought Haier many of the advanced refrigerator manufacturing skills that it needed to make better-quality products, and this quickly earned Qingdao Refrigerator the position of one of China's national refrigerator market leaders. Once again customers would be lining up in front of stores to buy Qingdao refrigerators. But this time, it was not merely because refrigerators were scarce; instead, it was because Qingdao Refrigerator's reputation was so much better than anyone else's in the industry.

Stage 2, 1991–1998: Diversification—Eating the Stunned Fish

Impressed by Qingdao Refrigerator's inspired performance based on its new business model and corporate culture, government officials at the provincial and national levels looked to Zhang

Ruimin and his colleagues to help turn other losing enterprises around. In this period, Zhang received numerous government requests to rescue many failing firms on the edge of bankruptcy—the so-called stunned fish—which he could not decline for risk of offending influential stakeholders. In China, it is important for companies to maintain good relationships with the local government, especially for a company like Haier with its origins as a collective company owned by the local municipality.

As a result, due to these requests, Qingdao Refrigerator acquired enterprises producing freezers, air conditioners, washing machines, irons, and televisions.[6] Although these acquisitions served to fill out Haier's product portfolio, many were poorly managed home appliance enterprises. Some municipalities even offered these needy organizations to Qingdao Refrigerator for free in exchange for a promise that the employees would be retained; this was hardly a bargain, but often a proposition that could not be refused.

Turning these dying firms around was not an easy task. Zhang's first reaction was to send experienced Qingdao Refrigerator managers to these firms to instruct them on improving their quality control. All too often, however, these visiting managers were perceived by the local workforce as outsiders and faced strong resistance. The result was that Zhang and his colleagues had to be tough in execution. For the first time, they realized how difficult it was to replicate their corporate culture in another firm. The attempted replication of Qingdao Refrigerator's star model in each of the stunned fish is illustrated in figure 3.4. What is not so obvious from the figure is how different each of these ailing organizations was and the efforts needed to turn them around. (There was no significant change in Haier's household appliance business model because of the stunned fish activities, and so we do not show a new business model canvas for this period.)

In 1991, in recognition that its product portfolio had moved well beyond refrigerators and that it needed to rebrand itself

Figure 3.4 Stage 2: Replicating the Star Model in "Stunned Fish"

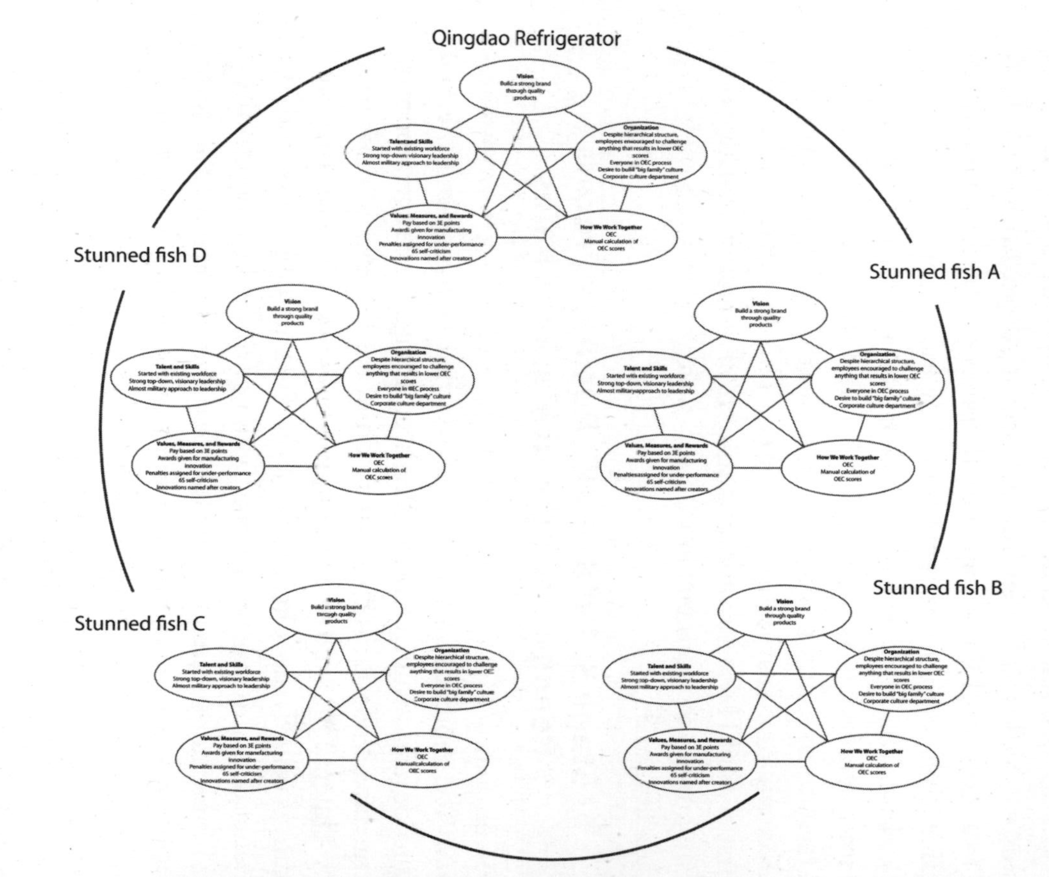

Note: Each smaller star figure is a replica of figure 3.3 for illustration purposes only.

in order to be a serious national, if not global, player, Qingdao Refrigerator officially renamed itself the Haier Corporation. The name reflected its German affiliation and was an effort to establish a more cosmopolitan edge to its corporate image. In 1992, this evolved into "Haier Group," and it adopted the brand logo of two young children, one blond and the other brunette, in an effort to broaden its market appeal beyond China.

By 2001, Haier's diversification had spilled out into unrelated fields such as finance, banks, and insurance companies. Haier took equity positions in Qingdao Commercial Bank and Changjiang Securities, for example. This was perceived as the first sign of Haier transforming itself from a manufacturing company into a service company.

Stage 3, 1998–2005: Business Process Reengineering and Market Chains

After completing its new acquisitions and in an effort to maintain the momentum for change that had characterized the first decade and a half of his leadership, Zhang turned his focus in the late 1990s to increasing internal management innovation at Haier. The catalyst for this initiative was China's entry into the World Trade Organization (WTO) in late 2001 and the belief that this was both a big challenge and a big opportunity if Chinese firms were prepared for what would come next in terms of increased competition. Clearly the competitive environment would change as a result of the WTO's intended liberalization of China's domestic markets, but it also opened up an opportunity for China to become a player on the global stage and have access to more resources globally. The immediate challenge for Chinese firms, however, was perceived to be the increased international competition in its domestic market.

Zhang was convinced that in order to survive, if not prosper, in the face of such an unprecedented competitive onslaught, Haier needed to move beyond being merely a manufacturing company into becoming a *customer-oriented organization*. This was both a big business model change and another ambitious cultural change as well. When Zhang thought about Haier, he recognized that there were many invisible walls between divisions and departments within the group, which could hamper it from meeting customer needs. Zhang believed that the best solution was to put everybody in direct contact with a market, so that all employees would understand the value of their services or products from the customer's point of view. This was the first step in a transformation of Haier's structure into an organization that increasingly used market-like mechanisms, but it was also a huge departure from the organizational culture that had been established around building a strong brand through quality products and would require yet another almost complete reinvention of the corporate culture.

Zhang's first step toward reinventing Haier's business model was inspired by his reading of Michael Porter's value chain idea and his belief that this could be taken into the organization through the creation of what would come to be called market chains.[7] Market chains in turn became the beginning of Haier's two-phase approach to business process reengineering (BPR), which would require yet another major cultural reinvention.

To Zhang, a well-running customer-oriented organization was really a value-adding process that could be portrayed as a market chain; in effect, he was recognizing the linkage that must ultimately occur among all of the value-adding activities that stretch from the customer to the back office. Every unit, every operation, and every employee could be linked directly to the customer in a market chain. At the same time, employees formed a chain of internal customers at each successive downstream activity as well. The design department, for example, is a customer of the environmental testing laboratory, product divisions are customers of the technical facilities department, and managers and employees are the customers of Haier University (for staff training). These internal transactions should work as in a marketplace. The two parties might even be encouraged to write a contract for the service or product provided and to reach agreement on specific items such as deadlines, specifications, and evaluation of service or product quality, including penalties in case of delay or poor quality.[8]

In order to support this market chain idea, Zhang's goal was to change the traditional pyramidal, hierarchical, and siloed structure of Haier into a project-based network structure so that the day-to-day workings of the organization would more closely represent the chained market interactions. He wanted to be able to start up projects when they were needed and be able to pull resources from the different divisions that had previously been isolated from customer-facing action. Unfortunately, the reality was that the existing organizational structure often made the progress of projects difficult because the project members' primary orientation was to their own division bosses rather than the project, thereby shifting allegiance away from the customer.

Matrix Structure

An initial effort to establish a direct market chain between customers and many Haier employees was unveiled in August 1999 when the organizational structure was completely redesigned into a matrix. Haier would now consist of four development divisions and six functional departments. The four divisions were closely related to the company's business development for all product lines: sales development, logistics development, finance development, and overseas development. The six departments were three development-supporting departments (R&D, human resources, and customer relationships) and three production-related supporting departments (total planning management, total quality management, and total equipment management). In addition, the factories were restructured into seven product divisions, each dedicated to manufacturing a specific product line: refrigerators, air conditioners, washing machines, information technology products, kitchens, baths, and electric, technology equipment, and direct affiliates such as communications, housing, and biological engineering.

The matrix structure facilitated the implementation of the market chain concept because each department or division now had much more freedom to provide services to other departments or divisions without going through their hierarchical superior as long as the two parties reached an agreement. This matrix structure remains at the heart of what has evolved into a form of self-organizing, essentially autonomous business teams, which have rearranged the former contractual relationship between divisions into a new market-based relationship among individuals. The goal has evolved into encouraging more internal competition that can forge a corporate culture based on internal reputation and performance. As in a real market, the more productive employees are and the more trustworthy they are, the more freedom they will have in setting up the contractual relationships with the people or divisions they want.[9]

Market Chains

Once the new organizational structure was in place, the second phase of business process reengineering (BPR) began in January 2001 with the idea of taking the market chains one step further.[10] Zhang's ambition was now to place not only divisions but also, ultimately, each employee into a market chain. He recognized that individuals are both receivers and providers of products or services and can be recognized as being their own profit center. Zhang's idea was to apply this logic to all departments at Haier, including managers and functional departments. Everyone at Haier was asked to fill out a strategic business unit (SBU) OEC form in Excel format daily. Using this form, employees were required to put in numbers that reflected their daily performance, such as sales and expenses. Their daily wages then appeared on the screen—in effect, creating their own individual profit-and-loss statement. Their performance could then be compared to their annual projected salary, which was also on the screen, so that the employee would know whether his or her performance exceeded or fell short of the expected salary.[11]

Putting such an abstract theory into practice was not an easy task because not every job's performance was easily quantifiable. Whereas an SBU might be a good organizational unit to track the performance of salespeople, it becomes much more difficult for departments such as the cultural center or human resources. By December 2010, Haier had established a management accounting research center at the University of International Business and Economics in Beijing in order to study and attempt to solve such problems.

The reliance on SBUs also faced resistance from some managers, who felt they were losing power because their employees were focused exclusively on their SBU OEC forms, which determined their take-home pay, and not on the leaders' objectives. As a result, the time that was being spent clarifying details was generating a lot of administrative costs. In an effort to reduce these costs, Zhang thought it was necessary to put a more powerful information system into place. The lack of timely and accessible performance information was frustrating the results that he had hoped for. Zhang thought that the lack of spontaneous communication also made sharing a common goal impossible because the divisions remained relatively isolated despite the matrix structure, each understanding the goals in a different way. He wanted a system that could link the whole company, from individual to division and from division to corporate, both top down and bottom up.

In an interview at the China Europe International Business School some years later, Zhang revealed that Haier had also implemented an enterprise resource planning (ERP) system in response to the need for processing massive amounts of performance data quickly, but, he said, it had been a failure. The reason, according to Zhang, was that the success of the ERP systems would have had to be based on the individual-goal combination (more details in chapter 4), which was absent in the system.[12] Without such data, the ERP investment could not work.

Haier's BPR efforts received considerable publicity outside the organization, as might be expected with such a bold and untraditional initiative. The reception was mixed. Many scholars and observers affirmed the theoretical benefits of individual SBUs, especially with respect to cost savings, and as the walls between departments were broken down, Haier's administrative costs were reduced, so customers truly benefited. In practice, the system also appeared to boost cooperation between factories and accelerated the standardization of certain components to save costs. The centralized finance department was able to leverage the financial resources of the entire company, which increased capital efficiency. And because every division and every individual had a market to serve, the concept of market chain became deeply rooted in the company's culture.

Between 1998 and 2002, Haier modified its company structure more than forty times in experimenting with improvements to the SBUs. The company needed time to learn from these mistakes and determine how they might work more effectively. For Zhang, an admitted believer in disruptive change, the initiative illustrated Haier's journey of self-improvement on the way to achieving the vision of becoming a totally customer-oriented company. For many managers, implementing these changes was difficult. The frequent strategic restructuring of the organization started to raise resistance and noncompliance among the employees, and managers began to question whether Haier's top management really knew what they were trying to do.

In addition, some skeptics in the public press doubted the wisdom and feasibility of Zhang's moves. The central question was whether the SBUs on both the department and individual levels were going to work. Operating the SBUs as autonomous market-seeking units was not cost free and could conceivably create higher administrative and transaction costs inside the organization: time costs, opportunity costs, and centralization costs, not to mention the strain that it had already created among employees. Zhang's belief in the initiative never wavered, however, and he continued to push BPR and the new strategic vision of customer orientation forward.

We have mapped the customer orientation business model (figure 3.5) and the associated managerial choices underlying the new Haier corporate culture established to support the customer orientation initiative in figure 3.6. What can be seen from these illustrations is that the business model changes that are represented by the new choices were still fundamentally inward looking, reflecting the centrality of the market chains and matrix structuring to this new business model, and the scale of managerial initiatives that were made to support this vision culturally; figure 3.6 is beyond anything seen in the first reinvention. It's also apparent from figure 3.5 that Haier was building on its previous business model reinvention choices rather than acting capriciously by making unconnected choices. The efforts required to create an internal market among the SBUs, which ultimately drove every SBU and individual to be market oriented, were both complex and demanding of resources, and it is not clear that they ever came together in a satisfactory and mutually supporting fashion at this point in time. Nonetheless, credit must be given for undertaking this immense effort because this upheaval created the launching pad for what came next.

In fact, the market chain theory, which integrates the consumer with individual roles deep within the organization, has come to be seen as a central part of the theme that consistently runs through Haier's evolution in its pursuit of getting ever closer to the customer.

Figure 3.5 Stage 3, 1998–2005: Business Process Reengineering and Market Chains

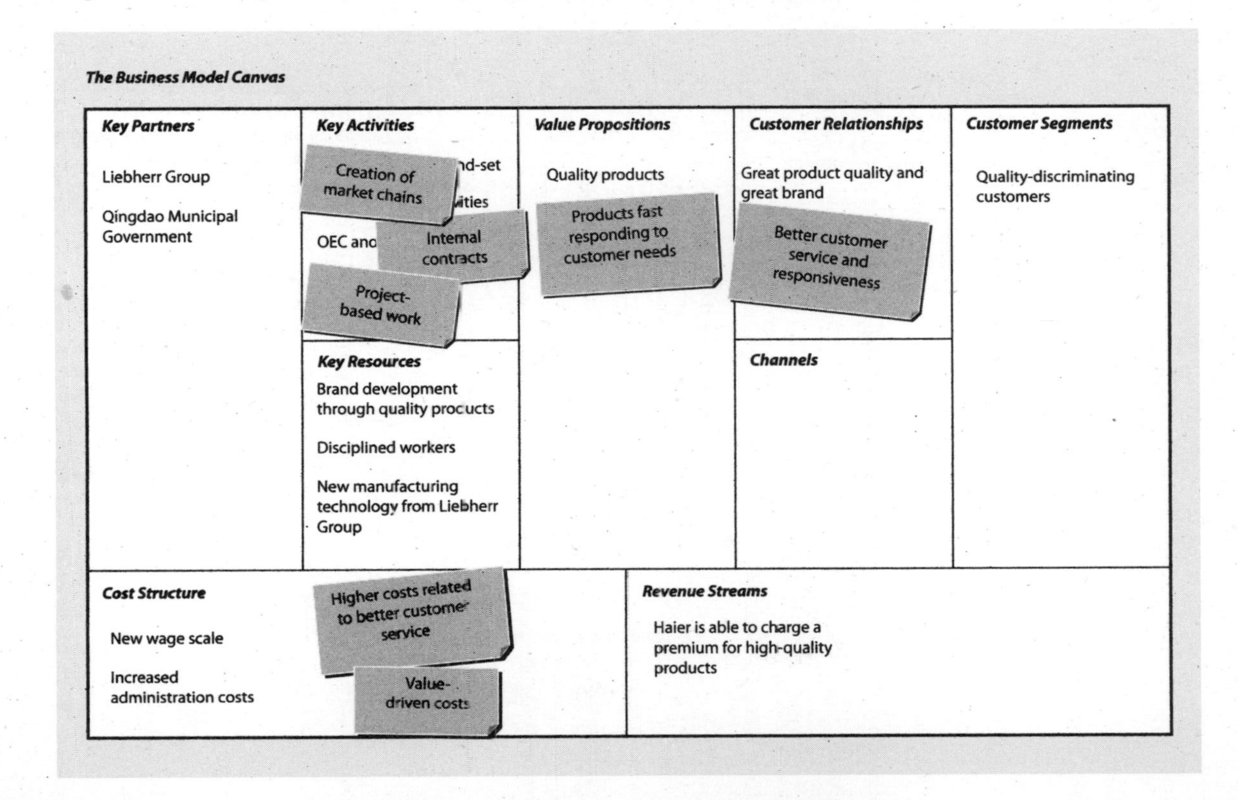

Note: The canvas is for illustration purposes. It is not meant to be comprehensive or exhaustive.

Figure 3.6 Stage 3: The Market Chain Era

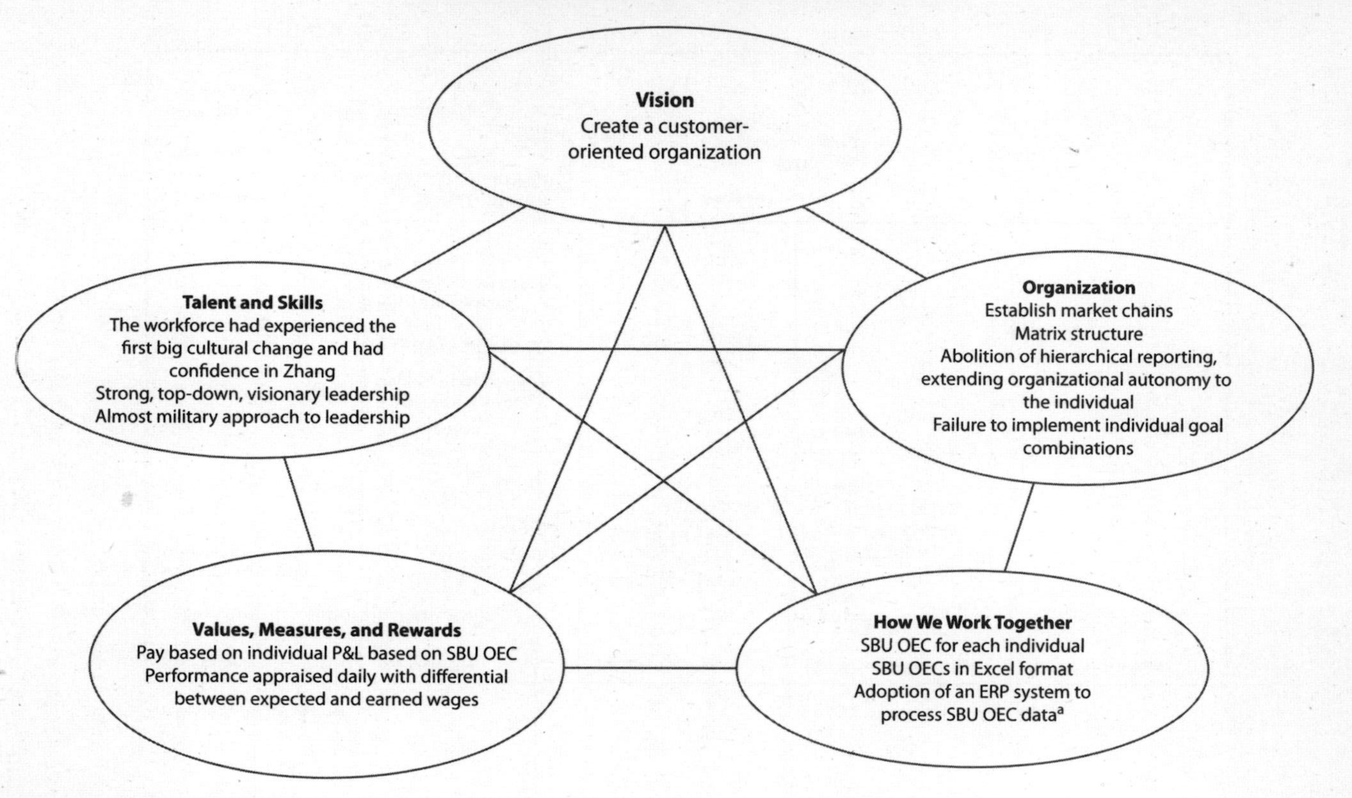

[a]The ERP system eventually failed.

Stage 4, 2005–2012: Zero Distance to the Customer—The ZZJYT

After the initial efforts to achieve a customer-oriented vision using market chains, Zhang decided that the next step was to invert the organizational chart, placing the customer at the top and creating autonomous business units inside the Haier organization that could act in whatever fashion necessary to best serve customer needs and, in the process, be better able to get the most out of the abundant talent that Haier employs. These autonomous business units are referred to as ZZJYTs (*Zi Zhu Jing Ying Ti*, literally translated as independent operation unit) and are the subject of much of what follows in this book. The ultimate aim was to link the customer directly to Haier's internal assets in an uncomplicated and natural fashion. To do this, Zhang believed that it was necessary to create a "pull" environment, with just-in-time production and delivery and with zero inventory. He also envisioned a company that was fully dedicated to customers, giving them both personalized products and services, all of which was encompassed under the metaphor of creating zero distance between Haier and its customers, in other words getting so close to the customers that Haier could anticipate their every need and desire. As Zhang said,

> Zero distance with customers is also referred to as "end-to-end" within Haier. On one end are Haier's customers and on the other end, Haier employees. If a customer has a need, we should have a very closely related mechanism within Haier to capture and satisfy this need straight away. For instance, customers in a village or in a community do not have the same needs. Haier employees integrate perfectly with customers by involving R&D people. In the past, R&D, manufacturing, and sales were all separate departments, each having their own agenda. Now, our salespeople put up a poster in R&D saying, "We don't design products, we design customers."

> In the past, R&D designed products; as long as the quality was good, the employee's job was fulfilled. Now, even if you design a good product, if it does not sell and create value for customers, your salary is affected. R&D, manufacturing, and sales have become a closely related team, which keeps close, inclusive relationships with customers.[13]

Haier was in transition from being a manufacturing company to a service company, which conceivably included a willingness to bond with the customers and sell services to them rather than products. Zhang said,

> In the past, selling an item was the end of the sales process. Now, selling an item is the beginning of the sales process. We want to bond with our customers. Now, we want all the products on the production lines in our factories to have customers, which means, even before the product leaves the factory, it already has a customer. We have a lot of information in our customer database. We hope we won't be selling products to them, rather, we will find their new needs and fulfill these needs. This is what we mean by selling solutions rather than products.[14]

Haier's vision of a customer orientation was illustrated by an inverted triangle concept in which the customer ruled from the top of the pyramid as the value receiver, the organization's assets existed to serve him or her (figure 3.7), and the "grassroots employees," in other words those on the front lines of customer engagement, were suddenly shifted from being on the lowest rung of the corporate ladder to being seen as being of utmost importance to the success of the firm.

Zhang believed that the way to operationalize this vision was to create independent functional units within Haier that would operate as small independent firms (within the boundaries of Haier) and have market relationships among themselves. These independent work units, the ZZJYTs, would be self-managed profit centers.

Figure 3.7 The Transformation to an Inverted Triangle Organization

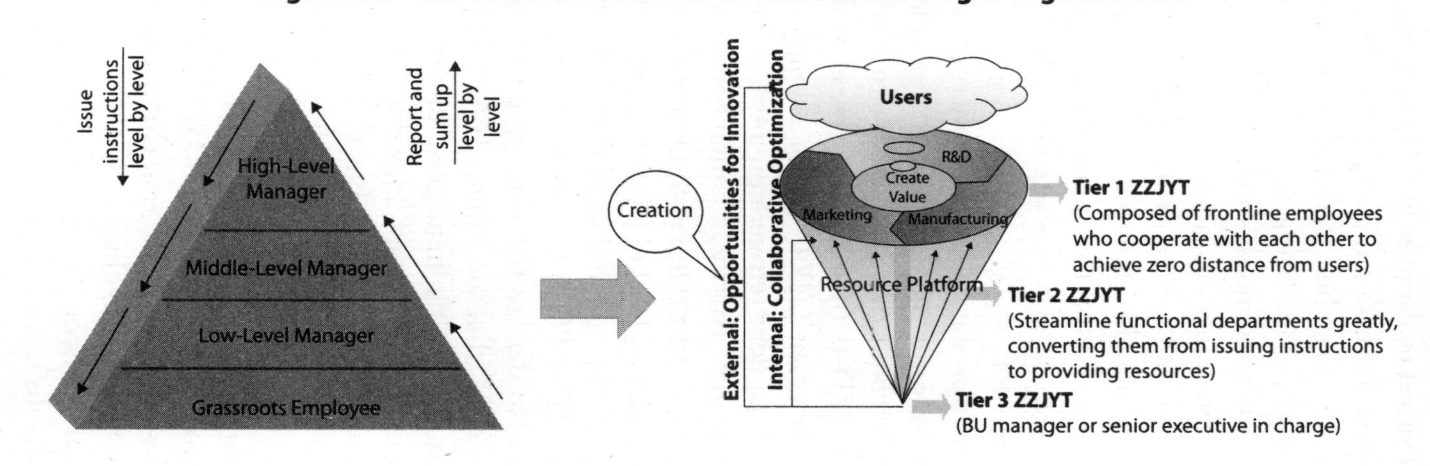

Source: Adapted from Haier internal documents.

They were the result of the evolution of SBU approaches that Haier had previously embarked on. ZZJYTs would not only have independent accounting, they would also have complete authority in matters of hiring and firing employees, setting rules about expenses, determining bonuses—and, in fact, almost any operational decision that could be made in an independent organization. A ZZJYT would not be an isolated functional or business SBU. Rather, it would be a virtual team (i.e., its offices are not necessarily physically together), composed of individuals from different functional and hierarchical levels, brought together for the same mission.

It was Zhang's belief that the demand for any type of activity at Haier should come from the market and pull a response from ZZJYTs along a market chain from the closest to the furthest from the market. The ZZJYTs that are the closest to the market are referred to as first-tier ZZJYTs. If, for example, there is market demand for a three-door refrigerator, a three-door refrigerator ZZJYT will be created. This ZZJYT then becomes responsible for all of Haier's three-door refrigerator activities: in charge of product design, research and development, budget planning, manufacturing planning, testing, product launch, and after-sales service—in short, from P0 to P6, as they were referred to within the Haier organization to denote the various levels back from the customer-facing ZZJYT that are required. Accordingly, the ZZJYTs have corporate planning managers, module development managers, and project managers. However, in a team of fewer than twenty people, it is impossible to have all of the knowledge that they may need. To obtain such specialized functional expertise, they turn to second-tier ZZJYTs, which are often organized by functional expertise. ZZJYTs on this level serve as consulting groups (resource providers) for the first-tier ZZJYTs, which are closest to the customers. (More details about how ZZJYTs work can be found in chapter 4.)

From the customer's perspective, Haier is a market-driven organization, responsive to customer pulls, while on the inside, it is a free labor market. It is indeed a labor market built so that personal reputations lead to a situation where, as one Haier manager told us, "Haier does not offer you a job. Haier offers you the opportunity to come to Haier and find a job." But, for the first time, we also can see that Haier's newest business model reflects both an internal and an external orientation, unlike the more internal approaches of its prior business models. With this new reinvention, Haier not only entered into new customer segments, using new brands, but also began to create new partnerships with its wholesaler partners in order to move Haier closer to its eventual consumers. Figure 3.8 shows the new business model elements on the canvas that address customer segments, channels, and partners, areas that had been essentially unchanged since the beginning of Qingdao Refrigerator's first steps at brand differentiation. Internally, there were many changes as well, reflecting the creation of the ZZJYTs and the establishment of market mechanisms across the organization. In fact, there is no cell on the business market canvas that has not been the subject of significant change as a result of this new business model reinvention. Moreover, it is also clear, once again, that Haier continued to make what appear to be radical jumps by building on prior choices rather than making new and unconnected ones.

The creation of an internal labor market within Haier recognized that every Haier employee was considered part of a companywide talent pool where individual reputation, based on skills as well as achievements, would define an employee's attractiveness, status, compensation, and career prospects. A new Haier employee in effect is entering a labor market where he or she may be employed (or fired) by a ZZJYT, which essentially becomes this person's actual employer. Each person's success or failure depends on his or her individual performance in this extremely energetic, motivating, and demanding work environment.

People who are entrepreneurial and results driven tend to find this an ideal platform to unleash their talent, which is precisely what Haier's new corporate culture is intended to achieve:

Figure 3.8 Stage 4, 2005–2012: Zero Distance to the Customer—The ZZJYT

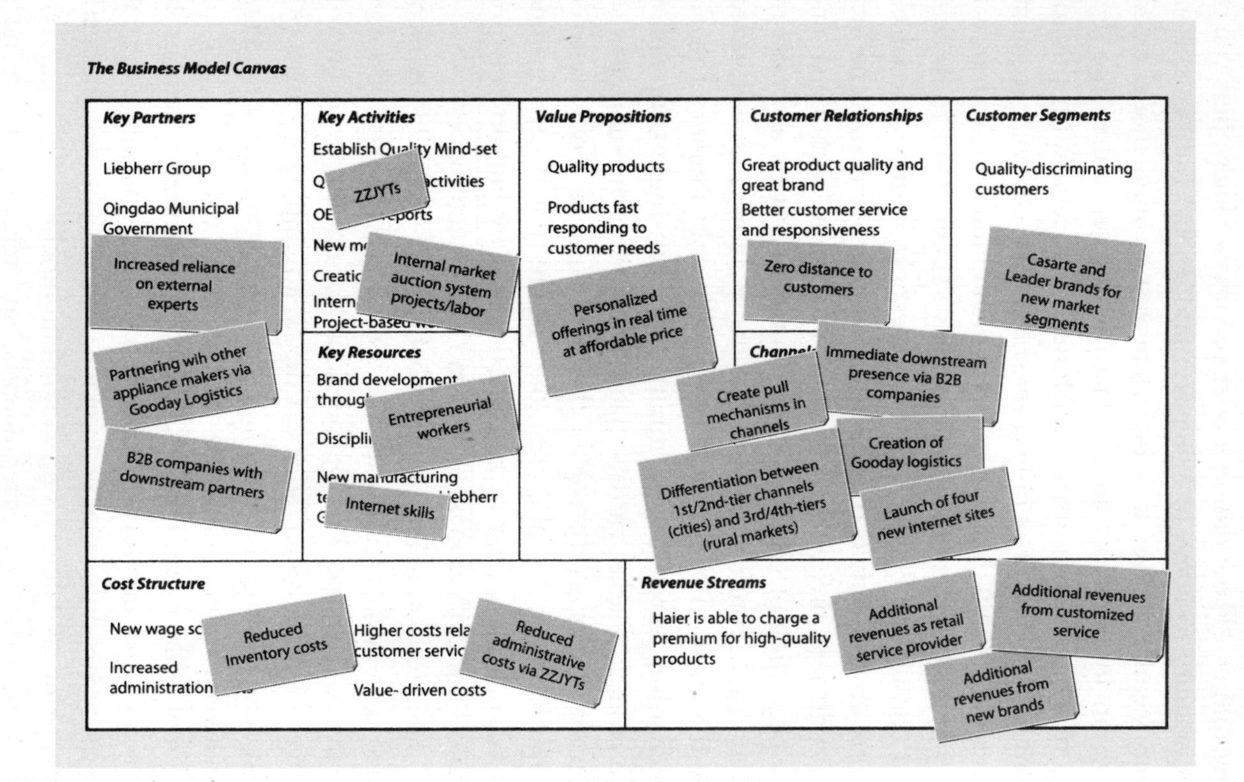

Note: The canvas is for illustration purposes. It is not meant to be comprehensive or exhaustive.

a platform for talent that creates value for both customers and employees. This reflects Zhang's long-held belief that "China is strongly influenced by Confucianism, which gives strong importance to family, but also to personal achievements."[15] As a result, he believed that linking an individual's compensation to performance was the best mechanism for managing the productivity of Chinese workers. Although Zhang has been an avid follower of Western and Japanese managerial thought, he has always believed that borrowing from foreign managerial theory without adapting these thoughts to Chinese culture leads to failure. As a result, the ZZJYTs employ a more Confucian approach to performance measurement and reward.

In addition, it was believed that the emergence of widespread Internet connectivity and increasingly sophisticated information systems would lead to more instantaneous communications both inside and outside Haier and that, as a result, it would be possible to forge the ZZJYT model to finally achieve Haier's goal of zero distance to the customer by leveraging all the other aspects of the star model (figure 3.9). What figure 3.9 reveals is that the new business model launched at this time (figure 3.8) requires, if it is to succeed, a broad-ranging set of bold managerial initiatives regarding how the work is performed, measured, and rewarded within Haier as well as changes in the nature of the workers that will be required to take the organization into this next stage of its development.

Thirty Years of Reinventing Haier Culture

What we have seen in this chapter is a relentless effort to reinvent both the business model and the culture of the Haier organization so as to be better prepared to address the ever-changing competitive requirements of a fast-moving business environment. Whether it is improving quality, creating a customer-oriented organization, or creating zero distance to customers, there should be little doubt that Haier has steadfastly sought to embrace

Figure 3.9 Stage 4: Zero Distance to the Customer—The ZZJYT

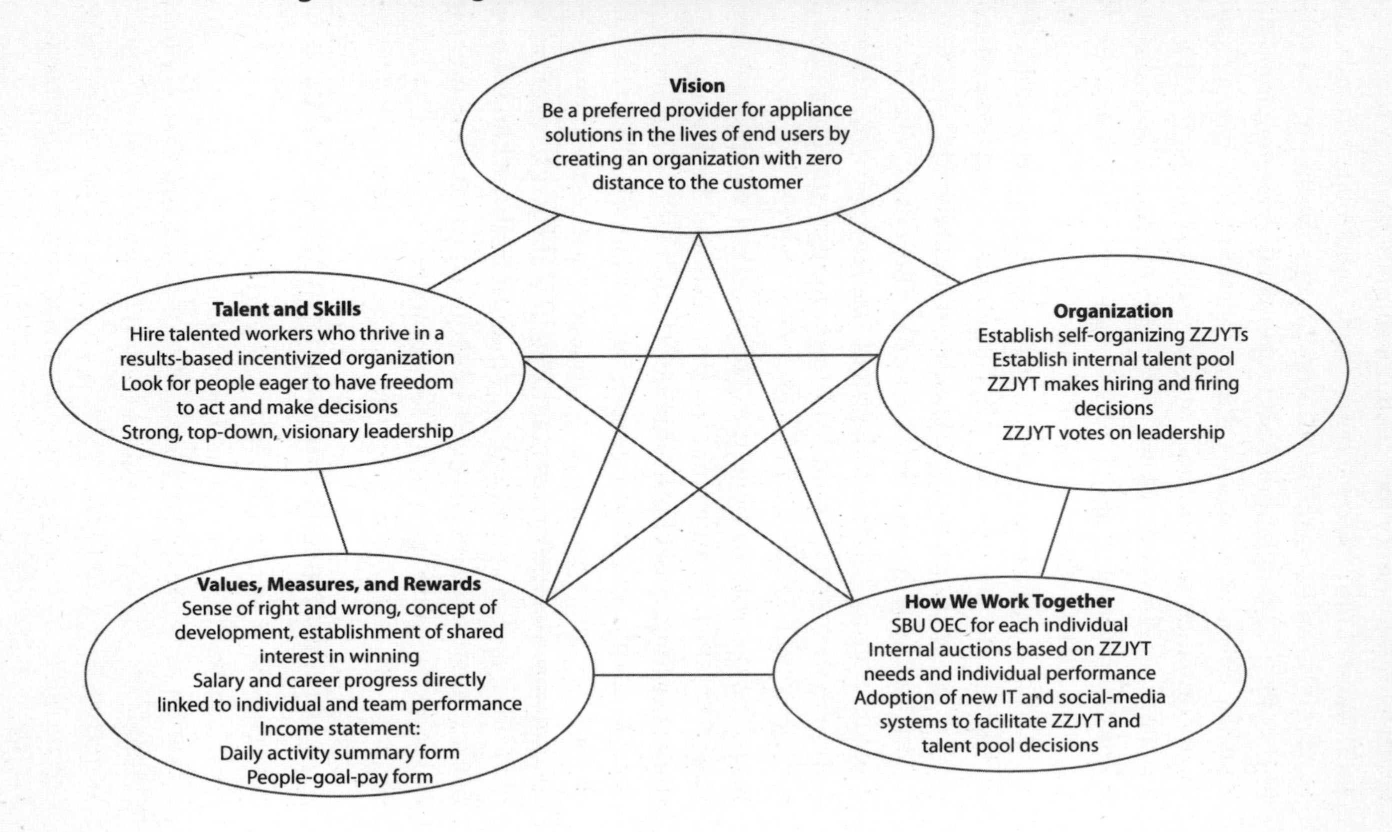

strategic visions that have been appropriate to the world around it. In addition, it has also made some big, ambitious, and challenging internal managerial choices in order to support its evolving strategic vision. Both observations are hallmarks of sound strategic management. Despite all of these changes, however, the continuous reinvention of its corporate culture has been at the root of Haier's success and achievements and has reflected Zhang Ruimin's belief that

> the soul of the growth of an enterprise lies in its culture, and at the heart of the enterprise's culture are its values. Haier's enterprise culture can be viewed as having three layers. On the outside is the material culture; seen as the company's growth speed, its products and services. Further inside is Haier's management system. At the core are the Haier values, the spiritual culture, so to speak. Most visitors to Haier [are] interested in Haier's management system, which was what they wanted to take away from here. Actually, it is the values that are more important. What kind of values a company has dictates the kind of system culture and management it has, which in turn decides its material culture.[16]

Haier's values are rooted in both Chinese and Western cultures—in the Confucian philosophy and market economy. They embrace seemingly contradictory concepts of community and individual performance, of strong leadership and the reduction of hierarchy. There can be no question that they are ambitious. Whether they can be deployed in a large, complex organization is the question that we turn to in the following chapters.

4

LIBERATING TALENT

Tapping the Entrepreneurial Spirit

Changing a corporate culture can be a fear-inspiring, enervating, and exhausting experience, and all too often it turns out badly. One only has to consider the trials and tribulations that have so recently characterized the efforts by Sony, Nokia, Yahoo!, Research in Motion, and Kodak to reinvent themselves to recognize how difficult it is to accomplish such a do-over successfully. It is not for the faint-hearted. Yet Haier has been in the midst of big cultural changes for nearly three decades. If Sam Palmisano's comments, quoted in the opening chapter, suggesting that "organizational culture thrives only to the extent that it is open to being re-created," are to be regarded seriously, Haier must be one of the most vital companies on the planet, and there must be management lessons for the rest of us from this experience.[1] We believe that Palmisano is right: organizational change is a constant, and Haier is in fact a study in organizational rejuvenation. In addition, it is clear that the first of the lessons to be taken from the Haier experience is that it is not change for its own sake that is to be pursued, but rather change in the pursuit of an overriding vision of what talent can achieve, what work can become in such a context, and what the role of employee participation is in that mission.

Since the beginning of his tenure as general manager of the Qingdao Refrigerator Company, Zhang Ruimin has consistently and relentlessly pursued his ambition of achieving greater customer satisfaction by unleashing the latent talent in Haier's employee pool. He has done this by successively redefining the definitions of how work is performed, how roles are assigned, how performance is measured and rewarded, and how leadership is expressed within the organization. In every one of Haier's reincarnations, these definitions have been reconsidered and redefined, and always in the service of directing employee talent to the pursuit of greater customer service.

We believe that if we distill the lessons from Haier as it moves through its cultural reinventions, there are six key themes that constitute the visionary engine that have been guiding its changes:

- *Haier thinks of itself as a service company*. Haier may manufacture household appliances, but it no longer thinks of itself as a manufacturing company. Manufacturing is a means of providing services to a customer, but it is merely one of a series of means that need to be mastered and coordinated in order that the ultimate ambition, providing outstanding customer service, can be achieved.
- *Service is best achieved if there is zero distance between Haier and its customers*. Distance of any sort—geographical, cultural, or temporal—works to frustrate the complete and timely achievement of customer satisfaction. In commodity markets, where everyone can produce the same thing at ever lower prices (and margins), customer satisfaction becomes the ultimate differentiator. Haier thinks of this as service and has worked relentlessly to anything that frustrates the achievement of its objective of zero distance to the customer.
- *The entrepreneurial energies of its own workforce are Haier's best means of achieving the service goals that it has set for itself*. Zero distance can be achieved only if the organization is in close enough touch with the customer and responds almost perfectly to customer desires. This in turn requires employees who feel empowered enough to act quickly and self-confidently in order to reduce the response time to zero. Such behavior calls for

entrepreneurs, not functionaries, yet entrepreneurship is not a familiar attribute of industrial organizations competing in commodity markets, especially when they have grown out of what were once centrally planned economies. As a result, leadership is required to take bold cultural initiatives in order to create an organizational environment that is hospitable to unleashing entrepreneurial energies. Haier's decision to adopt self-organizing, autonomous work teams as the basic organizational building block reflects the boldness that Zhang has resorted to in an effort to create a responsive and innovative culture within what could otherwise be a traditional commodity manufacturer.

- *Freedom requires control*. Fast response requires fast information, and fast information suggests the capacity for fast control. Attention to costs and delivery schedules are a critical part of customer expectations. Freedom and control, in the form of information signaling the appropriateness of entrepreneurial directions and the ability to quickly take corrective action, are essential and complement each other. In addition, Zhang has always harbored concerns over the loss of discipline that accompanied China's Cultural Revolution and the scars that it may have left on the popular mind-set with respect to a work ethic. As a result, Zhang sees a complementarity between greater entrepreneurial freedom for employees and greater accountability through better and faster control systems. A prior book by one of us, a study of exceptional team performance, concluded that optimal innovation occurs at the moment when team members believe that they have absolute freedom to contribute their talents and management believe that it is in complete control—both at the same time,[2] which is exactly what Haier is determined to accomplish.

- *Responsiveness can be facilitated by preestablished (Haier refers to them as* presets*) conversations and agreements*. One way of achieving speed in customer responsiveness without sacrificing control is through the development and use of preestablished conventions regarding targets and rewards. This means that promises and commitments are assumed to be fulfilled and that actions take place on that basis so that there is no slowing down to negotiate these once they are established. It's a faster way of working when you are only negotiating the variances rather than the entire set of targets. Haier, after all, is a company of eighty thousand people and there are no fixed salaries in the traditional sense. Each individual is budgeted by their ZZJYT for an annual salary (including a modest guaranteed municipal minimum wage plus expected bonuses, etc.), which for payment purposes is amortized over twelve months. This "salary" is not fixed but variable in the sense that it can be raised or lowered as the results are received over the course of the year and compared to the amounts that were preestablished (presets). This is true for everybody in the organization. For most individuals, there is little real difference between this situation and what would be the case with a traditional fixed salary because the preset estimates are reasonably close to what actually happens. But for some the variability can be keenly felt, up and down. Despite this, there is no high anxiety regarding compensation. This could not be achieved if it were not for preestablished expectations of outcomes and then an eventual settling of the variances associated with those outcomes. In much the same manner that a jazz combo can improvise to meet the moment on the basis of relying on a body of standard conventions, Haier can innovate faster on the basis of such preset understandings.

- *Value creation should be linked among customers, the organization, and the employees.* At Haier, the ultimate engine driving employees' efforts to satisfy customers is vested in the value created for all. Greater customer satisfaction should pay off for Haier and for the Haier employees who created this value as well. This is the ultimate market linkage and should serve as the basis for performance measurement and reward.

Each of these six themes is a critical part in the reinvention of Haier's corporate culture. We saw glimpses of each of them in chapter 3 as we traced the evolution of this cultural reinvention, but we have articulated them only in passing. In fact, we're not even sure how well articulated they have been within Haier, but it is clear that they have been consistent building blocks of Haier's culture for most of the thirty years addressed in chapter 3 and continue to be essential to the creation of the new Haier described in chapter 5. For that reason, we thoroughly examine them in this chapter.

Theme: Haier Thinks of Itself as a Service Company

Ironically, for a company whose defining brand image remains that of a vivid dedication to improving product quality (the smashing of the defective refrigerators in the 1980s), Haier now thinks of itself as a service company, with manufacturing merely one of the competencies that it needs to orchestrate in the pursuit of customer satisfaction. In much the same way that Apple has never thought of itself as merely a phone or computer device manufacturer, but rather the redesigner of customer experiences, Haier has steadfastly attempted to get so close to its customers that it can anticipate their needs, meet their expectations, and cocreate solutions with them. This is no longer (and in fact has probably never been) about low-cost manufacturing of commodity products. Rather, it is about defining success by the results of outstanding customer experience.

We saw glimpses of the service orientation mentality at Haier in the early 2000s, when it embarked on the concept of market chains, linking customers directly to each employee within the organization. The cathartic event, however, may well have been the 2010 decision to turn the corporate pyramid upside down in an inverted triangle and put the customer at the top. This is not a new concept. Many companies have depicted their relationship with their customers in a similar fashion. What distinguishes Haier from so many of these others is that its leaders took this seriously and were determined that this was more than simply corporate graphics; it was a profound shift in the way they thought of the organization relative to the marketplace: everything now depends on the customer, and everything—the organizational structure of the company, the skills of employees, the role of managers, and the way that they work together—is ultimately determined by customers. Being customer-centric is no longer only about products; it is also about how life is conducted in every aspect of the company's activities.

Service then becomes defined as the ability to achieve customer satisfaction, which is more than simply manufacturing and selling a product; in fact, there is a recognition that value can be created anywhere along the market chain—for example, in design, in a better retail experience, or in different business models. The organizational evolution of such recognition within Haier is quite revealing. Originally Qingdao Refrigerator essentially had a single focus: manufacturing. As Haier evolved and developed a reputation for listening better to the customer, it was often technical people who were doing the listening, which had the effect of making the manufacturing unit become customer facing (manufacturing ZZJYT in figure 4.1).[3] With the development of market chains, Haier began to expand its domain along its value chain and created a retail business (market ZZJYT in the figure) to complement its manufacturing business. This, then, was a second customer-facing unit, but in order to truly respond in a timely fashion, Haier needed yet another organizational unit, this one responsible for each product offered (module ZZJYT) and customer-facing in order to better understand customer desires (see table 4.1).

The module unit bridges the distance between manufacturing and retailing, and out of this, the "module" ZZJYT (the bridging organizational unit) was born. Haier now had three different customer-facing experiences taking place: distribution, manufacturing, and the unit responsible for each particular product, making the organization much more customer sensitive

Figure 4.1 Three Tiers and Three Types of ZZJYTs in the Inverted Triangle (BU Level)

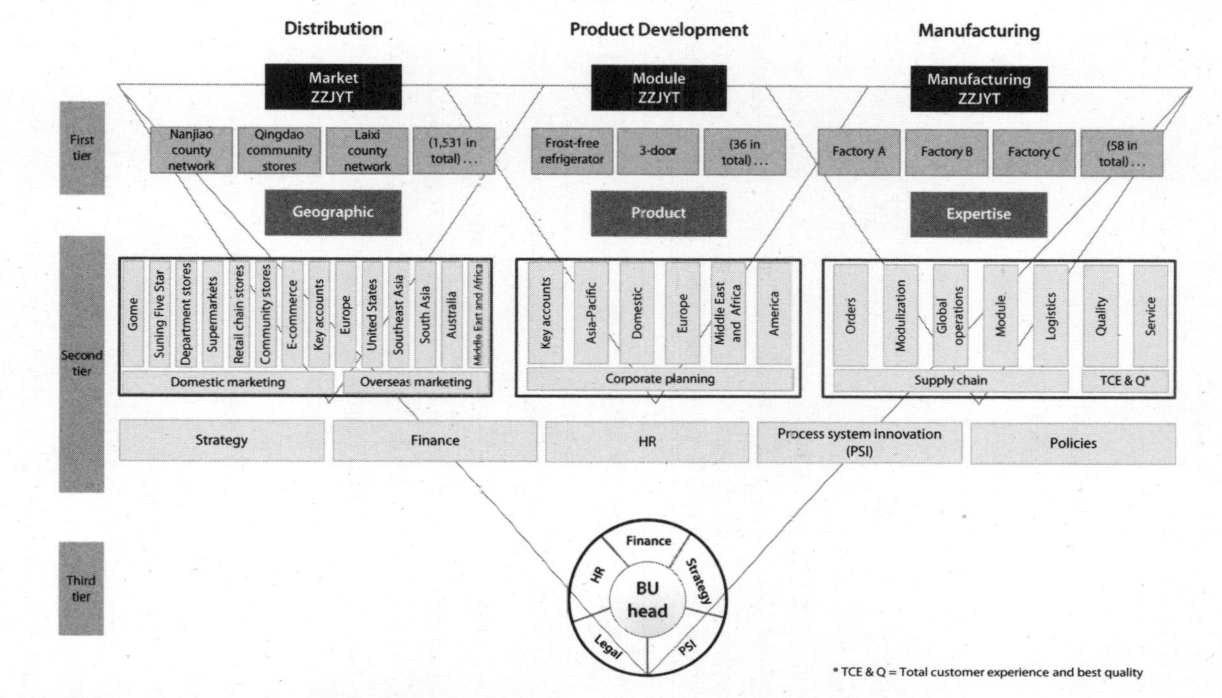

Source: Adapted from Haier company documents.

Table 4.1 Placement and Responsibilities of ZZJYTs in Haier's New Business Model

Three Tiers of ZZJYT (Distance from the Customer)	*Responsibilities of ZZJYTs at Each Tier*		
First tier (directly customer facing)	*Market ZZJYT*	*Module ZZJYT*	*Manufacturing ZZJYT*
	In charge of the regional sales of Haier products	In charge of the coordination of design, development, manufacturing, and marketing of new product modules	In charge of the manufacturing mandate for factory-floor production
	Tier 1 is the customer-facing edge of all operations and these ZZJYTs are at zero distance with end users.		
Second tier (one level back from the customer)	Tier 2 provides resources to tier 1, and because every tier 2 has contacts with many tier 1s, they also have the role of facilitating best-practice sharing and replication among the tier 1 ZZJYTs.		
Third tier (two levels back from the customer)	Tier 3 sets strategic direction of the company.		

than it might have been when almost anyone could think that "somebody else" had the direct customer responsibility. Module ZZJYTs are structured like independent companies whose task is to develop and sell a product or a family of products and improve the quality of these products and services provided to customers. Manufacturing ZZJYTs are the units that manufacture the products and have the purpose of lowering production costs and improving production processes and eventually provide the required service to module ZZJYTs. These activities became the base of the organizational pyramid (the long part). Now, however, the long part was the closest to the customer, not the furthest away. Suddenly the customer was on everyone's mind.

The way that this worked in practice was that in 2010, Haier created autonomous work units within the sales department

Table 4.2 Number of ZZJYTs at Haier in Each Category, April 2012

	Market ZZJYTs	Module ZZJYTs	Manufacturing ZZJYTs
First tier	1,835	78	107
Second tier	119 (including 31 first-tier functional units [support functions that provide expertise and guidance to the frontline ZZJYTs])		
Third tier	6		
Total	2,145 (excluding Haier Real Estate Group, investment, development, and so forth)		

Source: Haier company data.

only, organized on a regional basis and divided among markets in the different tiers of cities. (China is typically described by the various tiers of city sizes: Shanghai is tier 1, for example, and Dalian is a tier-2 city.[4]) Organizationally, these autonomous units were linked in a matrix structure where vertical business units interacted with horizontal functional departments that gave support to the what was at one point four thousand ZZJYTs, and has now been reduced to 2,145 (at the time of this writing). (See table 4.2.)

The original matrix structure has been reframed into a three-tier structure, depending on proximity to consumers: the first tier is the closest to consumers, the second tier provides resources for the first tier, and the third tier creates opportunities for development and strategic planning. The first-tier ZZJYTs are composed of frontline employees who implement zero distance from end users by interacting directly with the customers, capturing the market information and coordinating product design, sales and marketing, and production; the second tier has the task of streamlining the original functional departments, providing expertise and technical advice to first-tier ZZJYTs and the resources they need; the third tier defines strategies and looks for market opportunities and sets the strategic orientation of the company. All of this has the effect of linking every activity and every employee directly to the customer. The idea of a service orientation is now tangible to every employee at Haier.

Theme: Service Is Best Achieved with Zero Distance Between Haier and Its Customers

Great customer service is a mix of customer insight, anticipation of customer desires, and fast (and often innovative) responses to customer needs. Anything that gets in the way of complete communication with the customer or slows a response to customer needs diminishes the quality and effectiveness of customer service. If you define yourself as a service company, these disconnects threaten the very core of your self-image.

Somewhere around 2000, Haier's leaders realized that if they could use Michael Porter's concept of the value chain and build a market chain inside of Haier that linked every employee with the end customer, then they could harness the power of pull to increase the company's responsiveness to customer desires. Somewhat like the Japanese concept of just-in-time organization of physical flows, Haier's market chains went beyond a single focus on physical linkages and embraced all of the responsibilities and capabilities that the organization could bring to bear on serving the customer. It became an organizing principle in its own right. In this way, the functional centers of expertise, such as human resources and finance, could be directly linked to the customer-facing units to supply whatever expertise was needed whenever it was needed to satisfy customer needs.

In figure 4.2, the horizontal and vertical axes of the inverted triangle stand for different orientations: the horizontal axis (market, module, and manufacturing ZZJYTs) represents a focusing on the customer, and the vertical axis stands for efficiency (cost reduction, improvement of products and processes). As a result, we could say that the horizontal axis focuses on effectiveness (giving consumers what they want), whereas the vertical one

Figure 4.2 Haier's Business Model and the Inverted Triangle

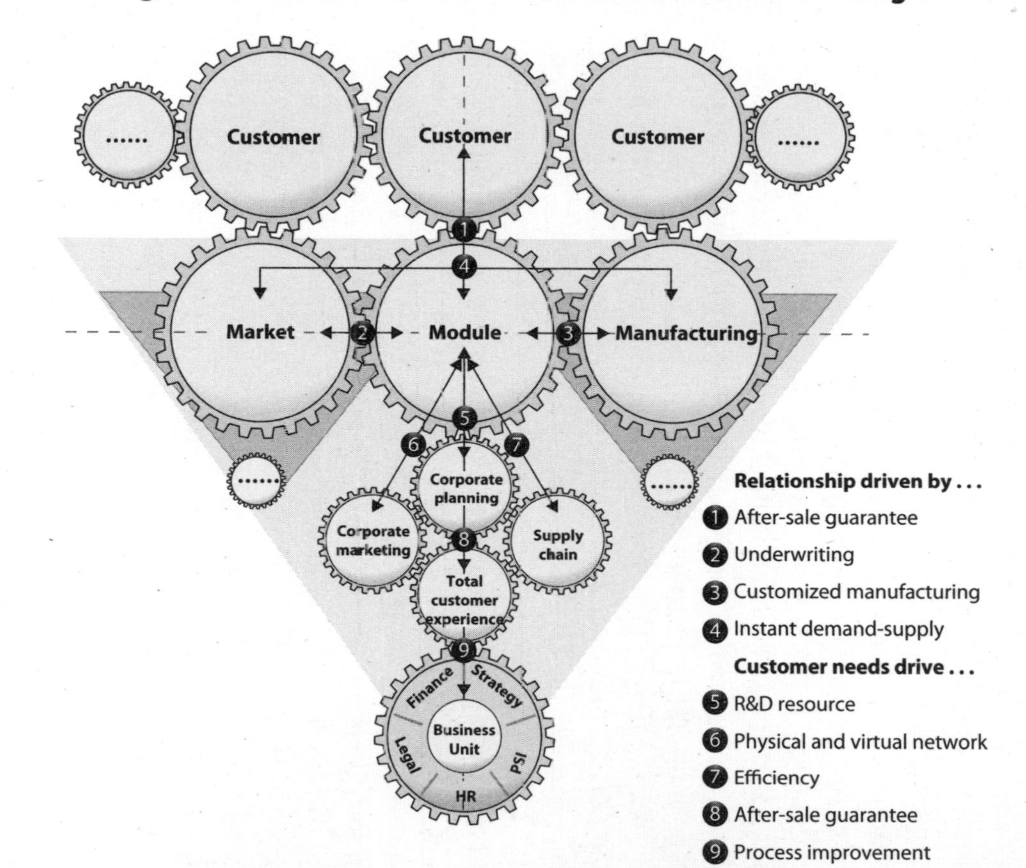

Source: Adapted from Haier documents.

focuses on efficiency (cost reduction, improvement of products and processes). In all of these cases, however, it is the organizational units, which are run as small businesses in their own right (the ZZJYTs), that make this system work.

First-tier ZZJYTs have the task of directly facing the market, understanding customer needs, and providing them with the right products. They have the power to define their own goals based on knowledge from both internal and external experts who provide information on industry average expected growth and sales conditions, so that their goals are competitive and realistic. These goals can change. If market conditions change significantly, the team will adjust its goals accordingly. This dynamically rolling system allows the teams to approach zero distance with their customers in both timing and response.

Second-tier ZZJYTs are responsible for supporting the first-tier ZZJYTs, providing them with the resources and the guidance they may need. These resources are not delivered on request, but should be planned with first-tier ZZJYTs by signing contracts between first- and second-tier ZZJYTs at the beginning of each year. (These are part of the presets discussed later in this chapter.) In this way, the compensation of second-tier ZZJYT members is directly linked to the success of the first-tier ZZJYTs.

Third-tier ZZJYT managers are the business division managers or functional managers (e.g., vice presidents and senior vice presidents) who are responsible for setting corporate strategies and direction for the whole group and providing them with resources. They are Haier's strategic planners: they identify new market opportunities, identify the best product mix for certain regions, and set new rules for improving overall efficiency. These managers communicate regularly with the first-tier ZZJYTs about sales targets and product mixes. Their compensation is partially linked to the performance of their business unit and partially to the strategic performance of the Haier Group.

Zhang Ruimin vividly described the system of ZZJYTs as tree branches: each ZZJYT comes from the trunk but is not isolated and thus maintains its vitality, as contrasted with a bouquet, which although pretty, dies as a result of its isolation.[5]

The ZZJYTs are constantly in a state of flux, some grow and others disappear, depending on market conditions. ZZJYTs with poor performance will be weeded out or merged with ZZJYTs with good performance, so the number of ZZJYTs constantly changes.

The next big breakthrough in the market chain concept was the realization that the linkages did not need to end at the company's walls; they could include many other external value chain partners, including customers, in order to better link Haier's internal corporate assets to customer needs and reduce the distance between Haier and its customers, a topic addressed in chapter 5.

Theme: The Entrepreneurial Energies of Its Workforce Are Haier's Best Means of Achieving Its Service Goals

Zhang has always believed in the entrepreneurial promise of Haier's employees, but he was also pragmatic enough to recognize that such promise would not bloom on its own; it needed the reinforcement of organizational support in order to develop. The ZZJYTs were Zhang's answer to this organizational support requirement. By creating self-organizing, relatively autonomous work units, he was essentially turning Haier's employees into entrepreneurs who were running their own small businesses, a mechanism long advocated conceptually by management gurus such as Tom Peters and Gary Hamel but rarely put into practice by organizational managers because of the enormity of the cultural change that would be required.[6] Haier, however, did it.

The ZZJYT is the basic organizational unit that Haier has established to achieve its goal of unleashing employee talent. Most ZZJYTs can be thought of as a team of cross-functional employees who have set their own goals and, essentially, determine their own compensation by virtue of their performance against these goals.

The concept represents the results of years of refinement and evolution of Haier's basic management model. In its early years, the primary emphasis of Haier's management approaches were mainly concentrated on control; by 1999, they had begun to focus on market relationships among different stages of the value chain; and eventually this evolved into the concept of the market chain (table 4.3). This concept has now been extended by linking it to market-oriented strategic goals (satisfaction of end users' needs) and personal incentives (personal compensation and career) in order to create a more powerful managerial tool.

The ZZJYTs are the soul of Haier's newest business model and required yet another reinvention of Haier's corporate culture. In July 2011, Haier issued its code of conduct for employees, which states some of the most important principles that underlie this new business model and the corporate culture needed to support it. The code states the new vision and mission for Haier: for the organization to become the industry leader and the preferred provider for (appliance) solutions in the lives of their end users. It recognizes that in order to achieve these goals, it must attract and develop first-class talent, essential

Table 4.3 The Three Stages of Haier's Management Mode Innovation[7]

Stage 1: 1984–1991 (Stage 2 represented the absorption of failed organizations and is not relevant to this analysis.)	Daily activity summary management method (OEC management model)	Everyone can manage something, and everything is managed.
Stage 3: 1998–2005	Market chain management model	Everyone is linked to the market, and everyone owns part of the market.
Stage 4: 2005–2012	Win-win mode of individual and goal combination	Everyone owns his or her own goals, and each goal is first class (first class designates the most challenging goals).

Source: Haier document.

to moving Haier closer to the customer. However, Haier also recognizes that if first-class talent is to accept and achieve first-class goals, they must be paid well. This belief has become one of the core value propositions at Haier at the heart of this latest incarnation of Haier's corporate culture:

- *A sense of right and wrong:* Always view customers as being right and yourself as being wrong.
- *Concept of development:* We will win in a commodity business on the basis of our entrepreneurship and innovative spirit.
- *Establishment of shared interest in winning:* Create a win-win culture of individual-goal combination (which links individual employees' rewards to their preestablished goals)

These three values clearly express Haier's newest vision for its business. The first value implies that Haier employees should always listen to consumers and try to respond to their needs, whatever they are. The business model structure is built on the basis of consumers' needs at the beginning of the value-creating process in the inverted triangle.

The second value is crucial for recruiting and developing the best people possible. Haier does not want traditional employees who merely take orders from their bosses. Haier's new business model requires that it hire innovative, entrepreneurial employees who regard themselves as their own bosses. There is no longer any room for mere order takers at Haier. Every employee is encouraged to take responsibility and act as an entrepreneur more than an employee. In fact, the ZZJYT structure is the most entrepreneurial structure in this large multinational corporation. This may seem natural for the reader in Western economies, where such aspirations are typical, but it is instructive to recall that Haier's culture in stages 1 through 3 (figures 3.3 and 3.6) accepted a more traditional form of employee than what the company aspires to in this latest cultural incarnation.

Finally, the third value speaks directly to the entrepreneurial character that Haier is striving to establish and is directly linked to self-interest: employees act entrepreneurially because they are entitled to claim residual rights on the outcome of their work. This is the essence of the win-win culture of the individual-goal combination: the link between the incentive and the goal, which is the satisfaction of consumer desires. In other words, the ultimate goal is the satisfaction of customer needs (the first value proposition), the mode is the entrepreneurial spirit used to accomplish this satisfaction (the second value proposition), and the incentive that drives everything is the self-interest of the employee (the third value proposition).

Haier also sees its business model as an open platform that can integrate outside resources (such as end users' ideas and suggestions) in order to create more value for its global consumers. The main challenge for most companies is that consumers' desires are always changing, and only when entrepreneurship is part of the makeup of the company can it guarantee the innovation needed to change at the same pace. It is essential to attract first-class talent if there is to be any chance of achieving such objectives. Haier maintains that assets do not produce value: they must be activated by people, and the same assets may have different results according to different people. But even the presence of talented people is not enough; they must be allowed to employ their talent in the service of satisfying customer needs, and it is the values of self-interest and the mechanism of the ZZJYTs that make this possible. Zhang quoted Peter Drucker, his long-time admired management guru: "The purpose of organization is to make ordinary people do extraordinary things." This sums up the ultimate achievement that the ZZJYTs aspire to.[8]

Theme: Freedom Requires Control

Although *freedom* and *discipline* appear at first glance to be contradictory, they are mutually reinforcing when it comes to innovation. There is a growing recognition within the management community that the freedom to innovate is best achieved with the support of discipline in many guises, including processes, senior management involvement, and performance accountability. At Haier, the introduction of a market mechanism (via the ZZJYTs) provides ever-present opportunities for senior management to feel as if they are in complete control without impeding the expression of entrepreneurial energies by the ZZJYT members.

Haier's control mechanisms are deceptively simple and are in fact essentially established by the employees themselves. In the very process of assigning work by inviting competitive bidding among employees for the right to pursue the development of market opportunities, whether they be geographic or product oriented, prospective ZZJYT leaders establish measurable targets that they and their team will be held accountable for if they are selected to be entrusted with the opportunity. Competitive bidders want to be ambitious enough to win the assignment, but not overreach for fear of failing to achieve the goal. Since it seems everything is measured at Haier all the time, there is ample reason for top management to feel secure in knowing what is going on. At the same time, employees are free to be as creative as they wish in the pursuit of winning an opportunity, or in delivering to meet a promise.

At the heart of Haier's control system, and its ability to define goals of both the ZZJYT as a unit and the individual members of that unit, is a tool referred to as the "strategic income statement." This is a framework to align market goals (end users' satisfaction) with the necessary human resources, planning activities, and personal incentives needed to achieve them. The strategic income statement is based on the following concepts:

- The market determines goals.
- There is competition for the opportunity to pursue a goal.

- Talent is screened as if in a funnel.
- Competition is introduced at the individual leadership level (the so-called catfish mechanism explained following).
- Strategic initiatives and the retention of leaders to pursue those initiatives at the ZZJYT level are based on mutual agreements between managers and team members.
- Individual rewards are based largely on individual performance against preestablished individual goals.

The Market Determines Goals

Haier wants all goals to be as ambitious as possible and for its employees to strive to reach them. Relying on a variety of information, including independent estimates of market size and growth, overall market targets are established and then distributed among the ZZJYTs and individual employees. Goals must be established by the employees themselves, not the managers. They are not fixed in the long run and can change every year, and even during a year, as market conditions change.

Employees Compete to Reach a Goal

Haier offers opportunities to those individuals who are most ambitious in their bidding to win new opportunities. Whether it is a new market, a new product, or a new manufacturing order, competitive bidding among Haier employees determines who will have the chance to pursue the opportunity. The goals that win the competitive bidding become, in turn, the business objective of the ZZJYT or individual who wins the bidding competition. This ensures that ambitious goals are assigned to motivated people who have won the right to pursue that goal on behalf of Haier. At Haier, competition is everywhere: there is competition for the leading role of any ZZJYT and competition among members of the ZZJYT for the best solutions to a problem.

The Talent Funnel

Unleashing the abundant talent that Haier believes it employs has been at the very heart of most of Zhang Ruimin's initiatives, at least since the "brand building through quality" era. And as a result, Haier's managers are encouraged to think about how they nourish and develop the talent that is available to them. One technique that they rely on is what they call the talent funnel. Every first-tier ZZJYT should establish a talent funnel, with the help of the second-tier experts in functional departments such as HR. The second-tier HR service ZZJYT recruits people by searching for talent worldwide and then presenting a list of the available talent to each leader of the first-tier ZZJYTs. That leader can then follow up with interviews. In this way, through a subsequent filtering of prospects, the number of candidates decreases until only the best ones are selected.

Creating Competition at the Individual Leader's Level: The Catfish Mechanism

There is an old Norwegian legend to the effect that the captains of fishing boats used catfish to keep their catch alive on the trip home, so they could charge more for these fish at the market. Introducing catfish into a barrel of other fish added an element of fear, which kept the other fish moving in order not to be eaten.

Haier's HR managers use this approach to motivate their ZZJYT teams so that each member feels strong competition and the entire team remains competitive. At Haier, this objective is usually accomplished by introducing a potential competitor for the role of the leader into the ZZJYT. This role is normally held by the runner-up of the competition for the leading role of the ZZJYT, although occasionally outside people can also be used to put pressure on the leader. The role of "catfish" is highly sought after by those who are ambitious and wish to rise quickly in responsibilities. They must qualify to become catfish. In fact, a "catfish rank" identifies the best leadership substitution candidates. Catfish role players are typically the best ZZJYT team members, and they can easily be transferred to other ZZJYTs as leaders. They must be independent of the leader because a ZZJYT leader cannot evaluate the catfish on his or her team. They are nominated through a voting system by members of the ZZJYT (or, more rarely, inserted into the ZZJYT by leadership or third-tier ZZJYT oversight) and are evaluated by the functional units (second-tier ZZJYTs, typically HR) with expertise in relevant areas of functional performance.

Choosing Team Leaders and Members

At Haier, a ZZJYT leader has the right and the means to choose the members of his or her team, but employees also have the right to choose which ZZJYT they want to work with, as well as the right to retain or dismiss their leader. There is an open market for talent and opportunity based on the incentives that a ZZJYT leader can offer to employees to induce them to join and remain with the team. These incentives are in turn a function of the talent that the employees can bring to the team. The talent market is also symmetrical in that there is a periodic evaluation when the leader evaluates the ZZJYT members and the team members evaluate the leader. A leader may thus be voted out by ZZJYT members and a new leader substituted.

The People-Goal-Pay Mechanism

Haier believes that the choice of first-class talent should lead to first-class goals, which will lead to first-class results and compensation. It is not enough, however, to choose the best people; Haier must dedicate great attention to targeting incentive mechanisms, so that worthy goals are established and met and to ensure that compensation and performance are in sync. To align these objectives, Haier uses the people-goal-pay mechanism, also called a strategic income statement. The key questions and issues for each of the four areas of the strategic income statement are set out in figure 4.3.

In the top-left quadrant, the ZZJYT should know its strategic positioning and goals and be able to articulate the execution details on the basis of which everything else follows. The ZZJYT should not only know its goals but also how to achieve

Figure 4.3 Key Issues in the Strategic Income Statement

Strategy: End-user resources	**People: Human resources**
• Know your strategic positioning and goals • Articulate the execution details • Know the resources needed from second-tier ZZJYTs • Know how anticipated profits can be distributed in the ZZJYT	• Match the right people to execute the strategy using tools such as bidding systems, funnel systems, voting systems, and competition
Execution: Zero distance between preset and result: close the gap • Detailed three-year, yearly, quarterly, monthly, weekly, and daily execution plans • Short-term adjustments based on external market changes • Tools such as weekly clear and daily clear to report the planned and accomplished tasks • Results for previous week, plan for the next week, and the next six weeks	**Pay: Close the gap and improve** • Individual compensation should be in line with goal achievement, which should be aligned with individual capabilities • Compensation is composed of base salary and bonuses

Source: Haier documents.

them, which resources to claim from second-tier ZZJYTs, and how the anticipated profits can be distributed among the ZZJYT members.

The top-right quadrant considers the people and the organization necessary to achieve the goals. It is the quadrant of the funnel system, of the voting system, and competition.

The bottom-left quadrant addresses the comparison between actual and forecast numbers on different goals and time dimensions, as well as the actions needed to be taken in order to reduce possible differences between goals and accomplishments. It serves to identify short-term adjustments during the execution of a strategy. This is also what we refer to as the preset quadrant because it represents the difference between what was agreed on beforehand and what was actually achieved, so it is the basis for improvisation and innovation. Typically, the strategic income statement shows results for the previous week, the following week, and six weeks into the future. The differences, if there are any, suggest the gap the team has to close for the previous week and the plan that needs to be developed to achieve the results for the next week and the next six weeks.

The bottom-right quadrant deals with the relationship between individual goals and compensation. Compensation should be in line with the achievement of goals, and the goals should be aligned with individual capabilities. Every individual who reaches his or her target goals should be assured of a target compensation that has already been established (i.e., preset). This compensation has both a fixed salary component (mandated by the government as minimum wage) and a bonus if the ZZJYT team member achieves his or her goals, which is essentially the majority of their compensation.

Haier has detailed procedures to guarantee that as many matters relating to performance appraisal as possible are preestablished, to ensure that the goals for both the ZZJYT and the individual are in line with overall corporate goals, and that both goals are ambitious enough. Haier itself does not impose these targets; they can be imposed only by the marketplace.

It is critical that the ZZJYTs ensure that the best people take on the most challenging targets and, if they are successful, earn good salaries. Individuals should be well matched with their goals and their compensation. It should be impossible for the best people to be poorly paid and for the worst-performing ones to be the best paid.

Theme: Responsiveness Can Be Facilitated by Preset Conversations

Haier's ultimate objective is to create entrepreneurial teams and entrepreneurial employees—"everyone is his or her own CEO"—so that customers are well-served quickly and efficiently.[9] Haier believes that it can accomplish these objectives more effectively if everything that can be preestablished is worked out and agreed on beforehand. This means that tasks must be carefully planned in great detail in order to provide sufficient precision to aid in ensuring that the goal is achievable. This resonates with ancient Chinese military strategic thought that a battle is won before it is actually fought.[10] In business battles, the metaphor is expressed in this way: *How can you win if you don't project and prepare for victory?* That is what the presets do.

Haier has an obsession with preparation: everything in Haier must be prepared in advance and preestablished for achieving the target. Since employees have much freedom in their everyday activity, presetting targets and resources is a form of attempting to control the company's activities in anticipation of whatever is to come. In a very real sense, the presets reduce the possible variance that comes with increased operational freedom at both the individual and ZZJYT levels.

The logic of the strategic income statement also enables a ZZJYT to assess why its results are not turning out in the

Figure 4.4 Strategic Income Statement Relationships

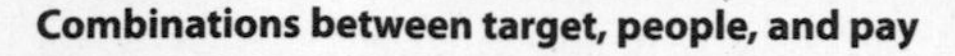

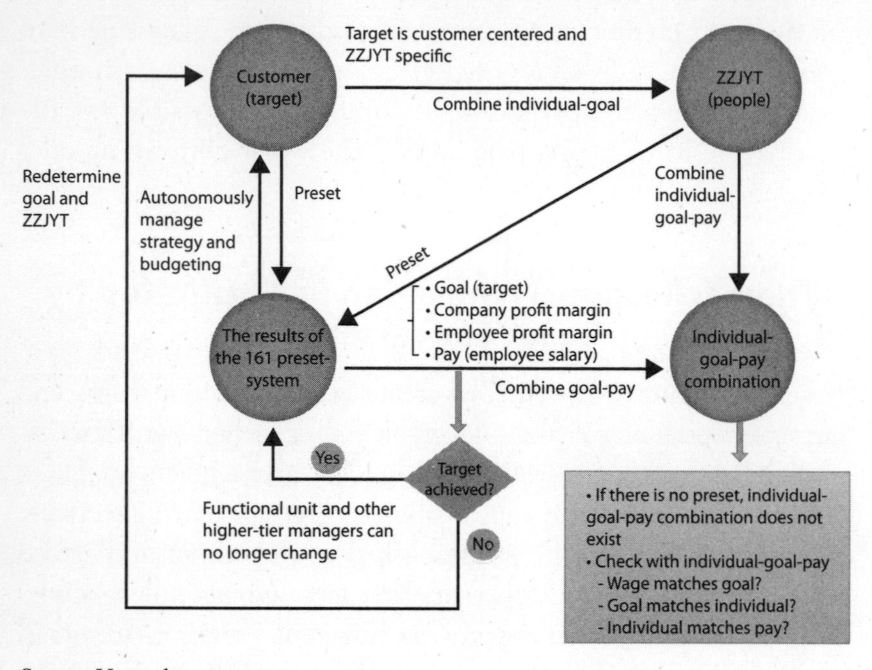

Source: Haier documents.

manner expected and what it might do to correct this. By examining various quadrants of the strategic income statement, a troubled ZZJYT can make a quick assessment (figure 4.4):

- Do we have the wrong target?
- Do our team members have the ability to achieve the target?
- Do we have the wrong presets?
- Do we have the wrong incentive system?

The procedure requires checking the appropriateness of the target first, then the team's qualifications (with consideration of the possible substitution of the leader or of elements of the team), followed by a consideration of the existing team presets and ultimately the individual incentives.

Theme: Value Creation Should Be Linked Among Customers, the Organization, and Employees

At Haier, all the group revenues are generated by first-tier ZZJYTs, while the second- and third-tier ZZJYTs supply resources to the first-tier on a contractual basis and are paid for what they provide. Haier's leaders realize that it takes more than frontline activities to satisfy the customer, and their intention is to see that everyone who contributes is rewarded. If the customer wins by receiving value, then everyone else should also win, including the organization's shareholders (through profits) and the employees who made it all possible.

Among the three types of first-tier ZZJYTs, the module ZZJYTs are responsible for developing specific product and service offerings and as a result are the principal generators of the large majority of the company's revenues. The output of the market and manufacturing ZZJYTs is to a large extent defined beforehand (i.e., preset) through contracts with the module ZZJYTs. Manufacturing ZZJYTs, for example, present a production proposal to the module ZZJYT. If the proposal is accepted, they are expected to deliver on their promises regarding delivery, costs, and quality. If the manufacturing ZZJYT can achieve a cost reduction below what it has promised, and thus a profit, then this profit belongs to the manufacturing ZZJYT. Similarly, the market ZZJYTs present their marketing cost proposals to the module ZZJYTs, along with their forecasts of sales. If they achieve either lower costs or more sales, they can also claim a profit.

The second- and third-tier ZZJYTs provide the resources, especially human talent. They are also evaluated on their results, which means the quality of resources and people they are able to offer to the first-tier ZZJYTs and, indirectly, on the performance results of the first-tier ZZJYTs. Expected results must be defined at the start. This emphasis on establishing presets is unique to Haier's culture. It facilitates the ability to improvise as necessary since employees are not reinventing everything but building on preestablished positions.

The relationship between the second- and third-tier ZZJYTs is also a contractual one. Second- and third-tier ZZJYTs are business units and offer their services to the first tier on a contractual basis. The finance function experts, located in a second-tier ZZJYT, support the finance people at the first tier and claim a fee for their services.

Figure 4.5 shows the contracting system among the three types and the three tiers of ZZJYTs. At the beginning of each year, every first-tier ZZJYT signs contracts with other first-, second- and third-tier ZZJYTs that specify all of the conditions (prices, timing of deliveries, penalties, and the like) that one would find in any typical contract between independent businesses. Responsibilities are clearly defined so that if things go awry, those responsible incur a penalty.

This system emulates a market system and is based on incentives: each ZZJYT has its own targets and its own incentives, and it must deal with other ZZJYTs on a contractual basis in order to achieve these targets. What is most remarkable is the fact that in such a large company, there are minimal signs of the use of hierarchical authority; contracts are used more than hierarchical authority to run the company and organize the relationships among the ZZJYTs. In this manner of relying on contractual arrangements throughout the organization to assess performance, all value creation is tied directly to customer satisfaction for all employees, no matter where they are located within Haier.

Figure 4.5 Contracting System among ZZJYT Types and Tiers (Qingdao Haier Corporate Level)

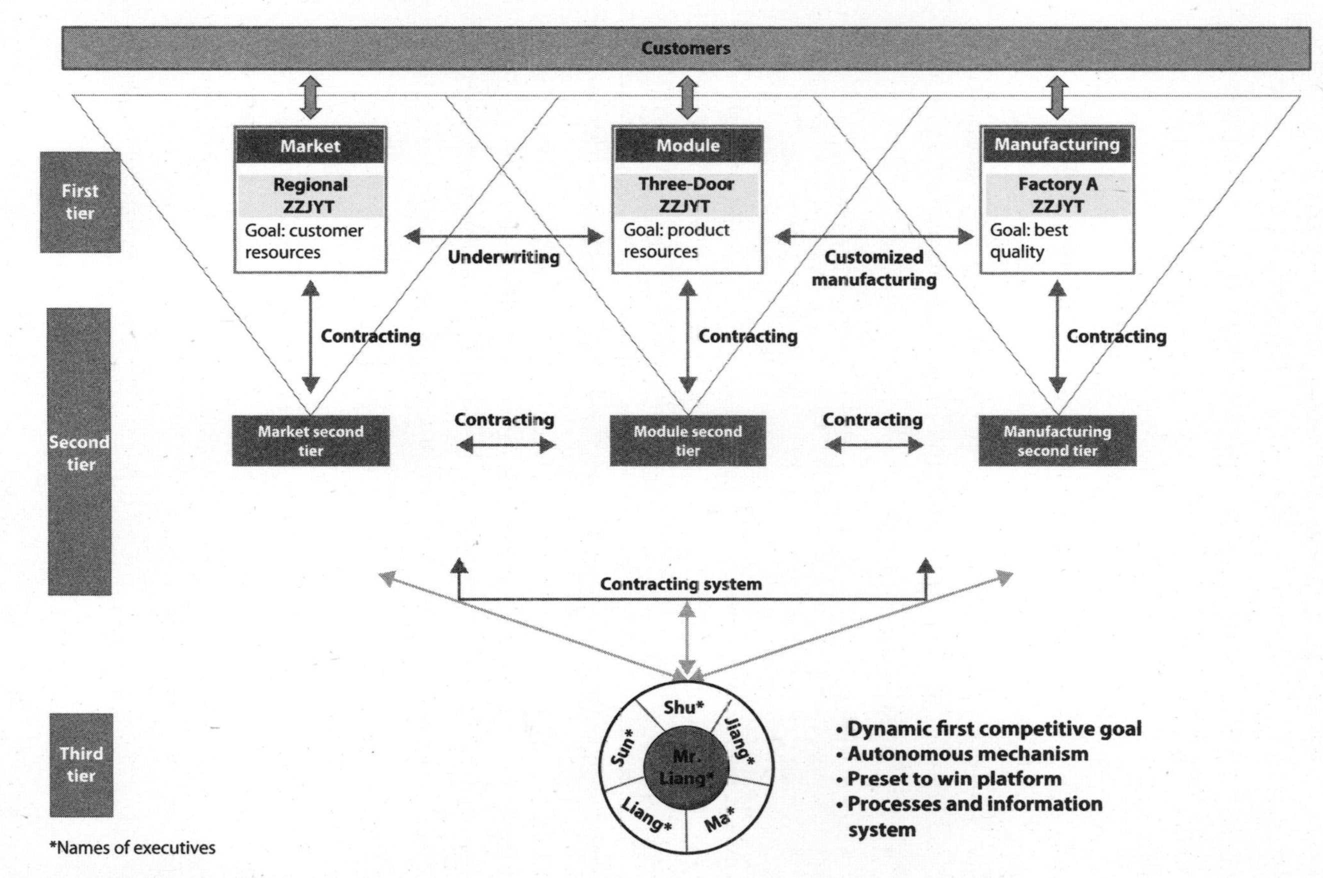

Source: Adapted from Haier documents.

Haier Today

Haier's success as a customer-centric service provider, global brand, and innovator is based on a high-performing organization of eighty thousand people working together on the basis of six principles:

- Haier thinks of itself as a service company.
- Service is best achieved if there is zero distance between Haier and its customers.
- The entrepreneurial energies of its own workforce are Haier's best means of achieving its service goals.
- Freedom requires control.
- Responsiveness can be facilitated by preset conversations.
- Value creation should be linked among customers, the organization, and the employees.

These principles are an essential part of the competencies that Haier established in its earliest days as Qingdao Refrigerator and has maintained and intensified over the subsequent three decades. These principles are also the basis for a number of managerial practices aimed at unleashing Haier's talent in the service of customers. How this works in practice and what it's like to work at Haier are the topics of the following chapter.

5

BUILDING A CORPORATE CULTURE FOR THE TWENTY-FIRST CENTURY

So how does it all really work? That's the fundamental question for those of us who are involved in the day-to-day management of complex organizations. All too often, these new initiatives sound great in theory, but it's in the details where the devil lurks. In this chapter, we get into the details and listen to the firsthand experiences of Haier employees.

Haier can be thought of as a universe of autonomous business units—ZZJYTs—that are bound together by common brands, strategic goals, values, and internal Haier organizing principles but otherwise operate as independent businesses coordinated by contractual relationships. We also know from prior chapters that there are several different types of ZZJYTs, which can be described by their distance from the customer, tier 1 being the closest:

- *Tier 1:* At the frontlines of Haier's customer engagement are two forms of ZZJYTs with direct, customer-facing responsibilities: module ZZJYTs, responsible for creating products that consumers desire, and market ZZJYTs, responsible for increasing Haier's market share within a particular geographical area. Parallel to these two customer-facing ZZJYTs, and directly responsible for producing the product that ultimately winds up in customers' hands, are the manufacturing ZZJYTs, responsible for producing the products that the module ZZJYTs have created.

- *Tier 2:* Supporting the tier 1 ZZJYTs in their customer-facing roles are a large number of functional ZZJYTs, which represent the various functional elements that make up any firm: R&D, marketing, HR, finance, and the like.
- *Tier 3:* These ZZJYTs define strategies and search for market opportunities.

This chapter explains how, why, and when these different types of ZZJYTs come together in Haier's universe of autonomous business units to support the firm's business model and define how Haier works as an organization.

Joining Haier's Three-Door Module ZZJYT

In order to experience ZZJYT life firsthand, one of us traveled to Qingdao to participate in the activities of a ZZJYT for a week. Arriving late one evening in blowing rain, Fang Liu was collected at the airport by a veteran Haier driver. As with so many of the other workers we have met at Haier, this driver not only had a long tenure at the company—twenty-two years, which turns out to be about the average for the company's drivers—but was also proud to be a part of the organization and knew many of the senior leaders for quite a number of years.

The Workplace and the Atmosphere

The next morning, after entering a gigantic industrial park, Fang arrived in the office of the three-door refrigerator ZZJYT, where she would spend the next six days with the team.

The three-door refrigerator ZZJYT is a module ZZJYT; its primary objective is creating consumer demand for a specific product—in this case, the three-door refrigerator unit.[1] Module ZZJYTs are structured as independent companies, each responsible for a specific product or family of products. Their job is to work as a small entrepreneurial business within the Haier organization and engage with other functions, such as R&D and marketing, to create products that are attractive to ultimate customers. Haier believes that product innovation creates consumer demand, but only if this innovation is based on consumer needs. The module ZZJYTs are not looking for breakthrough technological innovations as much as incremental product innovations that can improve the existing product to the point of making it the preferred choice of end users.

Haier's white goods division has thirty-one module ZZJYTs, including eight refrigerator ZZJYTs; the most successful is the three-door refrigerator unit. In 2011, the three-door refrigerator ZZJYT had the most impressive performance of all ZZJYTs within Haier, more than doubling its actual figures of units sold (figure 5.1). Its total revenues for 2011 were approximately RMB 7 billion (more than $1 billion), with a profit of about RMB 0.8 billion (around $100 million).

The three-door refrigerator ZZJYT is located within a large open space office that occupies hundreds of square meters that it shares with other teams. Its neighboring units are the French-style

Figure 5.1 Number of Three-Door Refrigerators Sold: Budgeted and Actual (in millions of units)

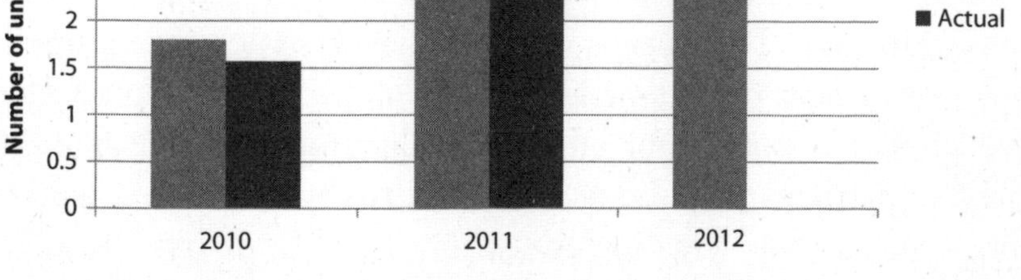

Source: Haier company documents.

refrigerator ZZJYT and the four-door refrigerator ZZJYT. Not all of the team members within the same ZZJYT work in the same space. The team that Fang worked with had eighteen people—both full-time and part-time members. (Part-time members work in more than one ZZJYT, say 50 percent of their time in the three-door ZZJYT and 50 percent in the six-door ZZJYT.) The R&D members of the three-door team also work in this open space along with the R&D forces of the other ZZJYTs, but other functional members (HR, finance, etc.) of the team are in another building, which houses their functional specialties. Although the team does not physically work in the same office, the communication is nonstop: they use their phone, e-mail, and weekly meetings and have lunch together as a team whenever possible.

The workday at Haier is long. The official work hours are 9:00 a.m. to 6:00 p.m., six days a week; however, the team seldom leaves before 8:00 p.m. During her stay with the group, Fang heard many stories about Haier's work heroes, including a project manager who did not go home for seven days in a row and another who essentially lived in a factory for a month because he had to supervise the production of samples for a new product launch and the factory was two hours away from his office. He thought that it did not make sense for him to spend four hours every day on the road. Although such legends are exceptional, it was clear that every minute Fang spent talking with the team would result in their having to work overtime to make up for the time lost.

How the Three-Door ZZJYT Was Created

One of the defining characteristics of ZZJYTs is that they are self-organizing. This means that whenever senior management proposes a new project or identifies a new market opportunity, the project is put up for an internal auction. Anyone has the right to participate in the auction, and the winner is responsible for recruiting and creating the team. That team has the right to change its leader if it feels that they are underperforming.

This self-governance characteristic is a central part of Zhang Ruimin's efforts to create a fast-moving, agile organization that has zero distance from its customers.

ZZJYTs are born in auctions, where aspiring ZZJYT leaders submit prospective business plans for a target market after carefully studying the potential of this market and formulating sales goals, a plan of attack, and a budget for the resources needed. These plans are reviewed by a committee of internal managers from the departments of finance, strategy, and human resources, as well as line managers from other business units and occasionally outside experts. The committee reviews the proposals on the basis of their objectives regarding timing, strategy, processes, and incentive system, as well as how the business plan agrees with Haier's overall strategy.

In the case of the three-door refrigerator unit, Haier's senior managers had been thinking for quite some time about launching a three-door refrigerator ZZJYT as a trial of one of the first ZZJYTs. In October 2010, they decided to go ahead with the idea and established an auction for a ZZJYT that would develop this concept into a product. It was not easy to find candidates at that time. According to Haier's head of HR, the auction policy was very new, and employees were reluctant to rush into this new practice. (The opposite holds now: everyone wants to be the head of a ZZJYT.) The perceived risks associated with participating in such an auction were vividly captured by the colloquial term Haier colleagues used to refer to it: "PK," which stands for "player kill," a term borrowed from Internet games characterized by competition to the death between two strong players.

Four people submitted proposals to create and lead the three-door ZZJYT: an employee from the two-door refrigerator R&D, a member of the domestic market planning staff, one from the supply chain function, and one from market research planning. All had been with Haier for more than ten years, and all had worked with refrigerators.

The proposal review committee conducted an intense discussion and careful examination of the four proposals and ultimately selected Pu Xiankai from market research planning. In addition, the three-door refrigerator ZZJYT was one of the first that would be allowed to recruit its own team. As the new team leader, Pu subsequently asked the candidate from the two-door refrigerator R&D (Li Gaojie) and the candidate from domestic market planning (Huang Yi) to join him as members of the new ZZJYT team.

Li was appointed the "catfish," or substitute. (Chapter 4 describes the catfish role in the organization.) He became the vice head of the ZZJYT, with the distinction of being designated to replace Pu if Pu did not perform well in his job by failing to meet the targets or as a result of losing the confidence of the team and being voted out. Haier believes that the idea of a designated substitute leads to higher performance because of the pressure on the leader, who knows that a substitute is standing in the wings. Li was an excellent candidate for leader or substitute: he had wide experience in the corporation, strong execution skills, and solid technical knowledge. Pu observed, "Every candidate in the auction competition had his own expertise field," and Pu did feel a sense of urgency because there was no guarantee that he would maintain his position. Performance would be the only key to his remaining leader. If he missed his targets for three consecutive months, an automatic company-wide reconsideration of his leadership would be launched. Although there was no certainty that Li would replace Pu in such a situation, he would be a strong candidate. So far, the head of a ZZJYT has been replaced by a substitute on three occasions.

The relationship between Pu and Li obviously is a complex one. They had competed for the same position; one won and the other lost. Now they have to work together on the same team. When Fang suggested that there might be high potential for conflict in their relationship, the answer that was given was quite straightforward: "Look at Barack Obama and Hillary Clinton. If they can work together, we can work together!"

Haier believes that the incentives for good team performance reward every team member, so solidarity comes before individual desires. When asked about his thoughts on this issue, "Catfish" Li smiled politely and replied: "Well, actually, this is not a problem for me because we are on a team. We work toward the same goal. If the team performs well, I receive more bonuses. I don't have any incentive to sabotage Pu's work." Subsequently, by talking to other Haier employees in China and Europe, it was confirmed that the absence of power play is indeed an important part of Haier's culture and the senior management team do not hesitate to let go those who spend their time fostering nepotism or cliques, or any other type of power play, rather than spending time on improving service and products for customers. This simple and easy work relationship is not very common in Chinese organizations, where *guanxi* rules the firm and large amounts of time and resources are thus wasted.

Building the Three-Door ZZJYT Team

The leader of the ZZJYT, who is ultimately responsible for the unit's results, has the right to decide which people should be hired and makes the final choices in their selection. Pu established the performance targets for the ZZJYT, and then, on the basis of the effort he thought necessary, he determined how many people he believed that the ZZJYT needed. In 2012, for example, he thought that the ZZJYT would need an additional seven people. He then wrote a contract with a second-tier HR functional unit to prepare a plan for recruitment. Pu's ZZJYT pays the HR department for recruiting services; HR then supplies the people the ZZJYT needs that year, offering a set of people each month from which Pu can choose the most suitable, a process referred to as the talent funnel (figure 5.2).

The recruiting process is bilateral. For example, the ZZJYT team leader asks the finance department for a finance specialist. The finance department then provides a list of candidates,

Figure 5.2 Using the Talent Funnel to Select the Most Suitable Candidates for the ZZJYT

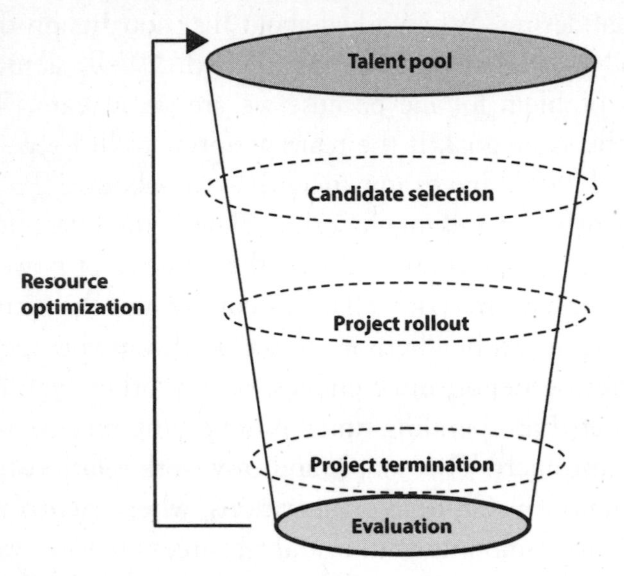

Source: Adapted from Haier documents.

both internal and external. An invited candidate has the right to refuse the offer. The employment relationship can be changed at any time if one of the two parties is not satisfied. Tan Lixia, chief financial officer and vice president of the Haier Group, explained:

> There is a strong reputation effect within the organization, as more skilled people tend to be asked [to join] by many ZZJYTs,[2] whereas less skilled people find it increasingly difficult to find work and are finally eliminated. In this way a hierarchy based on merit is created, and people who meet their performance target not only get extra compensation but also can enjoy a promising career path in the company.

This talent-sifting process goes on continuously in the search for the best people, and some ZZJYTs search so frequently that they have high employee turnover. Pu revealed that one person had been dismissed the previous year because of poor performance. But he also recognized the potential of some members of his team who he thought would become future leaders, and he was very proud of them.

Recruiting success is so important that it is monitored in the ZZJYT meeting held every Saturday afternoon, when Li (the "catfish") updates the team about where recruitment stands. In the meeting Fang attended, the team was still searching for experienced module managers, and recruitment was slow. As a consequence, in the absence of the talent that they were hoping for, the team was working overtime every day. Pu endorsed the idea of "going with no one rather than having somebody unqualified." He explained that he was most concerned by the motivation and skill of the prospective team members: "Sure, the best outcome is to have people who are motivated and skillful at the same time, but if I have to choose between motivation and skill, I will choose motivation, because skill can be learned, even if it takes longer than expected, but motivation determines how far you can go."

Haier's organizational culture is based on responsiveness and customer-centricity, and the company recruits individuals who show a high degree of entrepreneurial orientation. It is also important that those hired understand how Haier works and accept that a substantial part of their salary depends on how well they do their job. This acknowledgment should result in selecting people who are willing to accept the risk implied by a variable salary, by nature an entrepreneurial risk.

In order to train and educate people into the Haier model, Haier recruits college students. It invites third-year students to intern at Haier in order to become familiar with the Haier model. They are inculcated into the Haier culture, and when they graduate, they can come directly to work for Haier. Those hired must accept that their salary can vary depending on their performance, and they must show initiative and the ability to learn. Every newly hired graduate employed at Haier is required to have held a one-year internship in a factory or a retail chain. Those hired to work for a module ZZJYT must intern for two years. All of these internships include a salary.

In April 2012, the three-door ZZJYT team had eighteen members: four who analyzed market needs, five in R&D, eight working on specific modules (doors, cabinet, design, electrical parts), and one addressing quality control.

Haier's best practices state that the ideal size of a module ZZJYT is "10+*n*" members. Every module ZZJYT must have at least ten members: leader, project managers (the number determined by the number of projects), module managers (the number determined by the extent of use of the module), design managers, and functional managers. The number beyond that is flexible and is linked to ad hoc or part-time positions as needed by the project.

Haier encourages competition among the members of a ZZJYT whenever it is necessary to develop a plan to improve product sales. In 2011, the three-door ZZJYT had to prepare a plan for selling more refrigerators in a price range between RMB 2,500 and 3,000 (about $400 and $500). The ZZJYT member who presented the best plan was made responsible for this specific product line. The selection decision was made by the ZZJYT leader (Pu), the vice leader (Li), and outside consultants.

A Network of ZZJYTs

Each ZZJYT is embedded in a thick network of relationships with other ZZJYTs. The three-door refrigerator ZZJYT had signed twenty-two contracts at the beginning of 2012: eight with ZZJYTs dealing with domestic retail chains, six with ZZJYTs dealing with international retail chains, and eight with ZZJYTs dealing with manufacturers. Each contract specifies quantities for each type of refrigerator to be delivered, price, terms of delivery, terms of payment, penalties, and so on. Contracts with functional units that are necessary to produce these refrigerators also need to be signed. Retail chains in turn sign contracts with the market ZZJYTs (there is one for each geographical sales area).

All of the contracts are standard in form and are signed at the beginning of each year. Responsibilities are also clearly defined in advance. At the three-door refrigerator ZZJYT, at the beginning of each year a contract is agreed between the ZZJYT and a second-tier HR group for recruiting talent. There are, in fact, dozens of HR ZZJYTs from which to choose, and the contract that is ultimately agreed on specifies the objectives, processes, results, prices, deadlines, and penalty clauses in case the contract is not respected. Normally, when a ZZJYT signs a contract and fails to meet the obligations, it is forced to pay a penalty. This penalty is then debited against its future earnings and, as a result, becomes a penalty on the future bonuses that might otherwise be distributed to the ZZJYT members.

From the perspective of the three-door ZZJYT, all of the products that it sells are under its direct responsibility, from start to finish. All of the activities of the other ZZJYTs, including the marketing channels, represent a cost for the ZZJYT that should be subtracted from the unit price of the products sold (which is fixed in advance based on market research) to determine the ZZJYT's ultimate profit:

$$\text{Profit} = \text{Unit price} - (\text{materials} + \text{manufacturing costs}) - (\text{resources from second- and third-tier contracted ZZJYTs}) - (\text{marketing costs}).$$

Manufacturing costs for existing products are standard, whereas for new products, they must be negotiated with the manufacturing ZZJYT. Marketing costs are primarily associated with advertising. These costs are normally audited by the financial department in order to avoid costs that are not competitive.

Performance Evaluation

Haier's inverted triangle is premised on the desirability of driving strategic decisions down to the lowest level possible and then rewarding performance. Haier refers to this as the ZEUS model, or the individual-goal-pay combination model. This model operates at the ZZJYT level and serves as the basis for team and individual performance evaluation. It is the starting point as a ZZJYT puts together its action plan. (Figure 5.3 shows the ZEUS model and figure 5.4 a simplified version.)

The four quadrants of the strategic income statement introduced in the previous chapter provide the logic for how ZEUS works.

Strategy. The common theme that runs through everything that Haier does is the philosophy of connecting every employee to the market through the use of goals. The corporation, departments, and ZZJYTs set goals, and individuals set goals, and these goals should be aligned. Haier refers to the process of achieving these goals as "closing gaps," that is, reducing the gap between targets and outcomes. This also ties into the strategic positioning of product portfolios, strategic market opportunities, and the need for resources to support the ZZJYT.

People. The next step is to find the right people to execute the strategy, mainly using the services provided by the second-tier HR ZZJYT and the talent funnel system.

Execution. Once the strategy is clear and the right people are in place, execution makes the difference. Haier prides itself on both speed and agility, which are attributed to organization and focus. At every level, strategy is formulated into milestone targets—three-year targets as well as detailed yearly, quarterly, monthly, and weekly targets. For example, for the three-door ZZJYT, the targeted profits for the next three years are as follows:

Year	*Profit (million RMB)*
2011	581
2012 (target)	830
2013 (target)	1,000
2014 (target)	1,260

Figure 5.3 ZEUS Model: Individual-Goal-Pay Combination

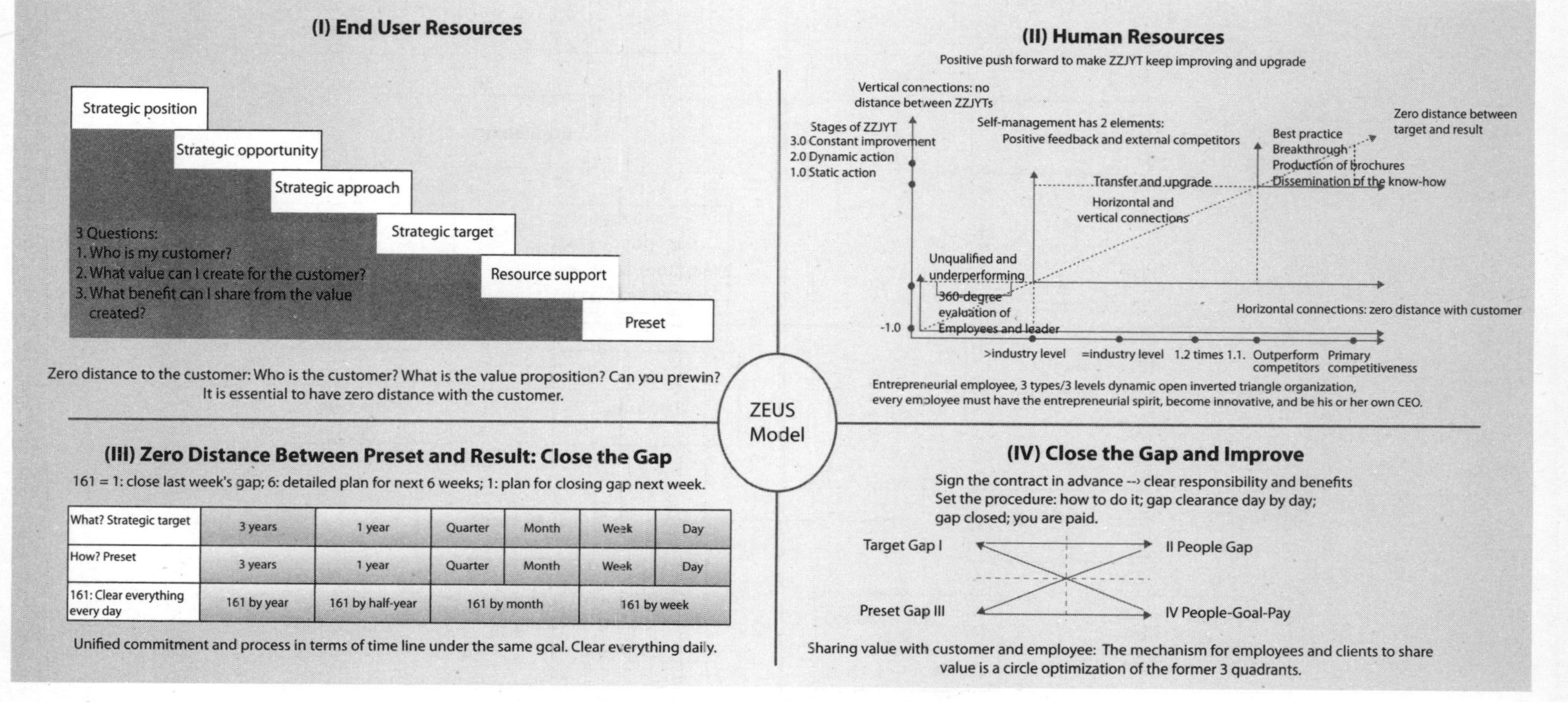

Source: Adapted from Haier documents.

Figure 5.4 Relationships in the Zeus Model

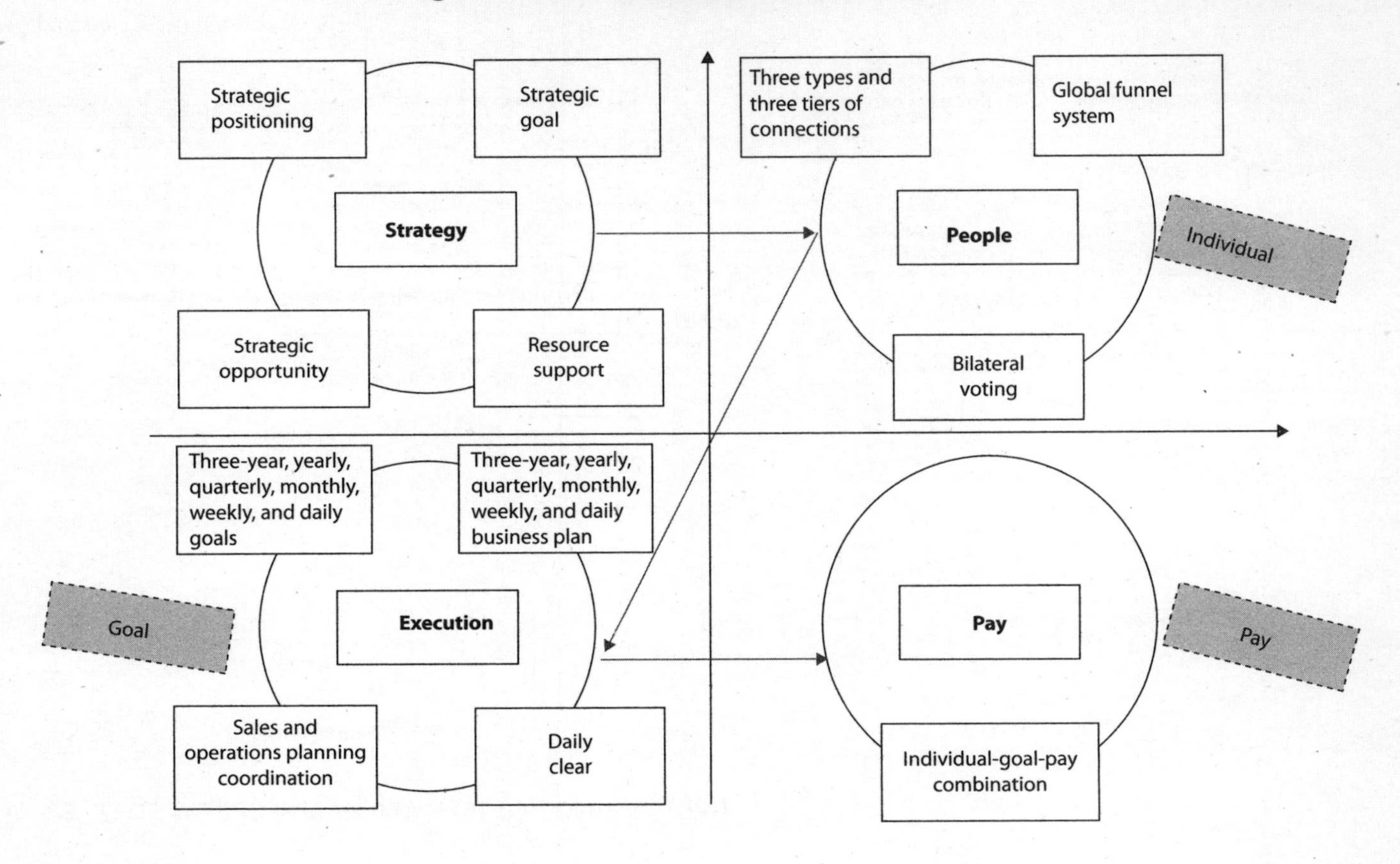

With these concrete target numbers in mind, the three-door ZZJYT then prepares an action plan:

- Gather consumer insights from both the Internet (website inquiries and search) and physical networks (customer conversations in showrooms, after-sale services, and other face-to-face interactions).
- Build a three-door ZZJYT module platform that meets customer desires and increases product component modularization so as to save costs and achieve higher efficiency.
- Work with supply chain partners, R&D, and procurement to set up a system to achieve the greatest operational efficiency.
- Work with manufacturing to create smooth connections with the market and manufacturing ZZJYTs.
- Formulate detailed plans about which milestones should be achieved at what time (i.e., year, quarter, month, week).

The speed of execution is also reflected on two reporting sheets referred to as the daily clear and the weekly clear. These two reports have existed from Haier's early days and have always been key tools for managers to know what employees have accomplished during the previous day or week, as well as serving as a useful guide for individuals in their own work planning. Each week team members present their weekly clear at the Saturday afternoon meeting. The purpose is to get needed help from within the team to close any gaps remaining from the previous week. At the meeting that Fang observed, it took thirty minutes to go through the weekly clear reports. The team mentioned that it typically takes each person between five and ten minutes to complete the daily clear or weekly clear.

Project progress reviews are also evaluated weekly at the Saturday meeting. The three-door ZZJYT typically has about twenty projects in process, both large and small, that need to be reviewed. Big projects might involve a brand-new refrigerator launch, while a small project could be changing the color of the door of an existing model.

Whenever it appears possible that a project might miss a deadline, Pu becomes concerned and calls the attention of all involved on how to avoid that. He might say, for example, "We are going to have two national holidays, one of three days and one of five days in April and May, plus Sundays. This is a lot of time lost. We should accelerate and meet the targeted deadline because time is short and our competitors can take advantage of the holidays to move their products to market before we can."

Pay. While establishing the ZZJYT's competitive strategy and finding the right people to execute with speed and agility are both essential parts of the targeting process, much depends on establishing the appropriate incentives. This means ensuring that employees' pay matches their performance.

At Haier, the team earns the rewards appropriate to the benchmarking between the target and the results, and these are then distributed to the individual team members according to their personal performance. If a team fails to earn a reward package in a particular month, then no extra profit is distributed; the team members receive only their contracted salary.

Haier's basic principle is that an individual's compensation is linked directly to his or her performance. In practice, however, the salary has to come from market results, so if a ZZJYT does not create sufficient profits, even well-performing teams are not paid in full. And when that happens, the team may ask for a new ZZJYT leader.

Haier's reward strategy is that good performance leads to good compensation, and extraordinary performance leads to extraordinary compensation. This intention is represented by an exponential curve rewarding achievement (figure 5.5). Given Haier's preference for presets, it is not surprising to find that it sets out its reward scheme at the beginning of the year.

Figure 5.5 The Accelerating Salary Scheme

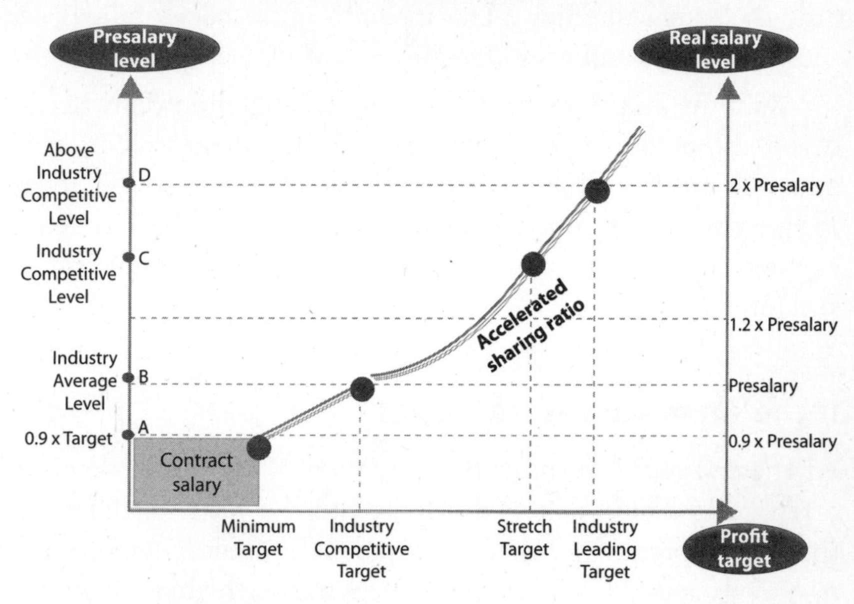

Source: Adapted from Haier documents.

In the case of three-door ZZJYT, rewards based on profits are characterized by four intervals:

Profit Target Interval	*Profit-Sharing Ratio*
A–B: Lower than industry level (0.9 × industry level) to industry average level	0 percent
B–C: Industry average level to industry competitive level[3]	0.5 percent
C–D: Industry competitive level to higher than industry competitive level	1 percent
D: Higher than industry competitive level	2–3 percent

The profit-sharing ratio accelerates as achievement advances relative to industry average levels. The better a ZZJYT performs relative to the industry average, the higher the profit-sharing ratio the team will enjoy. (The appendix at the back of the book shows how individual compensation is calculated.)

With the ZEUS model and the underlying philosophy of the inverted triangle, Haier is building a management process that puts into practice Zhang Ruimin's long-held belief that managing people requires processes. ZEUS allows every ZZJYT to react to the market in a dynamic way with less top-down intervention and ultimately adjust to market movements in an agile fashion.

If the Team Misses Its Target

At the end of the year, quarter, and month, each team receives a rewards package that is distributed to the team members. If the team's target is reached or surpassed, all team members are rewarded, and the cycle starts again with a higher target for the next cycle. (The appendix at the end of the book provides details on how this works.) If the team misses the target, it needs to go back to the other three quadrants of the strategic income statement and analyze the reasons. Is the strategy right? Are the people who were assigned to execute the strategy the right people? Have they executed in the right way? The answer must lie in one of these factors. This framework helps the team identify the gap between reality and target and how to fill the gap.

Individual Performance Evaluation

Haier's evaluation of individual performance involves both quantitative results and qualitative impressions. The quantitative evaluation part is determined by the individual ZEUS sheet, which is constructed on the same principles as the team performance evaluation. However, it has a more operational set of targets and execution commitments because of the specificity of individual assignments. Figure 5.6 is an illustration of an individual's ZEUS sheet for a midlevel manager in a module ZZJYT.

The individual's evaluation procedure, which is based on the strategic income statement, mirrors the questions raised by the ZZJYT itself:

1. Identify target gaps for the ZZJYT and for individuals. Why did they happen?
2. Identify ability gaps. Do individuals need to be educated? Do they need to acquire new skills?
3. Identify preset gaps. Are there errors in planning?
4. Identify incentives gaps. Are the incentives adequate to motivate people?

Every employee at Haier has a personal strategic income statement that is used to focus on gaps between actual and forecast performance at the individual level. For each quadrant, different key performance indicators (KPIs) are considered, each accounting for a certain weight in the final performance evaluation. The reward component for each quadrant is calculated by comparing each KPI (weighted by its importance to the individual's personal targets) to the person's achievement and is benchmarked against the previous year's performance on overall contribution to the ZZJYT's profitability. These are all quantifiable measures.

The second part of the evaluation is qualitative and reflects the general level of appraisal that a ZZJYT leader has for an individual. Although the objective of the individual-goal combination sheet is to quantify as many of the objectives and achievements as is possible, some aspects of performance appraisal defy quantification and will almost always remain qualitative. The head of the ZZJYT makes the qualitative evaluation. Pu has observed about this process, "Complete rationality is impossible. You might have stronger emotional attachment to the best performing individuals and favor them to some extent."

While he recognizes that total transparency is probably not achievable, he nonetheless works toward it. Pu employs a blind

Figure 5.6 Strategic Income Statement for a

ZZJYT: Three-door refrigerator			*Module manager*		*Name*	*Zhang San*
Quadrant	*Item*	*Undertaking tasks*		*February 2012*		
				Gap to be closed (task)	*KPI*	*Target*
I	End user resources (target)	Strategic goals	Responsible for the quality and cost of the module and product lifecycle management	Cost control of refrigerator door module	Cost	90% cost target
				Quality guarantee of refrigerator door module	Deficiency percentage during quality guarantee period	90% nondeficiency during quality guarantee period
				Product lifecycle management (PLM)	Product lifecycle management efficiency	95%
				Quantity target of refrigerator door module	Quantity	48
III	Close the gap	Planning: three-year, yearly, quarterly, monthly, weekly	Support the leading position as first-tier module ZZJYT	Cost reduction of refrigerator door module	Cost reduction	Implement six new cost reduction practicies and reduce cost by RMB 30
				Zero defficiency of refrigerator door module	Zero defficiency	Implement eight new practices
				Project progress	Project progress	Close twelve projects on time
				Leading innovation projects of refrigerator door module	Number of leading innovation projects	Close three new module development projects on time

Note: The figure identifies the goal (quadrant I) in terms of tasks, KPI, target, and the corresponding evaluation and bonus and specific tasks and KPIs. Then the performance of every task is compared against the goal, which finally determines the pay of

Module Manager in the Three-Door ZZJYT

Current	*Last year to date*	*Completion ratio*	*Bottom line*	*Evaluation*	*Weight*	*Source*	*Discussed weight*	*Final weight*
94%	85%	104%	85%	Fulfill No. 8 on bonus scale	104	PLM system	1.03	1.03
95%	82%	106%	85%	No. 8	106	PLM system		
97%	92%	102%	92%	No. 8	102	PLM system		
48	39	100%	39	No. 8	1	PLM system		
Done with cost reduction of RMB 32.6	/	/	80% completion	No. 8	109	Module development	1.02	
Done	/	/	80% completion	No. 8	1	Module development		
Done	/	/	80% completion	No. 8	1	Module development		
Done	/	/	80% completion	No. 8	1	Module development		

distribution part. The lower part of the figure corresponds to quadrant III, where every item in the goal is planned into executable the employee. Note that the weight of each KPI is different, which reflects the priority of each task for the team.

peer evaluation system within his team to reduce the chance of personal bias. Nevertheless, he is responsible for scheduling regular face-to-face meetings with each team member, and if he treats a team member unfairly, the team has the right to vote him out as the head of ZZJYT.

Market ZZJYTs

Haier has long been admired for its market acumen; in fact, one of the regularly cited reasons for its success in defending its domestic market against bigger-branded foreign competitors has been its ability to get closer to its customers, especially in rural areas, than others have been able to do. One reason for this success has been the development of market ZZJYTs, which are charged with developing a better market presence for the Haier brand.

Unlike a module ZZJYT, which is responsible for a particular product family and for its continuous improvement and success, or a manufacturing ZZJYT, which is responsible for making a quality product at an acceptable price, the role of a market ZZJYT is to increase its market share within a particular geographical area. By doing this, it increases the competitiveness of the Haier brand within that area.

A typical regional market ZZJYT has a team leader, three to five sales representatives for the different product lines, and several team members representing the functional units of finance, logistics, marketing and IT, and the like. A team has between ten and twenty people, with sales reps typically working on a full-time basis for one ZZJYT exclusively. The functional staff can work part time for one or more ZZJYTs. For example, eight hundred people in the finance department are allocated to two thousand ZZJYTs, which means that, on average, each finance employee works for two and a half ZZJYTs. In addition, Haier's corporate finance department at headquarters has 220 employees who carry out the conventional work of finance for the entire group.

Team members within a market ZZJYT assume different responsibilities. Salespeople are product-area managers for different product lines (e.g., refrigerators) and are responsible for exploiting new market opportunities. The best-performing sales reps are often recruited by other teams. They are also potentially strong candidates for leadership positions in new ZZJYT auctions. Those in finance analyze the performance data for the whole team and for each team member in order to help achieve better performance. The logistics person is responsible for time-to-market of the ZZJYT's products and follows products from order to delivery. Those in marketing help retail customers win the loyalty of the ultimate product purchasers and give them better service.

Market ZZJYTs are created on a regional basis and have exclusive rights in their own region. Zhou Yunjie, the senior vice president (SVP) of marketing at Haier, has indicated that the potential for conflict between different ZZJYTs in fighting for customers is virtually absent as a result of this geographical exclusivity.

A Market ZZJYT in Jiao Zhou

The Jiao Zhou market, in the suburbs of Qingdao in Shandong province, provides an example of how a market ZZJYT works. When it became available as a target market for a ZZJYT, seven people bid for it by presenting their business plan. The winning bid was that of Miao Shuqiang, who subsequently formed a team of sixteen people: seven full-time salespeople (one county head and six county managers) and nine part-time employees from different essential functions (three from supply chain, three from marketing, one from finance, one from human resources, and one from after-sales service).

The task of this new ZZJYT was to assist stores in the county market that were already selling Haier products by helping them in virtually every activity that they were engaged in as retailers, from budgeting sales to logistics to marketing and after-sales support.

There was already a Haier dealer in Jiao Zhou, Yang Hong Gang, who owns two retail stores in the town. Besides being a retailer, Yang also acts as a wholesaler for stores located in the rural satellite towns in the area of Jiao Zhou, and through these stores he supplies eighteen rural villages in the surrounding countryside. Yang is an exclusive dealer of Haier products for all of Jiao Zhou, so Haier's relationship with him is very important to the company.

Yang buys products from Haier at a discount of around 20 percent. He then resells these products to the other eighteen shops he serves, with a 3 to 5 percent margin included in the price that they pay him. In return, he guarantees them three basic services: sales support, logistics support, and after-sales service.

Yang also provides training to rural shop owners to improve their sales skills, including teaching them how to use Haier products. He is supported in these efforts by Haier through the market ZZJYT, which provides sales assistance (marketing campaigns), logistics (delivery and inventory), and after-sales service (repairs and maintenance). Haier's market ZZJYT also assists Yang with his own budgeting in order to help him maximize his profits. All of the shops in Yang's network sell their products at prices recommended by Haier within a discretionary markup range of 10 to 15 percent.

Yang takes the orders from the eighteen stores that he serves and then places a consolidated order with Haier through the market ZZJYT. Normally the suburban shops carry a large variety of products, including all of the high-end products that Haier offers, whereas stores in the smaller towns that serve rural villages tend to offer a more limited range of products.

The rural shops buy from Yang but are also directly assisted by Haier people from the market ZZJYT. The main task of these stores is to go to rural villages to look for customers. The owner of one of these shops in Lige Zhuang, a small rural town, estimates that he spends around 80 percent of his time looking after customers in rural villages (there are forty in the region). Originally two rural stores were assigned twenty of these villages each, but the reality is that if one shop is more aggressive, it can take some sales away from the other.

Sales in the villages are organized through Haier village representatives; about sixty of them operate in these forty villages. The representatives are villagers with good local reputations and strong personal networks, who are also good word-of-mouth promoters. In fact, Haier believes that villagers often buy Haier products simply because they trust the representative. In such cases, the representative is awarded a percentage of the sales revenue generated. In one rural village that we visited, the representative we spoke with was earning 1 percent of the product price for each product sold. If he sold more than five products in a year, he received a bonus of RMB 300. This is why there is often competition among people in these villages to become Haier sales representatives. The shop owner transports the goods sold to the ultimate customer and absorbs the cost.

The village representatives also handle after-sales service. If a customer reports a problem, the representative tries to solve it. Only when the situation is beyond his or her capabilities will this representative ask for help from technicians. In this manner, Haier conserves its after-sales resources for the most significant problems without sacrificing customer attention.

This organization of market services is typical of Haier across rural China (figure 5.7). Jiao Zhou has roughly 1 million inhabitants. The two shops in Lige Zhuang had gross sales of RMB 900,000 in July 2011. There are twenty small towns like Lige Zhuang under Jiao Zhou and twenty-eight counties like Jiao Zhou in China, so the potential sales for Haier are enormous, and the amount of customer learning that takes place at a very minimal cost is profound.

Figure 5.7 The Sales Hierarchy for Haier in the Qingdao Area

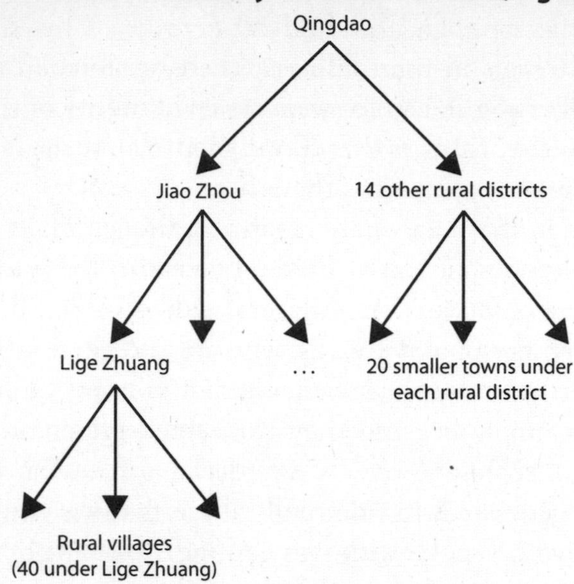

Performance Evaluation in Market ZZJYTs

At the root of the ZZJYT concept is the idea that the goals for critical performance measures such as market share, revenues, and profitability should not be assigned by managers who are not in the market but by the employees who are close to the market and the customers. Once a ZZJYT's goal is approved, it becomes the team's key performance measure. Individuals are then assigned their individual goals in support of the overall objective, and their performance is constantly measured based on their personal strategic income statement.

One of the unique characteristics of Haier's ZZJYT performance measurement approach is that the performance of salespeople is measured not on revenues but on profitability, or as Haier refers to it, the value that an individual brings to the company. Basically, all Haier products are categorized into four grades: A, B, C, and D. A products generate the highest profit, B products are a bit lower but still profitable, C products do not generate any profit, and D products generate losses. Obviously salespeople try to promote A and B products primarily. In the past, when salespeople were measured by revenues, they would trade off selling A and B products if the sale of C and D products was easier (as it was, especially in the rural areas).

AB grade customers (distributors or dealers) or consumers are those with the largest purchases of the more profitable products. Haier views them as its most valuable and loyal customers and consumers. As a result, if AB grades make up a high percentage in the portfolio of a salesperson, he or she will be considered a star employee and receive a higher bonus.

The total amount of profits earned is ultimately shared between Haier and the salesperson. A fixed preset level of profit belongs to the corporation, and the salesperson keeps the remainder. If the salesperson does not generate enough profit to meet Haier's target, the amount that should have gone to the corporation will be noted in that person's income statement as a "profit payable" in the next assessment period; the salesperson is required to pay it back as soon as he or she is generating profits again. Salespeople do have some discretion to set the prices of the products they sell as long as the target is to generate higher profit. Similarly, they have discretionary power to recruit salespeople, without approval, provided that they have determined that hiring more people will generate a positive return.

Profitability, however, is not the only performance measure. Market share, new product development, and customer satisfaction are taken into consideration as well. Haier uses the percentage of A and B customers over the total number of customers as a measure of satisfaction and loyalty. Market share is a secondary measure. Haier's target is to increase the AB customer overall percentage to 70 percent. In the past, like many other complex manufacturing organizations, the company also had serious cost problems associated with inaccurate sales forecasts, which led to excess inventory. Overstock charges did not seem to help, as the penalty for exaggerating forecasts was much less than the possible reward of having a product on hand to sell. The incentive for sales reps to reduce inventory remained low because they were more afraid to stock out than to pay for excess inventory, CEO Zhang recalled: "It was like a vicious circle: when cutting inventory, sales revenue would be reduced; when loosening the control on inventory, sales revenue would be increased, and so would the inventory."[4]

In June 2010, Haier attempted to address this problem in the refrigerator division by evaluating employees based on value creation for the customer. Three key performance aspects—order forecast accuracy, inventory turnover days, and inventory overdue percentage—were rated weekly and added to performance evaluations of the sales force. Salespeople with unsatisfactory performance would lose their right to place orders during a period of time, which would affect their sales volume and ultimately their compensation. The result was that salespeople began to go to the frontline of the market more frequently to discern the true demand of consumers. In the process, they also collected market intelligence firsthand. One salesperson discovered that the reason that brown washing machines were not selling well was that many users thought the color was "not clean." The feedback was sent back to R&D in order to improve the products according to such market reactions.

Eventually the refrigerator division incorporated these three criteria—forecast accuracy, inventory turnover, and inventory overdue—into its ABCD grading system. The new grading system resulted in the dismissal of four salespeople who did not improve their performance within a fixed time period. Haier sees evaluation of employees based on value creation for customers as a big step in pushing its just-in-time and zero inventory philosophy and embodying the essence of individual-goal combination. This approach has now been replicated in all the market ZZJYTs at Haier.

Income Statements for Sales Representatives

Each morning when Haier's salespeople open their computers, they see their performance in terms of sales and profitability as well as what their current order portfolio looks like. They therefore know where and by how much they should be improving their performance. They can also see their expenses, which are based on a forecast of the next two weeks and the next six weeks. They are also informed, based on promotion-activity plans, how much they should be planning to spend over the next six weeks in order to achieve their budgeted performance targets.

All of this information comes through Haier's enterprise resource planning system, which means that it is available on mobile phones as well. Haier's salespeople also receive daily text messages telling them how much they have gained or lost that day, which is important to their personal income. At any time, all sales reps know how much they are making.

Next Steps for Market ZZJYTs

The ZZJYT model is still young, put into practice only two years ago, and is not yet fully developed. Nevertheless, Haier is already thinking beyond ZZJYTs and experimenting with new forms of governance.

In Jiaonan, a small village a few kilometers outside Qingdao, Haier is conducting an experiment: creating a direct sales channel made up of Haier people (ZZJYT members) and local store owners. This business-to-business (B2B) unit will control several stores in the area and sell both products and services. It is the prototype for a new organizational form. Business-to-business companies jointly owned by Haier employees and shop owners could eventually replace all of Haier's market ZZJYTs. These will be independent companies, outside Haier's corporate boundaries, created and owned by ZZJYT employees and local dealers together. They are viewed as the next stage in the evolution of the inverted triangle and zero-distance concepts. Haier believes that transforming market ZZJYTs into independent companies, with direct responsibilities for revenues and costs and a direct equity stake for employees, will reduce the distance between it and its customers even more.

While it is envisioned that the ZZJYT employees, along with their local dealer partners, will purchase equity in these companies and thus become owners, they will also remain Haier employees. Challenging traditional norms regarding conflicts of interest, the former ZZJYT employees will continue to be responsible for performance on their internal Haier strategic income statements, including the possibility of being promoted within the Haier Group. Their fixed wages will still be paid by Haier, and their variable compensation will still depend on the sales of Haier concessions to a large extent (these companies sell Haier products on concession). Estimates are that the ratio of the fixed salary paid by Haier to the variable profit from the company could be around 20:80. As shareholders in the B2B companies, ZZJYT employees will also be able to take profits from the B2B company's earnings.

While legally the B2B companies are different corporate entities, from a managerial point of view very little changes with respect to the original ZZJYT structure and operations. Haier will not be a shareholder in these companies, which will be owned exclusively by the Haier ZZJYT employees and the independent store owners. However, it will keep tight control over these B2B companies. The companies will be connected to Haier's enterprise resource planning system so that Haier knows everything about their activities and can become involved in their management if necessary, controlling their growth or forbidding a possible sale of non-Haier products, for example.

The main advantage of the evolution to B2Bs for Haier is that whereas the costs of the ZZJYTs are 100 percent Haier's costs now, the expenses of these B2B companies will no longer be on Haier's income statement. In addition, the B2Bs will be independent companies, motivated to control their own costs and pursue economies of scale.

The ownership structure of the B2B companies will ensure Haier a high degree of control over them. Haier employees will control 75 percent of total shares and the local dealer the remaining 25 percent. As far as Haier employees are concerned, first-tier market ZZJYT members could collectively own around 50 to 60 percent of the capital, whereas second-tier ZZJYT members could collectively own around 15 to 25 percent. There will also be rules about the percentage of shares that each individual can have. For example, the general manager of the B2B company will be entitled to a maximum of 12 percent of the shares, while regular employees will be able to own 2 to 3 percent. Employees will not be forced to buy the shares or even to set up such companies. However, Haier believes that ambitious employees will be strongly attracted to buying such shares, whereas employees who have poorer performance will be averse to this change, and this has convinced senior management that this is the right way to go. It has been estimated that the payback period for the investments that Haier employees make should be around two years.

The B2Bs will be restricted to selling Haier products exclusively, and these products will actually be sold directly by the Haier Group. The B2B companies will be only service companies: they make the sale and provide services to customers. They will receive a 5 percent margin on gross revenues and will have the right to charge customers for their services. B2B companies will seek a sales mix that increases profits (both Haier's and their own), as well as aiming to provide consumers with more value-added services, over which they have full control (even regarding prices). Haier will not charge for services in which it is not directly involved.

Implementation of this ambitious next stage requires the resolution of two problems. The first is the balance between short-term and long-term profitability. Store owners tend to focus on short-term, immediate profitability, whereas Haier has a greater interest in increasing its long-term competitiveness, and in developing and exploiting its consumers' networks. The solution, for the time being, is devising specific KPIs to promote user interaction and development of consumer networks. These new KPIs, which have been formulated at the individual level, are envisioned as providing the company with an additional margin (on top of the 5 percent).

The second problem is the measurement of the individual's contribution to profitability. Haier believes that even if the companies are legally separated from Haier, it is necessary to define precise goals for everybody; otherwise there will be a natural tendency to free-ride. Haier thus makes an effort to create a target for every employee and to measure each contribution from different perspectives (not only profitability). The goals for the B2B companies are primarily to expand sales by serving an increasing number of stores in their area. This exclusive right to a geographical area has been developed in order to exploit the full potential of every area, pushing companies to go up against competitors within their own assigned areas and avoid competition among different areas.

Manufacturing ZZJYTs

The ZZJYT concept has also been widely practiced on production lines at Haier, where each of its 107 production lines is a ZZJYT, with an average of ten to thirty people per line. When a production order is received, it is put into an auction. The heads of the manufacturing ZZJYTs can bid to obtain the order on the basis of the performance indicators that they propose that their team can achieve. The internal transfer price at which the products are "sold" is preset each year, so normally there is not much bargaining regarding that number unless there is an increase in sales volume or the product line manages to improve its productivity. Given the preset price, however, a team that can propose the highest quality or fastest delivery may be chosen. The difference between the price and the costs is the margin that the manufacturing ZZJYT can retain; it is shared by all of the team members. Haier believes that this encourages the manufacturing ZZJYTs to be in continuous pursuit of greater efficiencies and cost-saving innovations to increase their profitability.

The relationship between the manufacturing and module ZZJYTs is based on a fixed price. The manufacturing ZZJYTs serve as an original equipment manufacturer for the module ZZJYTs. The evaluation of their performance is thus based on quality, cost, and delivery time. The aim for a manufacturing ZZJYT is to become the most competitive manufacturing factory in the world.

Manufacturing ZZJYT members are given efficiency targets based on the rate of their output. From such calculations, they are assigned a certain budget. If they remain below budget, they make a profit, which the ZZJYT members share. A manufacturing ZZJYT that can reduce labor costs due to innovation is entitled to keep the savings as the labor compensation associated with its proposed output is fixed and preset.

Second- and Third-Tier ZZJYTs

One step removed from the customer-facing frontline ZZJYTs are the second- and third-tier ZZJYTs, which mainly consist of functional managers. Their role was dramatically changed with the implementation of the newest Haier business model and the ZZJYT organization. As Tan Lixia, head of finance for Haier Group, reports, "They have had to change their behavior radically. They are no longer order makers but resource providers, meaning that they have to listen to those that were [formerly] listening to them."

Managers in second- and third-tier ZZJYTs can be divided into line managers (directly supervising salespeople) and staff managers (supervising functional professionals, such as finance, HR, and strategy).

Line Managers

Before the introduction of the ZZJYT model, managers were evaluated on market share gained, revenues, profits, and customer satisfaction. Today, with the inverted triangle in place, these KPIs are now used to evaluate only first-tier ZZJYT leaders. Second-tier managers are evaluated on the performance of the first-tier ZZJYTs that they supervise, as well as on the quality and the incentives of people engaged in supporting these activities. As an example, a second-tier sales manager is responsible for supporting the first-tier ZZJYTs in achieving their sales goals. Every day these managers should know the performance of every ZZJYT they are responsible for. In particular, they are responsible for checking each ZZJYT's incentive system. These second-tier managers have the power to change the system, should they realize that it is not working or that it is not adequately motivating people. They are also responsible for the performance of employees of first-tier ZZJYTs, and for substituting people if appropriate. Normally, it would seem as if this responsibility would be that of the first-tier ZZJYT leader, but that leader has a narrow market focus, whereas the second-tier manager oversees many ZZJYTs and can compare performance among them and so suggest to ZZJYT leaders that they consider replacing some members.

Staff Managers

Since most of the people employed in functional positions are assigned to activities within the ZZJYTs, the goals for the staff managers are fairly clear: nurture and develop excellent functional specialists who can perform well in the ZZJYTs. In addition, these staff managers make suggestions on how to improve the performance of ZZJYTs. Finance staff managers can evaluate a ZZJYT's performance by talking with the finance people who operate within it, and they can, together with HR, give suggestions to first-tier ZZJYT leaders as to the attractiveness of merging their unit with other ones if they see the advantages of doing so.

Evaluating Functional Staff Using the Strategic Income Statement

While evaluation of first-tier ZZJYT staff is facilitated by the objective numbers from market results, this is not the case for Haier's functional staff. Located in second-tier ZZJYTs, their situations, evaluations, and compensation have to be handled differently. For example, a finance member embedded in a ZZJYT receives a base salary from the finance department and a variable salary from the ZZJYT that he or she serves. The latter compensation depends on the profitability of the ZZJYT. If a team does not produce profits, the second-tier expert is simply paid his or her base salary for up to three months. After that, the person undergoes additional training and tries again in another ZZJYT. If there is a second failure, that person would be fired.

Preliminary Conclusions Regarding the ZZJYT Model

ZZJYTs are still relatively recent, but preliminary results of this approach appear promising. Haier believes that ZZJYTs have improved efficiency and infused the entire corporation with a strong entrepreneurial spirit. Since their implementation, Haier has become the world's biggest white goods company. However, there is no disputing that the ZZJYT concept has not yet evolved to the point where it is perfected. Although it has been easily implemented in the market, module, and manufacturing teams, it has proved more difficult to appraise the value of employees in functional departments. There is also the challenge of attracting talented individuals who embrace the mind-set of internal entrepreneurship, and there is a potential disconnect between the desire to unleash young talent and the perceived loss of power and status of middle managers who, with the ZZJYTs, may perceive themselves as little more than mere resource providers. Changing this mentality has proven to be a challenge. At the time of this writing, Haier announced new progress on the inverted triangle.

The next step for Haier could be to eliminate the second-tier ZZJYTs (they will be integrated into first tiers) and transform the company into one that will have no more middle managers—a node-based structure. (Please refer to the postscript for more information.)

On a more strategic level, there is an inevitable tension between the powerful market incentives of this model and the more stable requirements of corporate strategy. There may be trade-offs between individual objectives and corporate strategy. Done well, the model requires a strong commitment to aligning individual goals with corporate goals, which may be the most critical determinant of the approach's effectiveness. The approach should be extremely powerful when incentives are well aligned but may prove precarious when, for any reason, individual and corporate incentives lose alignment.

Looking Forward and Looking Back

Haier has built one of China's leading brands, a brand that has generated enormous national pride. As a metaphor, Haier's path can be seen as a reflection of China's path. Haier, one of the oldest collective firms, has passed through several phases of development that mimic the development phases that all of China has undergone. It began life as an unbranded OEM and established its success through product quality. It next took this established domestic brand and grew rapidly thanks to internal demand and the acquisition of companies that were failing. Eventually it moved abroad, first by export and then by direct investment, to become a global company. Now it is implementing a strategy of zero distance from end users, switching its emphasis from manufacturing to transforming itself into a service company All of these phases parallel the rise of China as a global power: the country established itself as the "factory of the world" in the mid-1980s and is now turning to the imposing challenge of creating global brands.

What Haier is embarked on represents the next frontier in the development of complex organizations: unleashing employee talent in such a way that large organizations can meet the needs of their customers without sacrificing the achievements of efficiency that they have won in less customer-centric eras. Haier's win-win approach to connecting employee energy and ingenuity through individual goal combinations, the core of Haier's business model, should be as interesting an approach in the new economy of Silicon Valley as it is in making household appliances in Qingdao. It represents the new frontier of organizational development. In many ways, it is a simple yet powerful idea that requires a vastly different way of organizing economic activity within firms.

6

HAIER AS A HIGH PERFORMER

> I have a dream of organizations that are capable of spontaneous renewal, where the drama of change is unaccompanied by the wrenching trauma of a turnaround. I dream of businesses where an electric current of innovation pulses through every activity, where the renegades always trump the reactionaries. I dream of companies that actually deserve the passion and creativity of the folks who work there, and actually elicit the very best that people have to give.[1]
>
> *Gary Hamel*, The Future of Management

The dream that Zhang Ruimin has been pursuing for the past three decades is an elusive one but not an entirely new one. There are precedents against which we can compare Haier's ambition and achievement, and it is instructive to do so. It is also an interesting commentary on the company that Haier is keeping, as the organizations that we consider in this chapter are all well respected for their dreams and their pioneering spirit. It is sobering to think that we are seriously including a Chinese company that makes household appliances in this set, but most of the companies that we review are not competing in what is fashionably referred to as new-economy industries; they are all in unfashionable, competitively challenged old-economy industries, and it is the pressure of such situations that has driven them to dream bigger than most of their rivals in a bid to not only survive but also flourish.

We begin with the notion that no matter which industry we are in, the future will most likely be profoundly different from the past; in fact, we can already experience it. Our lives have changed; we communicate differently, more frequently, and with more and different people; we work at jobs that would be unimaginable to our grandparents; we work in different places and learn different things than our forebears did; and our homes and personal lives are nothing that could be imagined even a few decades ago. Such changes are startling, but they are not as incongruous as the notion that the same organizational logic that has been relied on for centuries—command and control—will continue to provide the optimal organizing template for the future. Yet that is exactly what is happening. Most organizations today look exactly like the organizations of the past. Not much has really changed with the art of management. There has not been much to speak of when we consider managerial innovation.

Yet organizations matter. In many respects, they are the engines that drive our economies and societies. They are the motors that are responsible for taking raw materials, including human talent, and converting them into outputs and outcomes of higher social value. They, more than any other type of social instrument, are relied on to satisfy human wants and needs. If anything should be given careful attention in terms of its running condition and suitability for use, it should be organizational design.

To be sure, the contributions of organizational design have been recognized and appreciated in many settings and for much of recorded history. People have employed organizations as tools for leveraging labor, machinery, knowledge, power, and authority since prehistoric times. Professionalization began early with the development of hydraulic societies in Asia, the imperial bureaucracy of dynastic China, and the Roman Catholic church's need to maintain discipline and consistency over wide geographical areas, and it evolved to such sophisticated commercial organizations as the European East India Companies (British East India Company, 1600) and the Japanese commercial organizations (e.g., Mitsui in the early seventeenth century) that were complex multibusiness businesses that performed on a global scale.

Ultimately there appears to be uniform agreement with the idea that the organization of work, especially the development of the modern organization in the West, has been a major contributor to the ascendancy of Western economies over the past five hundred years. John Micklethwait and Adrian Wooldridge write:

> *The company* has been one of the West's great competitive advantages: . . . The [Victorian corporate laws of the mid- to late-nineteenth century] ushered in an organization that has been uniquely effective in rendering human effort productive.
>
> ". . . The limited liability corporation is the greatest single discovery of modern times," proclaimed Nicholas Murray Butler, one of the great sages of the Progressive Era; "even steam and electricity would be reduced to comparative impotence without it."[2]

It would seem natural, therefore, to assume that if we had so long enjoyed the benefits of a tool as productive as organization, we would also have long studied the nature of that tool so as to extract every last bit of potential benefit out of it. That has not been the case. Modern organizational studies go back only a relatively short while. One might argue that it was Max Weber (1864–1920) who began modern organization studies with his inquiry into bureaucracy as the organizational analog for the sorts of breakthroughs that industrial engineers, under the leadership of Frederick Taylor, were making. Whereas Taylorists were reengineering the shop-floor and man-machine interactions, Weberites were reengineering administrative structure in the same pursuit of rationality and efficiency. In both instances, however, the emphasis was almost purely structural, as if understanding and improving the processes that worked would be enough to realize the full power of the organization.

Subsequent generations of organizational designers—scholars and students such as Elton Mayo, Douglas McGregor, and Herbert A. Simon and James G. March, to name but a few—added bits and pieces of human relations and decision sciences until we arrived at the 1960s and the work of Alfred Chandler Jr. Chandler was unequivocal in his opinion that the modern complex enterprise is the "underlying dynamic in the development of modern industrial capitalism."[3] In Chandler's mind, the key to all of this was placing organizational structure in the service of organizational strategy:

> At the core of this dynamic were the organizational capabilities of the enterprise as a unified whole. These organizational capabilities were the collective physical facilities and human skills as they were organized within the enterprise. . . .
>
> But only if these facilities and skills were carefully coordinated and integrated could the enterprise achieve the economies of scale and scope that were needed to compete in national and international markets and to continue to grow.[4]

So it is more than merely structure and, as Chandler noted, this is where leadership comes in. To Chandler's credit, he did not disconnect the behavioral and cultural nature of the organization from the more structural aspects of organizing and governing, but for the most part, the nature of the change that he described, until at least the mid-twentieth century when he was writing, appears to today's observers to be remarkably linear in nature: almost as if the rate and direction of future growth could be anticipated based on the extrapolation of past success, and the expectation of a continuation of these same business conditions into the future. In fact, however, Chandler himself admitted that in the middle of the twentieth century (the 1960s, to be precise), the world began to change. We started to see intense competition on a global scale, along with the development of new technologies that were changing nearly every aspect of the managerial role.

Since the 1980s, a lively field of inquiry has flourished, examining what new managerial roles should look like that will take our organizations and the strategies that drive them into the future. There has evolved, in fact, a mythology of modern management that, while not scientifically satisfying, does speak to the art of leadership and reflects inherited wisdom gained from practical experience. With the appearance of a path-breaking study by McKinsey & Company entitled *In Search of Excellence*,[5] which addressed the underlying sources of corporate excellence, management students began to turn their attention to what it was within these structures and governance models that made some organizations outperform. The book was wildly successful and was followed by a long and continuing line of studies, each of which tried to answer essentially the same question with ever more ambitious means.

Despite their widespread acceptance and commercial fame, these studies of corporate success, including some of the most popular business books of all time, have to be treated very carefully, as there is a general theme of casualness in the research methodology that runs through the literature and might well negate the power of the lessons they propose to offer. Phil Rosenzweig of IMD has written in great detail, and with piercing critical analysis, in his book *The Halo Effect*[6] about the dangers of relying on such flawed research, as has Michael E. Raynor and his Deloitte consulting associates in their work on the determinants of organizational performance.[7] Part of the essence of these arguments is that we have socialized managers to attribute certain "successful behaviors" in explaining their own success, so what we obtain from interviews with managers in exceptionally high-performing companies may not be so much what really happened, but what they believe happened as a result of the ex post rationale that they construct for explaining their success. Raynor, Ahmed, and Henderson suggest that despite such problems, there is still some value in this "success studies literature":

> This doesn't mean that you should necessarily dismiss the advice offered in success studies. The authors are savvy observers of the

> business world. Their recommendations can be useful. . . . Success studies should be treated not as how-to manuals but as sources of inspiration and fuel for introspection. The value is not in what you *read* in them but what you read *into* them.[8]

So what can we, in fact, read into these studies?

The Mythology of High-Performing Organizations

If we collect the best known of the success story literature and look for the commonalities that might well reflect what Raynor, Ahmed, and Henderson suggested are sources of inspiration and fuel for introspection, a number of lessons are worth noting:

- *Change is ever-present and needs to be continually adjusted to*. One of the themes running through all of these books is that change is constant and that the outperforming organization needs to be continually appraising the world around it and changing accordingly. Rosenzweig has noted that all too often today's "excellent" organizations are tomorrow's "average" performers and has characterized this as "High-performance is real, but fleeting." He has also observed that regression to the mean is the typical fate of most organizations that cannot, or do not, continue to change.[9]
- *Speed may be the most important competitive differentiator*. One of the common lessons from the emerging mythology of high-performing organizations is that they are more agile and more responsive and, as a result, faster.
- *Ambition matters*. It appears that the companies identified as being successful are those that dream big, are proactive, and are not afraid to be ambitious.
- *Being in touch with the world around the firm*. Another theme that runs through nearly all of these stories is that of the utility of an organization's being in touch with the world

around it, and of ensuring that it is aware of and responds in a timely manner to events that are unfolding around it, its industry, and its value chain partners.

- *The value of self-awareness*. Knowing who you are and what you stand for and then emphasizing that awareness appears to be of considerable importance. In nearly every success story related, the exceptionally focused firm—which might include a culture of strong discipline to make the organization's self-awareness reliable—was the high performer.
- *Autonomy, risk taking, and entrepreneurship*. The ability to respond rapidly, take risks, and think differently marks exceptionally successful firms in many of the success stories. Frequently the descriptions that accompany such examples cite entreprencurship as part of the corporate culture.
- *Unleashing talent*. Being able to attract great people and then unleash their talent is associated with exceptional performance in many of the success stories.
- *Strong, self-confident, people-based leadership*. Strong leadership need not be a death sentence for inclusive participation in forging the future of the firm if the leaders are self-confident enough to be close to their people and to trust them to get on with the job. In fact, it might only be strong leaders who are self-confident enough to allow others to be included in key decision-making roles.

Creating the High-Performing Organization of the Future

For the most part, the mythology of successful organizations has concerned itself with the reported attributes of these organizations at the time of their success. What goes underexplained in too many instances is how these attributes were achieved. Yet there is some vivid instruction in this regard from different sources.

The High-Performing Success Story Literature

Tom Peters and Robert Waterman, *In Search of Excellence* (1982)

Jim Collins and Jerry Porras, *Built to Last: Successful Habits of Visionary Companies* (1994)

Jim Collins, *Good to Great* (2001)

Richard N. Foster and Sarah Kaplan, *Creative Destruction: Why Companies That Are Built to Last Underperform the Market—and How to Successfully Transform Them* (2001)

Donald Sull, *Why Good Companies Go Bad, and How Great Managers Remake Them* (2003)

Yves Doz and Mikko Kosonen, *Fast Strategy* (2008)

Jim Collins, *How the Mighty Fall* (2009)

Jurgen Appelo, *Management 3.0: Leading Agile Developers, Developing Agile Leaders* (2011)

Nearly fifty years ago, the great leadership scholar Warren Bennis, writing with Philip Slater, argued that "whenever a social system is competing for survival under conditions of chronic change," it becomes necessary for that social system to develop the following organizational behaviors, which suggest instrumentality for achieving the attributes described in the success story literature:

- Full and free *communication*, regardless of rank and power
- A reliance on *consensus* rather than the more customary forms of coercion or compromise to manage conflict
- The idea that *influence* is based on technical competence and knowledge rather than on the vagaries of personal whims or prerogatives of power

- An atmosphere that permits and even encourages *emotional expression* as well as task-oriented acts
- A basically human bias that *accepts the inevitability of conflict* between the organization and the individual but is willing to cope with and mediate this conflict on rational grounds[10]

More recently, work by Yves Doz and Mikko Kosonen has provided some additional empirical insights into how effective organizations of the future might behave.[11] They refer to these organizations as "strategically agile companies" or, in the case of Jurgen Appelo's *Management 3.0*, as having "agile management" and they characterize them as having five elements of operating that reflect much of what we heard in the success studies:[12]

- *Strategic sensitivity:* This recognizes that strategy starts outside an organization and, to be successful, an organization needs to establish the ability to generate both foresight and insight, that is, the ability to see further faster than its competitors and then interpret strategic meanings. Such vision is critical for future success. Typically this requires looking outside traditional knowledge communities for insights, probing and testing through experimentation and prototyping, creating the capacity for confrontation to test new ideas, and involving more rather than fewer knowledge contributors in the decision process. All of these will characterize new ways of working in the future.
- *Speed of change:* In competitive markets characterized by chronic uncertainty, successful organizations of the future will succeed in part because of their speed of response and adjustment. It is increasingly difficult to aspire to the completeness of knowledge that formerly characterized optimization approaches to organizational decision making. Tomorrow's organizations will no longer pretend to be knowledge holders. They instead will have to succeed by discovering ephemeral knowledge through testing and revising and then will have to be able to

execute on these insights without assurance that the initiative is the correct one but with confidence that they can respond and revise in a short time span.

- *Resource fluidity:* Organizational responsiveness by definition requires the ability to move resources—people, funding, technology, brands, and so forth—to wherever in the firm's portfolio of activities they might be needed. This is the complete breakdown of traditional fiefdoms and the recognition that all assets belong to the firm not the strategic business unit. It is an essential complement to the sorts of learning that will be required for achieving speed of change.
- *Collective commitment:* Fast-response, nontraditional learning and similar undertakings frequently require support from the top of an organization's hierarchy.[13] Doz and Kosonen found that this was associated with leadership teams with strong CEOs, shared agendas among the leadership team, and mutual dependencies. As natural as this might appear, for coauthor Mikko Kosonen, a long-time senior Nokia executive, it was an eye-opener: "That's probably, to me . . ., the biggest finding and learning from our research: this whole notion of leadership unity and its critical importance, and how companies really need to pay deep attention to the mechanisms that sustain leadership unity."
- *Strong people-based leadership:* Increasingly, competitive success goes to organizations that have the best ideas and can learn and respond the fastest. This is a talent issue, and organizations that emphasize strong, people-based cultures are more likely to get the most out of the talent that they employ.

Benchmarking Against Trailblazing Talent-Liberating Experiences

The attractiveness of the success-story ideas can be found in several notable attempts to design organizations that could succeed in competitive markets by virtue of unleashing the rich talent that they employ, which inevitably meant adopting Bennis and Slater's types of approaches to the design of these organizations. We look at several of these and then benchmark them against what Haier is trying to achieve with its journey of unleashing its talent in fulfillment of customer desires.

Oticon

Oticon was for many decades one of the world's leading producers of hearing aids. Danish by origin, the company had enjoyed nearly seventy-five years of success as a worldwide market leader before losing half of its market share in a single year.[14] Having enjoyed the inertia of market success for such a prolonged period, Oticon found itself unwittingly relying on old products, with out-of-date design and technology, employing uninteresting value propositions and distribution channels, and costly manufacturing approaches, and suddenly the organization was on its way to bankruptcy and extinction. In fact, hearing aids were a traditional industry undergoing profound changes in the areas of, for example, customer demographics, marketing channels to reach new (younger, more hip) customer segments, advertising shifts from medical information to "lifestyle," new technologies (analog to digital), miniaturization, new product design (from behind the ear to in the ear), and new manufacturing technologies. In addition, low-price competitors were emerging, leaving Oticon with no place to feel secure on the changing competitive landscape.

A new CEO, Lars Kolind, was brought in from outside the industry and posed the challenge as "how to reinstall hearing into a deaf company . . . how to make a conservative company innovative and flexible, how to carry through a paradigm shift." The new paradigm that Kolind was referring to was a different way of working that he believed would revitalize Oticon and restore its competitive vigor despite the fact that many of its most talented employees had already left what they felt was a dying organization. According to Kolind:

> There are four basic, common aspects for organizations that can continuously adapt to changing environments and continuously apply knowledge in new ways to create innovations in products, processes, and services [these are remarkably similar to the arguments of Doz and Kosonen already set out in this chapter]:
>
> - They have a meaning, which goes beyond that of making a profit or being the industry leader.
> - They involve a fundamental partnership between management and staff, and they do not look upon the two as opposites. The partnership also extends to suppliers, customers, and other partners outside of the organization.
> - They are organized for collaboration—that is, less structured and more organic and chaotic than a conventional business.
> - They are led by people who base their jobs on shared values rather than authority and power.[15]

Building on this set of beliefs and following a short interim respite where Oticon appeared to be recovering simply by working harder but not smarter, Kolind employed "shock therapy" to transform the old culture into a radically different one. Among the initiatives he unleashed were these:

- Creating a new organization vision that encouraged "thinking the unthinkable"
- Emphasizing the need to not only dream big dreams but also to make the numbers at the same time so that the organization was solvent
- Changing the concept of a job to better match the talents of each individual
- Discontinuing the old hierarchical departmental structure and replacing it with a project-based organization

- Selecting project leaders to run the projects based on the quality of their project proposals
- Creating an open and inspiring workplace with no walls or partitions
- Creating a talent pool within the organization and market-based bilateral hiring and acceptance processes to staff the projects
- Peer appraisal of performance[16]

In addition, Kolind made absolutely certain that his initiatives were all focused on the objective of creating a new and successful Oticon business model and that each of the initiatives reinforced the others. Most of these initiatives were launched simultaneously so that there were no dangling initiatives that might be picked off by forces of resistance to change. Figure 6.1 illustrates the Galbraith star representation of how the Oticon culture appeared as a result of these initiatives.

The results were remarkable. Annual sales rose over a five-year period by an annual average of 19 percent, return on sales reached 15.4 percent from a starting point of 1.8 percent, and profitability reached an all-time high of 23.3 percent. In addition, a depleted R&D pipeline was restocked, and Oticon won a number of prestigious innovation and design awards.[17] All of this was accomplished with essentially the same workforce as before (minus some of the most talented employees, who had already left the company), indicating that the culture of the old Oticon was actually diminishing the talent that the organization had rather than unleashing it.

Morning Star

You don't need to do an industry analysis to appreciate that vegetable processing is a challenging industry to make money in.[18] Morning Star's CEO Chris Rufer understood that, and yet, compared to average industry growth of approximately 1 percent a

Figure 6.1 Galbraith Star for Oticon

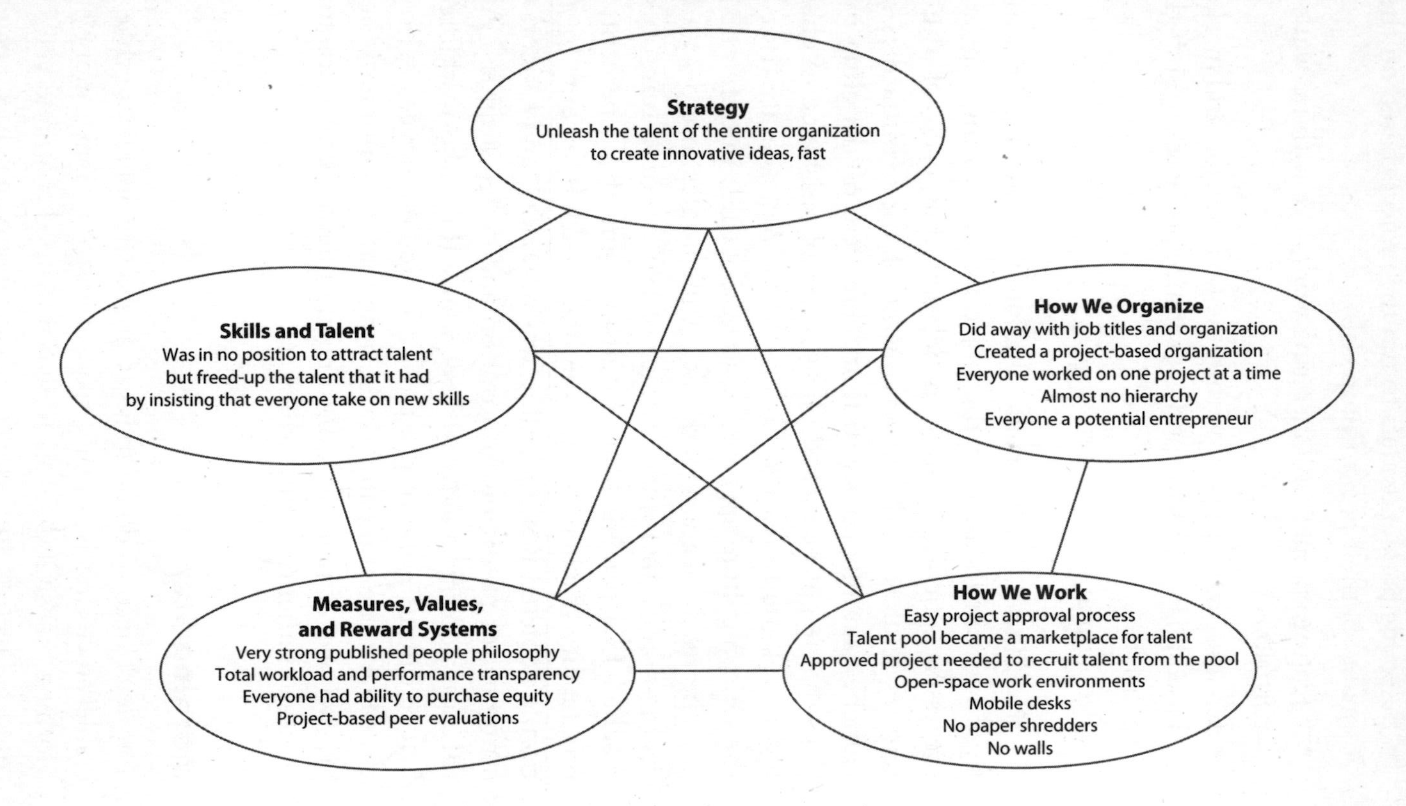

year, Morning Star's volumes, revenues, and profits have all grown at double-digit rates over the past twenty years. Clearly it is doing something different.

Management guru Gary Hamel has been following Morning Star for inclusion in his book *What Happens Now?* and in a *Harvard Business Review* article, "First, Let's Fire All the Managers."[19] He characterizes Morning Star as a "positive deviant"—an organization that is a "large, capital-intensive corporation whose sprawling plants devour hundreds of tons of raw material every hour, [and] where dozens of processes have to be kept within tight tolerances" yet where:

- No one has a boss.
- Employees negotiate responsibilities with their peers.
- Everyone can spend the company's money.
- Each individual is responsible for acquiring the tools needed to do his or her work.
- There are no titles and no promotions.
- Compensation decisions are peer based.

The objective of Morning Star is "to create a company in which all team members 'will be self-managing professionals, initiating communications and the coordination of their activities with fellow colleagues, customers, suppliers, and fellow industry participants, absent directives from others.'" This is achieved through a variety of managerial choices such as the daily disaggregation of the company's goals into personal mission statements; annual negotiation of colleagues' letters of understanding, which are shared understandings of what formal relationships mean, will accomplish, and how they should be measured; customer-supplier agreements negotiated annually between Morning Star's twenty-three business units; transparent information availability for all; mediation of disputes between colleagues; peer appraisal of strategic business unit (SBU) performance; and a host of other specific choices targeted directly at achieving the corporate vision and are all also mutually reinforcing.

According to Hamel, managers do what markets cannot: they amalgamate thousands of disparate contributions into a single product or service. They constitute what business historian Alfred Chandler Jr. called the *visible hand*. The downside, though, is that the visible hand is inefficient and often ham-fisted.[20] By making everybody a manager, Morning Star has avoided the trade-off between either market or hierarchy, creating "neither a loose confederation of individual contractors nor a stultifying bureaucracy; [Morning Star is] a subtle blend of both market and hierarchy"—a mix of a *socially dense marketplace* and many *naturally dynamic hierarchies*.[21]

ABB

Asea Brown Boveri is the celebrated combination of what were originally two venerable European power companies: Swedish Aesa and Swiss Brown Boveri. Well-known management scholars Chris Bartlett and the late Sumantra Ghoshal considered ABB at the time of its formation in the 1990s as one of the most intriguing examples of what they saw as an emerging new organizational model:[22]

> We believe that the management of ABB . . . is premised on a set of basic assumptions on the part of its managers regarding organization structure, decision making processes and, ultimately, human behavior that are significantly different from those that underlie the economic and behavioral theories that currently dominate academic analysis of business organizations.[23]

The premise paid off in the postmerger period from 1988 to 1993 when CEO Barnevik built ABB into a federation of national companies composed of thousands of companies within Europe. ABB decided to use English as its working language and the U.S. dollar as its accounting currency. With only one hundred employees in its headquarters in Zurich and a profoundly decentralized structure, ABB claimed, "We are not homeless. We have many homes," and then proceeded to create structures and processes designed to make "many homes" an advantage rather than an administrative nightmare.[24] To many observers of the organizational scene, ABB was the first true effort to build a complex global commercial organization, rather than settle for remaining multidomestic, and it worked well for a while because of the thought that went into how it was to be designed and the way it would pursue the benefits of spontaneity despite having an industrial DNA that valued linearity and regularity over nearly everything else.

ABB's mission, values, and policies at the time stated that "our guiding principle is to decentralize the Group into distinctive profit centers and assign individual accountability to each." ABB described this as "radical decentralization," indicating that it believed that its firm was profoundly different from a traditional corporate entity subdivided into separate divisions that were coordinated and directed from the top. Instead, at ABB, the SBUs were "self-contained and manageable units with strategic overview." ABB organized this as a federation of approximately thirteen hundred companies, each structured as a separate and distinct business unit. On average, each of these companies employed around two hundred people in order to gain the advantages inherent in smaller organizations.

Underneath these business units, monthly performance data were collected on forty-five hundred profit centers. These frontline companies were given complete responsibility for their balance sheet. As ABB's 1991 mission, values, and policies document also stated, "A decentralized organization will only work effectively with a good reporting system that gives higher level managers the opportunity to react in good time." To facilitate this, ABB implemented a fully automated system, ABACUS (Asea Brown Boveri Accounting and CommUnication System), which served as the nervous system for the entire organization. On the fifth of every month, each of the forty-five hundred profit centers sent their profit-and-loss reports to the Zurich headquarters. Senior management then reviewed their performance and compared them against the SBU's budgets and forecasts. The system allowed ABB to aggregate and disaggregate the data by segments, countries, and regions to create meaningful comparisons within ABB's matrix structure's two dimensions of geography and product lines.

The reporting changes were in line with ABB's philosophy of valuing speed more than precision. In an interview with the *Harvard Business Review* at the time, CEO Percy Barnevik said: "Why emphasize speed over precision? Because the costs of delay exceed the costs of mistakes."[25] (Recall that speed is also one of Haier's core competencies.) To have speed and communication, that is, clear and quick communication, is vital in big companies like ABB and Haier. ABB used to have fifteen thousand middle managers around the world, and Barnevik believed that their role needed to be dramatically redefined from being implementers of top-down decisions to primary initiators of entrepreneurial actions. Middle management at ABB would then exist primarily to coach and support the front managers, while top managers would be expected to develop broad sets of objectives and establish stretch performance standards.

ABB had become, in fact, a totally decentralized federation of national companies on a worldwide scale and, as a result, a pioneer in the willingness to reinvent a corporate culture at an early stage of globalization. When Göran Lindahl replaced Barnevik in 1997, the matrix organization was restructured as a multidivisional network to put more focus on product than on geography. Over time, a combination of misreading the Asian currency crisis then unfolding, a controversial decision to move out of heavy-industry engineering and reconceptualize the company as a knowledge company, and the fallout from the Combustion Engineering unit's asbestos liabilities all conspired to bring Barnevik's influence to an end and reduce the firm's propensity for organizational experimentation.

ABB's matrix organization and decentralized federation of national companies under Barnevik had shown, however, that it was possible for a giant global company to become a "dancing giant." Among the keys to this achievement were these:

- "Thinking global, acting local," ABB's philosophy of achieving synergy on the global scale while still adapting to local customers' needs. Barnevik thought that an ABB company in France should fully serve its French clients because it understood its customers better. While this exact strategy might no longer apply in today's extremely globalized environment, the core of the strategy, local adaption, still matters.
- In order to achieve global-level synergy, ABB also created centers of excellence, where one company is selected as the exemplar for others for its best practices in each specific field.
- ABB created an internal labor market to facilitate the internal transfer of employees so that they could share best practices with teams in different product lines and regions.
- The ABACUS information system served as a necessary reporting tool for senior management to keep track of what was happening on the front lines. It not only quantified performance measures but also took into account some qualitative indicators and long-term impacts of certain difficult-to-measure activities.

Amid the carnage of ABB's crash following Barnevik's departure and the falling out of fashion of the "*CEO as Superman* school of thought" (Jack Welch's retirement at about the same time led to Barnevik and Welch, and a few other über-leaders, being characterized as belonging to the same school of leadership thought), ABB became a much-studied case history.[26] Between 1988 and 1996 under Percy Barnevik's leadership, ABB's revenue grew from $17.5 billion to $33.8 billion and the company's market capitalization increased fivefold. It was undeniable that decentralization generated a high level of entrepreneurship in a giant organization. Its global matrix structure was also one of the first trials in the global era to resolve the contradictions that existed in many global companies of being global and local, big and small, and decentralized and centralized. In 1995, Barnevik received Ernst & Young's Global Growth Award and the European CEO of the Year Award.[27]

Nash Confectionery in India

Nash Confectionery is one of the largest fast-moving consumer goods companies in the world. (Nash Confectionery is a disguised example.) European based, it has a global reach and a wide portfolio of local and international brands in a mature industry. It employs approximately fifty-five thousand people and is a high flyer in the equity markets. India should be an important market for the company, but it has historically struggled there.

In 2005, a new country manager, Dale Johnston, was appointed to India. What he found there was chronic average performance in a market that should have been promising. After spending the first one hundred days asking questions, Johnston concluded, "The business was run based on past beliefs, not current market data. We missed big shifts in consumer preferences and the aggressive moves of competitors. It appeared to me that we didn't know the business that well."[28]

After employing external consultants to read the market more accurately, Johnston established stretch goals—including making a public promise to earn profits within three years that were approximately 22 percent above what the already-stretched targets (14 percent) were set at—that went well beyond what anyone, including corporate headquarters, believed was possible. On the basis of internal HR surveys, Johnston also believed that the organization had squandered the talent that it employed and that if the leadership team could somehow unleash this talent, a heroic turnaround was indeed possible.

Armed with this ambition and following the same star logic of Jay Galbraith described in chapter 3 of this book to map cultural interventions and used in this chapter to describe Oticon, Johnston began to change virtually every aspect of the corporate culture, including

- Relying on fact-based market data for decision making rather than allowing personal opinions to determine choices
- Dissolving functional silos and moving to a project-based organization
- Moving key decision roles from headquarters to the field
- Establishing transparency in HR decision making so that everyone knew everything at the same time
- Abandoning the former informal organizational "caste" system, based on schooling and rank, to one in which everyone was counted on to be an idea contributor toward achieving the new, ambitious goals
- Adopting new measures that better captured performance
- Making a public promise, if successful, to offer an extraordinary bonus, which, at the lowest levels of the organization promised three years' salary as an immediate cash bonus, in addition to the "normal" bonus scheme, if the objectives were reached on time.

With Galbraith's star chart on his wall guiding every move so that each was aimed specifically at the overall objective and also mutually reinforced the other moves, Johnston and his team achieved their objective and completely turned the Indian operation around, based not on new people or new products, but on making better choices to unleash the talent that Nash had always had in that market.

Several years later, reflecting on the enormous success of the venture, Johnston's "number two" shared several lessons that speak to the issues in this book:

- We always talked about talent, the best people; but we had never actually managed explicitly toward that goal:
    - I now believe that you shouldn't hire if you can't fire.
    - You have to allow the people to whom you give responsibility to make the calls. . . . Don't move those choices to somebody else.
    - Tolerance of poor performance is now out.
    - Rewarding the wrong people is not the right thing.
- People should be rewarded in the way that they'd like to be rewarded—with rewards that matter to them.
- Honesty: being absolutely honest about what works and doesn't work is necessary.
- Taking risks: asking for forgiveness not for permission.
    - And, go public with it [beforehand], so that everything is transparent.
- Senior leadership has to understand what it stands for and what it wants to accomplish:
    - I want to make changes; not be a bureaucrat!
- Everyone in the organization should have a personal "blueprint for success."[29]

Markets, Hierarchies, and the Future of Management

Despite their disparate origins—hearing aids, tomatoes, power engineering, and confectionery these examples are all strikingly similar in a number of fascinating ways. The companies profiled are all struggling to deal with an uncertain future—faster, more complex, more unpredictable—despite their being in old-economy industries. And they are all trying to accomplish this by taking fuller advantage of their employees' talents than the old hierarchical models of organization would allow. To return to the lessons learned from the success stories mythology, this is an acknowledgment that change is ever present and needs to be continually adjusted to and change is a direct outcome of being in touch with the world around the firm.

All of the firms are hugely ambitious, with objectives, visions, and goals that go well beyond industry norms, and all of them invite their employees into critical discussions about the future, with the result that they are probably more self-aware than anyone else in a similar situation in their industry who relies instead solely on managerial wisdom for a sober appraisal of the organization's competencies. One common outcome that they all share is that of speed: they are faster than their competitors and are constantly in motion. Another common trait is that they all have encouraged autonomy, risk taking, and entrepreneurship among their workers, who are now colleagues rather than employees. Yet at the same time, there is in every instance discipline built into the way of working so that there is never a loss of control or accountability. And we think that it is safe to say that each of these situations is characterized by leaders at the top who are smart, strong, and self-confident; without these leadership traits, it is unlikely that such experiments in reinvention would ever be considered, much less acted on. As a result of all of these attributes, each of these organizations is remarkably agile, despite the old-economy nature of their industries and the ever-present fear of commoditization that characterizes their competitive arenas.

Comparison with Haier

When we compare these attributes to Haier, it is easy to see the many obvious similarities in both intentions and approaches. As with Haier, all of these organizations are aspiring to outperform in mature industries flirting with commoditization, by making full use of the talent they have employed. Like Haier, their quest for talent utilization takes on the form of decentralizing the organization into units closer to the customer, giving those units more accountability for their profit and loss, creating more transparency in managerial information and results so that better decisions can be made, creating market-like conditions for the movement of talent, and rewarding performance. Although there is a spectrum of activities ranging from regularity to spontaneity, as well as a spectrum of instruments ranging from hierarchy to markets, it seems safe to say that all of these examples, including Haier, are relying more on markets to achieve spontaneity than would be true for their competitive peers.

It is equally instructive, however, to note that Haier's experiences differ in some fundamental ways from those of the companies we have just reviewed:

- Haier is the only example where the size and direction of the experiment has been increasing. Nash was essentially a one-time effort in a regional context, although subsequent efforts in both the Indian market and elsewhere were less successful and occasionally retrogressive. At both ABB and Oticon, subsequent efforts were more modest and, like Nash, the ambitiousness of these later initiatives had diminished in some ways as well. Morning Star's commitment to the experiment has been relatively long-lived, but it appears to have been more steady than experimental.
- Haier, along with ABB, is the largest. This is no small feat: the challenge of reinvention is probably exponentially associated with organizational size.
- Haier is the most customer-centric of the companies. The upending of the triangle to place the customer experience at the top of all ambition is the most vivid linking of external outcomes to internal organizational changes among the examples considered.
- Haier has been the most ambitious in taking the idea outside its own organizational boundaries. By stretching the

market chain concept to include both distributors of Haier's products and possibly customers, Haier has broken through traditional organizational walls and attempted to capture the power of pull.

All of these firms must balance the cost concerns that call out for regularity in work approaches with the desire to accommodate as much spontaneity as is possible in their work life in order to gain the advantages of responsiveness. One way of thinking about this is to suggest that these firms, like all other firms, exist on a spectrum that stretches from regularity to spontaneity in their approach to decision making (figure 6.2):

Figure 6.2 Different Approaches to Decision Making

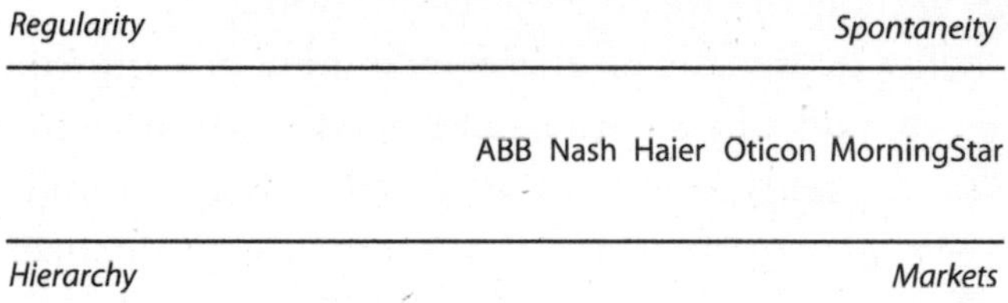

Regularity					*Spontaneity*
	ABB	Nash	Haier	Oticon	MorningStar
Hierarchy					*Markets*

Nash and all of the other examples to its right along the spectrum have employed projects as the key organizing theme in order to gain responsiveness. What is also clear is that from Haier to the right along the spectrum, the explicit theme of relying on market behavior between the project teams has been chosen over a reliance on hierarchy. In such situations, we see large industrial organizations attempting to harness the power of what John Seely Brown and John Hagel have called *pull* in order to unleash the power of human talent in the face of ever more complex and unpredictable market dynamics.[30]

David Bollier has written that as the world moves from episodic punctuations to a more continuous acceptance of change, organizations have to adapt as well. In his words, "Pull platforms harness the passion, commitment, and desire to learn of their participants, thereby enabling the formation and functioning of distributed communities that can rapidly improvise and innovate. Pull platforms tend to be able to mobilize and deploy social energies more effectively than bureaucratic, standardized push platforms."[31] This has also been the message that we saw with Doz and Kosonen, who argued that as the speed of market change increases, strategic planning fails, and as the complexity of that change increases and becomes systemic rather than merely linear, entrepreneurship is simply not enough. Their conclusion is that such fast and systematically complex business environments need organizations that behave differently from the way they did in the past; the biggest changes will have to be the acuity with which the organization senses its environment, the way that it builds a fully committed team culture, and its ability to move ideas, resources, and talent around the organization quickly.[32]

We believe that all of these examples are illustrations of why more-market-like solutions are needed in order to reestablish the power and insights of all of the informed and capable stakeholders in organizations that have too long been under the tyranny of hierarchies. Stanford University economist John McMillan warns us, however, that "markets are subtle organizations. The mechanisms that underpin transacting are intricate—and they are in everlasting flux." McMillan suggests that well-structured markets require five essential elements:[33]

- Information flows smoothly.
- Property rights are protected.
- People can be trusted to live up to their promises.
- Side effects on third parties are curtailed.
- Competition is fostered.

He then adds, "The platform for a market in large part evolves by trial and error."[34]

To a greater or lesser extent, we believe that all of these illustrations are trials aimed at achieving a more equitable balance between market advantages and hierarchical legacies. Each of them offers glimpses of what Seely Brown, Hagel, Doz, Kosonen, and McMillan are speaking about. In the innovation literature, it is quite common to speak of trailblazers who are trying to invent the future when almost everyone else is content with the present. It is our opinion that what we are seeing with the companies profiled here and with a small but growing number elsewhere, including Zhang Ruimin's Haier, is that very act of trailblazing.

7

A TRUE HYBRID

How to Fashion a Strategically Agile Organization

Simplicity is almost always a good idea in organizational design. Such is the lesson from nearly one hundred years of managerial observation and at least one Nobel Prize in Economics. Yet it is hard to deny that what we have seen in the previous chapters has been the addition, rather than the reduction, of complexities to normal everyday work life at Haier. If the Haier model is to be adopted by other companies, then this apparent contradiction between how more complexities can yield greater organizational agility must be addressed. That is the purpose of this chapter.

Haier's radical rethinking of its business model and the implications for its corporate culture are so wide-ranging and so comprehensive that there should be little doubt of the high stakes that are involved with these initiatives. What has not yet been addressed, however, is the wisdom of what Haier is attempting to do from the perspective of economic logic. In fact, it may well be that the trade-off between the cost efficiencies of reduced complexity versus a heightened ability to achieve a desired corporate strategic outcome through the introduction of increased complexity is the ultimate determinant of the attractiveness of Haier's new strategy. In this chapter, we turn our attention to an economic analysis of that trade-off.

Haier's Business Model and the Governance Structures of Economic Activity

Ronald J. Coase was the first economist to address the issue of the nature of the firm and its boundaries; he published "The Nature of the Firm" in 1937. In that article, he questioned the existence of firms and compared the Western economic system based on markets with collective systems based on internal planning.[1]

Coase posed several problems that remain at the very heart of contemporary economic thinking (and for which he received the Nobel Prize in Economics in 1991). While discussing the nature of the firm and the industrial system in the Western world, Coase questioned the possibility of running an economic system as one big factory (a model close to the one aspired to by the central planning mechanism of the former Soviet Union), or as a sum of different factories, each of them accomplishing only a limited part of the production process (as might be closer to the Western market economies).

Coase, who believed in specialization and the division of labor (as originally formulated by Adam Smith), was puzzled by firms that move away from specialization and asked: "When is moving away from specialization more efficient? Why is it that costs can be lowered by grouping together certain activities under one control, as might be found in a planned environment, as opposed to allowing them to remain independent, as would be ascribed to a typical market approach?"

Coase argued that the legitimacy of the firm in a contemporary economic system is defendable only if it is possible for transactions to be organized within the firm at less cost than would be incurred if the same transactions were carried out through the market. If this is the case, however, one could ask why all economic activity is not carried out by only one firm. In other words, where is the limit between the economic activity carried on within the firm and that carried on outside the firm?

It is generally assumed that the commercial relationships between independent firms should be regulated by an arm's-length market mechanism, which provides the best resource allocation mechanism between stages.[2] In other words, through the price mechanism, the market is assumed to allocate resources between suppliers and customers more efficiently than alternative (e.g., administrative) forms of governance. Only when the market does not work properly and is inefficient in this allocation does the firm (hierarchy) emerge as an alternative and more efficient governance model.

Following this formulation, Oliver Williamson considered markets and hierarchies as two alternative modes of organizing transactions, implying that the most efficient mode will prevail.[3] A transaction is said to occur "when a good or service is transferred across a technologically separable interface." The study of transaction cost economics "recognizes that there are a variety of distinguishably different transactions on the one hand and a variety of alternative governance structures on the other. *The objective is to match governance structures to the attributes of transactions in a discriminating way* [emphasis added]."[4]

According to Williamson, exchanges that are not repetitive and do not require specific investments are likely to take place in a market. In a market, each firm is specialized in the production of a limited part of the final product (or service), and the relationships among firms are regulated by price. In a perfect market, information is freely available, buyers and sellers are easy to come by, and there are no carry-over effects from one transaction to another. Markets offer choice, flexibility, and opportunity: they are a form of noncoercive organization with coordinating but not integrating effects.

Neoclassical economists believe that in the beginning was the market. However, in particular cases, transaction costs, which arise mainly because of opportunism, bounded rationality, uncertainty, and asset-specific investments, block the formation of markets. Such market failure leads to the development of hierarchies. Hierarchies arise when the boundaries of the firm expand to internalize transactions that were previously conducted in the marketplace between independent parties. When this happens, the visible hand of management substitutes for the invisible hand of the market. In hierarchies, coordination is achieved not through a price mechanism but through an authoritative fiat.

Hierarchy as a governance form is particularly well suited to highly repetitive mass production, but when it is confronted by sharp fluctuations in market demand or unanticipated changes, its limitations are exposed: "Given its bureaucratic disabilities, hierarchy is the organizational form of last resort."[5]

From an economist's perspective, the balance between market and hierarchy is reached when the firm has expanded to the point where "the costs of organizing an extra transaction within the firm are equal to the costs involved in carrying out the same transaction in the open market, or to the costs of organizing by another entrepreneur."[6] In other words, a firm will integrate a transaction (thus shaping a hierarchy) when the external cost of a certain product (price, P) plus the transaction costs (TC) is higher than the internal cost of production (PC) plus the administrative costs (AC): $P + TC > PC + AC$. On the contrary, when $P + TC < PC + AC$, the firm will not integrate the transaction. Firms that do not follow this rule are expected to be less efficient than their competitors and will eventually be driven out of business (assuming that price, and hence efficiency, is the only determinant of firm success).

In the case of Haier and other large producers of mass-consumed items, most of the internal activities of the firm have traditionally been transacted using a reliance on hierarchy, which should take advantage of the highly repetitive nature of such transactions and organize them in such a way that the unpredictability and transaction costs of market relationships would be minimized, if not negated. Yet as Williamson has argued, hierarchical transactions do not work well under conditions of high uncertainty and have the unfortunate result of reducing the firm's agility in dealing with changing market conditions. What Haier is attempting to do is relax the shortcomings associated with hierarchy without incurring too many of the additional transaction costs associated with market relationships.

Interfirm Networks, Partnerships, and Alliances in the Market-Hierarchy Debate

The debate contrasting market and hierarchy, which are seen in the economic and strategic management literature as two alternative ways of organizing economic activity, has been vigorous. Scholars have long debated market and hierarchies as governance structures, and this has brought a recognition that Williamson's contribution, although vital from a theoretical point of view, cannot be naively translated into practice, since many of the governance forms that are found in real life are not plainly recognizable as either pure market or pure hierarchy.[7] Furthermore, there is a popular market rhetoric in the Western economies that, while recognizing some of the advantages of administrative control that are possible in firms, has always considered hierarchy as the weaker choice—the second-order option. Therefore, a large stream of literature from Europe, the United States, and Japan has concentrated on integrating some of the advantages of hierarchies into what are essentially market transactions. As a result, interfirm networks, strategic alliances, partnerships, and cooperative ventures have become popular concepts in both strategic management and economic theories.

Interfirm networks are a form of governance structure that resembles neither arm's-length market contracts nor the ideal of vertical integration.[8] Interfirm networks have become widely popular in the last thirty years as an alternative to the model of the integrated firm.[9] Italian industrial districts and Japanese *keiretsu* were extensively studied by scholars of different disciplines (economics, management, sociology, technology) as a market alternative to the hierarchically integrated firm. These networks have been classified using a transaction-costs economics framework. Some authors argue that economic changes can be arrayed in a continuum-like fashion with discrete market transactions on the one side and the highly centralized firm on the other.[10] In between, there are the intermediate or hybrid forms of governance, among which are interfirm networks. One possible way of thinking about what Haier is doing is to consider that it has borrowed from the idea of interfirm networks to emulate such relationships, while still staying within the boundaries of the Haier family.

Transaction Cost Economics and Interfirm Networks

In transaction cost economics (TCE) language, interfirm networks have been classified as a mixed form of market-hierarchy governance structure. They "have most of the characteristics of a hierarchical relationship [and] yet the contracting parties remain as independent organizations, with few or no points of contact along many dimensions."[11]

Williamson has contributed to this debate by introducing a third form of governance, intermediate between market and hierarchy, which he names *hybrid*.[12] Williamson, while contemplating frequency, uncertainty, and asset specificity as primary variables for the choice of the most efficient governance structure, focuses mainly on the last: "[The critical dimensions with respect to which transactions differ] include the frequency with which transactions recur, the uncertainty to which transactions are subject, and the type and degree of asset specificity involved in supplying the good or service in question. Although all are important, transaction-cost economics attaches special significance to this last."[13]

According to Williamson, hybrids are forms of governance that minimize transaction costs in situations of intermediate asset specificity. When asset specificity deepens, a condition of strong bilateral dependency is created. In this situation, there is a trade-off between transaction costs induced by the level of dependency related to asset specificity and the bureaucratic cost implicit in hierarchies. For low levels of asset specificity, the market is the best governance structure, as actors can effectively adapt to disturbances without incurring additional (bureaucratic) costs. For high levels of asset specificity, transaction costs overcome bureaucratic costs, and hierarchy becomes the most effective form of governance. For intermediate levels of asset specificity, a hybrid form of governance appears as the most effective, as the sum of transaction and bureaucratic costs implicit in this form of governance is lower than either pure transaction costs sustained in the market or pure bureaucratic costs sustained in hierarchies. In other words, the more elastic contractual regime, which supports hybrid forms of governance, allows better treatment of bilateral dependency without adding the bureaucratic costs of hierarchies.

Hybrids are intermediate between markets and hierarchies in many respects. Whereas markets support high-powered incentives and display adaptive properties to disturbances of an autonomous kind, they are poorly suited with respect to longer-term and cooperative adaptation (see table 7.1). Hierarchy has weaker incentives; it is comparatively worse at autonomous adaptation but better with respect to cooperative adaptation. Hybrids emerge when bilateral dependence and the need for cooperative adaptation build up. When the need for cooperative adaptation increases to a certain point, hybrids give way to hierarchies.

Hybrids, in sum, are an intermediate governance form that displays elements of both the market and a hierarchy. According to Williamson, the hybrid mode displays intermediate values in all four features: autonomous adaptation, coordinated adaptation, incentive intensity, and administrative control.

Table 7.1 Distinguishing Attributes of Market, Hybrid, and Hierarchy Governance Structures

	Governance Structure		
Attributes	*Market*	*Hybrid*	*Hierarchy*
Instruments			
Intensity of incentive	++	+	0
Administrative controls	0	+	++
Performance attributes			
Autonomous adaptation	++	+	0
Cooperative adaptation	0	+	++
Contract law	++	+	0

Note: ++ = strong; + = semistrong; 0 = weak.

Source: O. E. Williamson, "Comparative Economic Organization," *Administrative Science Quarterly* 36 (1991), 281.

Trust and Interfirm Networks

A fundamental critique of strategy scholars' positions regarding interfirm networks was developed by a group of economic sociologists who felt that the description of external context in competitive terms assumes an atomistic notion of firms evaluating alternative courses of action and does not take into account the actions of other firms or the relationships in which they themselves are embedded.[14] For them, the governance structures presented by Williamson—market and hierarchy—are both under- and oversocialized. The efficacy of hierarchy is overplayed, resembling Hobbes's sovereign state (apropos of the world of executive authority), whereas the market resembles Hobbes's state of nature (apropos of the world preceding governments).[15] To test the suitability of these models, economic sociologists turned to TCE analysis but noted several concerns about that approach.

One of the limitations of analysis is that context and people matter in how relationships work. According to Granovetter, Williamson's concept of markets neglects the role of social relations among individuals in different firms in bringing order to economic life. He maintains that the economist's market is only a theoretical construction: "I argue that the anonymous market of neoclassical models is virtually non-existent in economic life and that transactions of all kinds are rife with the social connections described" and that economic relations are intertwined with social ones, so that a certain degree of trust permeates economic life: "Without it, you would be afraid to give the gas station attendant a 20-dollar bill when you had bought only five dollars' worth of gas."[16]

At the same time, Granovetter criticizes the TCE representation of hierarchies, saying that Williamson vastly overestimates the efficacy of hierarchical power within organizations. In his view, hierarchies are exposed to coalitions, malfeasance, and opportunism on the part of employees, which can lead to inefficiency. Therefore, a high level of order can be found in the market (i.e., across firm boundaries) and a correspondingly high level of disorder within the firm, where social relationships are thought to play a higher role, given the frequency and familiarity that characterize such dealings within a single firm. Whether these inefficiencies actually occur, instead of what Williamson expects, depends on the nature of personal relations and networks of relations between and within firms. Order and disorder, honesty, and malfeasance have more to do with structures of such relations than they do with organizational form.

In summary, according to Granovetter, the behavior of people in economic life is better explained by personal relations than by the form of governance under which they act. Personal relations account for the development of correct behavior among distinct economic actors and for the development of opportunistic behavior, even among actors belonging to the same organization. Granovetter introduces concepts such as frequency of relationships and reputation as basic principles on which the relationships among economic actors should be grounded in order to obtain effective organizational structures. Frequency of relationships and reputation lead to the development of trust, which reduces friction and opportunistic behavior among economic actors. Trust, in fact, is defined as the willingness of a party to be vulnerable to the actions of another party based on the expectations that the other will perform a particular action important to the truster, regardless of the ability to monitor or control that other party.[17]

Powell maintains that trust is the pivotal point on which networks are based. In his view, network-like organizations are a distinct form of coordinating economic activity, based on neither price, as in the case of markets, nor authority, as in the case of hierarchies, but on a different mechanism of coordination: trust. In networks, transactions occur neither through discrete exchanges nor by administrative fiat, but through networks of individuals engaged in reciprocal, preferential, mutually supportive actions.

Other scholars maintain that "reliance on trust will emerge only as a consequence of repeated market transactions between the parties, affirming the observance of norms of equity by both parties" and that the greater the ability to rely on trust, the less inherent risk there will be in a transaction, ceteris paribus.[18] For these reasons, networks may emerge in situations of high risk (high transaction costs) among economic actors when a corresponding level of trust is also present. In the absence of this level of trust, economic actors are forced to internalize transactions, thus shaping hierarchies.

In sum, trust is seen as the agent that can help firms to develop strong ties while at the same time remain separate business entities. In the absence of trust, firms would be forced to internalize transactions.

Some Preliminary Comments

The interest in interfirm networks has been inspired by the success of Japanese firms, especially in the automobile industry, and to a lesser extent of Italian firms in industrial districts operating mainly in clothing and fashion-related industries. These models have been compared to the North American model of the integrated firm.[19] For a time, they were thought to represent, at least within the strategic management literature, a viable alternative to the integrated firm. The main rationale beneath the interest that they raised could be found in the fact that whereas the integrated firm is the epitome of the widely caricaturized, soulless, and inefficient hierarchy, network-like firms are much more like a market than an organization and were considered more agreeable and efficient than the integrated firms. In some sense, it is possible to think of the interfirm networks of Japan and Italy as arriving at a hybrid governance solution that offered strategic flexibility without the burden of significantly higher transaction costs by coming from the "outside of the firm and working in," while Haier might be thought of as trying to achieve the same hybrid balance, but "working from the inside of the firm, out." At any event, at some point in these experiments there should be a form of convergence, and this is what makes interfirm networks so interesting to us in this study.

Some scholars go as far as to say that interfirm networks are more "democratic" than integrated firms because power and wealth are distributed among a larger number of economic actors, none of whom controls a significant part of the economic activity. Moreover, the market forces, as well as the social forces (reputation, trust) that operate among the economic actors, force them to be competitive in costs and quality and cooperative with their economic partners at the same time. This is a much better, more democratic solution than would be found in the predatory behavior of large corporations that try to consume their competitors and to gain monopolistic rents by dominating the entire value chain of which they are a part.

However, fairness is not the purpose of capitalism, and even if there is much merit in the idea of having networks of small and medium-sized firms rather than gigantic firms that control a large part of the economy, this model is not emerging as the dominant model. First the crisis of Japan and then later, more convincingly, globalization have tested the limits of such a model and severely diminished the attractiveness of the idea of a world of interconnected small and medium-sized firms as an alternative to the world of large corporations. In fact, what we observe in real life is a growing number of industries where the power of large corporations is increasing through mergers and acquisitions.[20] Perhaps the search for control—monopolistic power or the ability to secure unique or rare resources—is a stronger incentive than those granted by specialization and market transactions. If so, maybe we need to restate some of the assumptions that we have widely used in economic theory, such as the one that sees hierarchy (the firm) as the organizational structure of last resort.

Indeed, hierarchy seems to be the first, rather than the last, choice of practicing managers aspiring to increase profitability. It is somehow distressing to see that even if economic theory has considerable merit in highlighting problems and inefficiencies of large corporations because it focuses the attention on the possible resolution of these problems, in fact most managers do not follow its recommendations. Is the managerial theory of the firm more realistic than the economic theory of it? Empirical evidence argues that managers choose to internalize transactions rather than the opposite (at least, in normal times) and, only then, perhaps to introduce in the hierarchy some of the elements that make the market so efficient.

We are not the only observers so concerned. Coase, in quoting his correspondence with Ronald Fowler, says that Fowler is puzzled by vertical integration, since he sees it as an inefficient reversal of the process of specialization: "If one is of the opinion that there is a general tendency towards vertical integration, one has got to admit that there is a general tendency to eliminate the middleman, in other words that in competition two middlemen are more efficient that three middlemen. It really amounts to denying the greater economy of specialization."[21] In fact, however, this is exactly what we observe in many industries: a reduction of specialization as a consequence of the increasing size and power of buyers and sellers that tend to eliminate the middlemen in order to streamline the supply chain. Are such transformations the result of higher transaction costs within the supply chain, or are they the result of deliberate strategies of the most powerful economic actors to increase their control over that supply chain? If the former, then we should assume that integrating the activity to protect a firm from transaction costs should itself come at a cost: the cost of losing specialization and the increased cost (bureaucratic) of using the hierarchy.

The integration of supply chains and the reduction of time to market can actually reduce the costs of the processes involved if the integrating firms can achieve economies of scale or eliminate cost duplications (i.e., inventory costs). Moreover, if the elimination of middlemen is promoted by manufacturers, it allows them to have better control over operations and more information about their customers. In other words, reducing specialization, and thus integrating activities within the firm, is not necessarily bad: it can reduce interface costs; reduce the time to market, which in some industries is a crucial competitive issue; allow manufacturers to gain more information on the ultimate customers of their products; and allow retailers to exert their influence over upstream operations.

Of course, not all transactions could be beneficially organized within the same firm: the disturbing idea of one big firm organizing all economic activity collides with any appeal associated with diminishing returns from the internalization of transactions. Coase affirms:

> As more transactions are organized by an entrepreneur, it would appear that the transactions would tend to decrease as the firm gets larger. This furnishes an additional reason why efficiency will tend to decrease as the firm gets larger. Inventions which

> tend to bring factors of production nearer together, by lessening spatial distribution, tend to increase the size of the firm. Changes like the telephone and the telegraph which tend to reduce the cost of organizing spatially will also tend to increase the size of the firm. All changes which improve managerial technique will tend to increase the size of the firm.[22]

It is shocking today to read Coase's statement, made in 1937, and to realize that we have spent most of the time since he wrote it taking the market as the "preferred" or "natural" state of economic affairs and considering as aberrations those circumstances where deviation from market transactions (the base case) can economize on transaction costs. More than seventy years ago, Coase claimed that information technology (even if it was only the telephone and telegraph at that time) is a major force to increase the size of the firm. And, now, in the era of globalization and a booming growth of information and communication technology, when industries are concentrating and corporations are becoming bigger and bigger as a result, we still instinctively consider firms (hierarchies) as the organizational form of last resort.[23]

Consistent with this "hierarchy as second class" view, the last twenty years of academic debate have revolved around the idea of the market as the most efficient governance structure and the firm as a second-order organization. To be sure, a large part of the debate, especially in the strategic management literature, has concentrated on the various governance forms that are in between pure market and pure hierarchy: interfirm networks, such as partnerships, and strategic alliances that seem to combine the advantages of the market (incentive) with those of hierarchies (control), which provide management with a way to enjoy some of the advantages of a hierarchy while at the same time maintaining transactional efficiencies in the market. The presumed superiority of the market lies at the core of TCE analysis. But we have seen that managers and firms do not share the same ideas and that hierarchies have become bigger and bigger over the past twenty years. Notwithstanding this fact, a comparatively very small debate has evolved over the idea of the organization as a viable governance structure and over possible ways to internalize in the firm some of the powerful incentives that work so well in the market.

From Interfirm Networks to Intrafirm Networks

Economic theory and strategic management have been studying interfirm networks as governance forms that are intermediate between market and hierarchy but that are, in essence, market forms. At the same time, CEOs and managers were struggling to bring market mechanisms into their firms, namely to infuse entrepreneurship in their hierarchical forms.

Chandler's M-Form Organization

The first and most notable evidence of what firms were trying to achieve dates back to economic historian Alfred Chandler's study of the multidivisional organization structure.[24] What Chandler referred to as the M-form organization emphasized the decentralization of responsibility to operating divisions, which previously had been coordinated by a strong corporate management.

Chandler concluded that companies driven by market growth and technological change to develop greater diversity in their products and markets were able to manage their new strategies efficiently only if they adopted a multidivisional organizational structure. He showed that the management process created by this organization allowed companies to apply their resources more efficiently to opportunities created by changing markets and developing technologies. Also, Chandler recommended a reliable information system to support the line of authority: "A decentralized organization will only work effectively with a good reporting system that gives higher level managers the opportunity to react in good time."[25]

Chandler's view, which he arrived at from the observation of a few large American corporations, gives evidence of the first attempt to break down organizational hierarchy into smaller and more agile units that are strategically relatively independent but still loosely coordinated by headquarters by means of a reporting system. Each unit is in charge of a specific product–market combination and has specific resources and performance targets.

Chandler saw this translation from the more traditional functional organization (U-form) to the M-form as testimony to corporate management's need for strategic business units to become closer to the market with less bureaucratic, more flexible structures. Put in transaction cost terms, these managers were trying to infuse their traditional U-form organizations with market elements, curbing some of the rigidities of hierarchy with stronger, more market-like incentives. One could, of course, ask why these managers didn't go all the way toward externalizing such activities. Transaction cost economics will answer that they did not do so because of transaction costs inherent in the market approach. We prefer to adopt a more managerial approach and say that the benefits in terms of market power to a large organization were (and are) larger than the costs of an apparently suboptimal allocation of economic activities—in other words, impact, or organizational power, triumphs over market efficiency in much of corporate planning.

Nonetheless, the advantages of a market governance mode in terms of efficiency and incentives, even if they are not enough to offset the advantages of size and ownership of assets, are still strong. This is the reason that corporations, while willing to maintain economic activities within the boundaries of their firm, are increasingly trying to run these activities in a market-like, more efficient fashion. They are simply trying to add the advantages of market efficiency to the advantages of market power. To a large extent, however, these advantages are conflicting: the larger the corporation and the higher its market power, the higher the probability of stronger administrative controls, bureaucracy, and inefficiencies. There is a clear trade-off between market power and economic efficiency, and corporations strive to find a balance between the two.

Haier, rather than solving this trade-off with a blend of market incentives and administrative controls, has raised it to the upper tier of its business model. It has become a combination of different product-market combinations. It could well be considered an extreme form of a conglomerate corporation, employing powerful market incentives so that employees can be considered entrepreneurs and independent units can be seen as being similar to independent firms in many ways. However, before coming to the Haier business model, we should first consider some other examples of infusion of market attributes into hierarchies.

Bartlett and Ghoshal: Beyond the M-Form

Bartlett and Ghoshal, in their important article, "Beyond the M-Form: Toward a Managerial Theory of the Firm," have in fact gone beyond Chandler's M-form. They describe the organizational structure of one firm, Asea Brown Boveri (ABB), which they consider to be an example of an emerging organizational model that they have studied in many other corporations as well.[26]

Bartlett and Ghoshal began their analysis with a statement about the value of economic theory in interpreting reality, which may appear shocking for an observer of business life but is perfectly in line with what we have said here. They wrote:

> We believe that the management of ABB, and of a number of the other companies we studied, is premised on a set of basic assumptions on the part of its managers regarding organization structure, decision making processes and, ultimately, human behavior, that are significantly different from those that underlie the economic and behavioral theories that currently dominate academic analysis of business organizations. As a result, these theories are of limited usefulness for analyzing the behaviors of and within such companies. This is a serious handicap for management scholars and a major reason for the widening gap between existing management theory and emerging management practice.[27]

Unlike Bartlett and Ghoshal, we do not believe that we need a new theory to explain the behavior of ABB's management (which we saw in the preceding chapter) or Haier's management. Both portray the trade-off between the search for market power and for superior resources that only size can guarantee and the contrasting search for efficiencies that only market incentives can provide that shapes these new organizational forms. It is a mix of these two objectives that can provide competitive advantage, and that has always been on the agenda of top managers. Whereas economic theorists compete to explain management behavior and are generally mutually blind in accepting others' findings, real managers in their everyday practice behave in a way that combines ideas and theories to make their companies more powerful and more efficient.

One of the most important goals that managers have long pursued worldwide is that of infusing their organizations with entrepreneurial spirit. The nightmare of every top manager is to have underused, undercommitted personnel. Transaction cost economics has argued that this problem is typical of large hierarchies and is virtually absent in markets because of the powerful individual incentives that markets can offer. Managers have therefore tried to import these market incentives into their hierarchies. As Bartlett and Ghoshal reported, ABB's mission, values, and policies say, "Our guiding principle is to decentralize the Group into distinctive profit centers and assign individual accountability to each." That is a remarkable analogy with Haier, where every individual is a profit center and has individual accountability.

From the ABB Model to the Haier Model

We saw in the previous chapter several other success stories of radical decentralization, employee empowerment, and individual incentives: Oticon, ABB, Morning Star, and Nash Confectionery. All of these stories teach a similar lesson: if a company can unleash its talent and reward it, it can significantly increase its chances of success. We have also seen that in order to achieve this aim, companies have to overlook traditional hierarchical organizational structures and develop new forms of governance where market incentives play a very important role.

Whereas Oticon, Morning Star, and Nash Confectionery were interesting case studies, their breadth is limited since the extent of their endeavor was limited by their size. ABB is the only case of a large multinational company trying to achieve radical decentralization on a global scale, and therefore we compare the ABB and Haier business models here.

ABB described its approach to organizational design as radical decentralization, meaning that the firm was something different from a corporate entity subdivided into separate divisions that were coordinated and directed from the top. Instead it chose to create its organization around "self-contained and manageable units with (corporate) overview." In Haier, these are the ZZJYTs and they have much the same purpose.

The translation from Chandler's divisions to Haier's ZZJYTs is a matter of the degree of decentralization and the nature of control. ABB is intermediate between the M-form and Haier's

ZZJYTs, or we could say that Haier's independent units are the extreme consequence of the decentralization process that started with the M-form and was carried on by ABB's organization model.

ABB was organized as a federation of approximately thirteen hundred "companies" structured as separate and distinct business units. On average, each of these companies employed around two hundred people. In Haier, there are now over two thousand ZZJYTs, each employing between ten and thirty people.[28]

Whereas ABB had strongly reduced the hierarchical structure above the individual company level in order to streamline the organization, Haier has moved the hierarchical structure below the first-tier ZZJYTs as a result of its inverted triangle organization (figure 7.1). Indeed, it is the end user who sits above the top of Haier's inverted triangle, with ZZJYTs in the top layers, immediately facing end users, and managers in the bottom layers. Managers are supposed to provide the ZZJYTs with the resources that they require in order to satisfy their customers and consumers.

The analogies with ABB are remarkable, even if at Haier the decentralization is pushed to a much greater degree. For example, whereas at ABB each frontline company was given responsibility for its complete balance sheet, in Haier this responsibility is given to each employee. With the "individual-goal combination win-win mode," every ZZJYT defines its own goal (subsequently approved by managers), and this goal becomes one of the key performance measures. Every individual within the ZZJYT has goals to reach, and performance is measured daily with three instruments: the personal income statement, the daily activity summary form, and the people-pay incentive form (this form links the individual's work to compensation).

Clearly, when such a complex system is implemented, there is a risk that everything will turn chaotic as employees look after their own interests rather than those of the company. It is crucial,

Figure 7.1 Haier's Organizational Structure: From "Pyramid Hierarchy" to Inverted

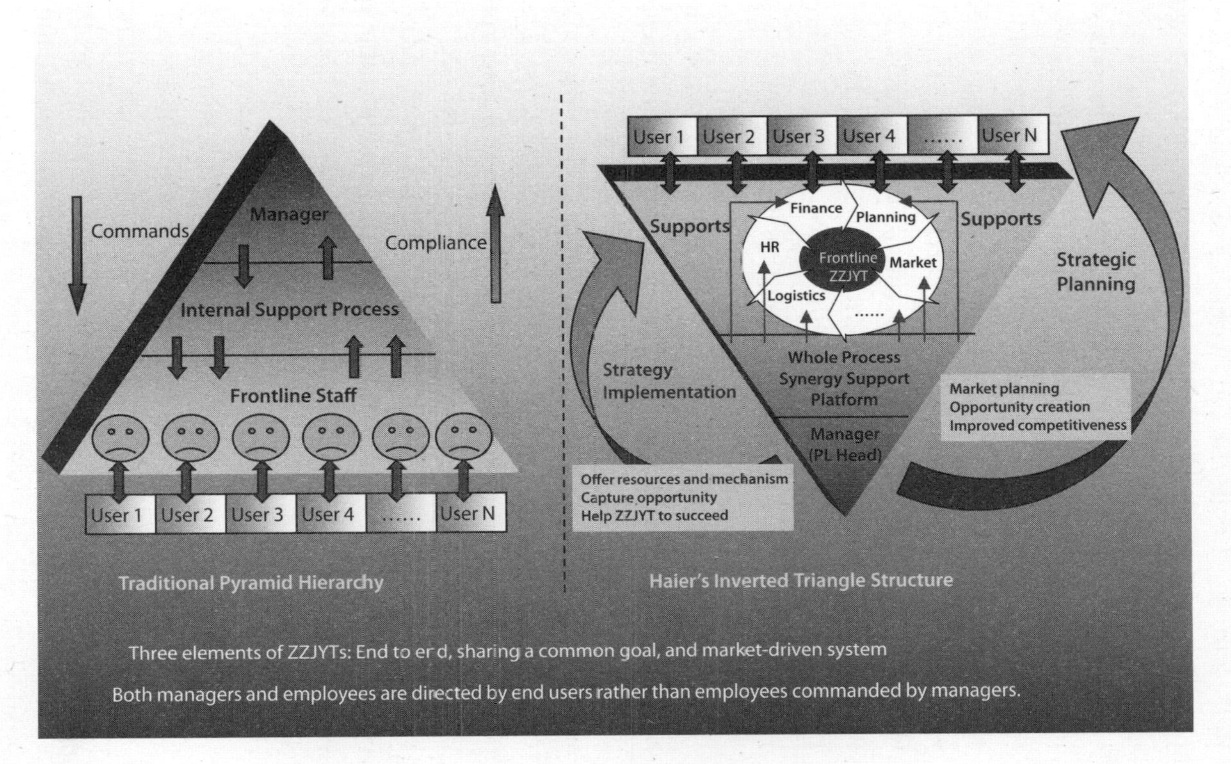

Source: Haier company information.

therefore, to align individual goals with the company's goals and to craft incentives that can achieve this objective. Haier calls its incentive scheme the "individual-goal combination win-win mode" to signify that individual goals are combined with the company's in a way that is mutually beneficial.

It is also crucial to align and control a large number of different operations, which requires an efficient information system. As ABB's 1991 mission, values, and policies document states, "A decentralized organization will only work effectively with a good reporting system that gives higher level managers the opportunity to react in good time." Whereas ABB implemented a fully automated system, ABACUS (Asea Brown Boveri Accounting and CommUnication System), Haier has implemented its system on SAP. Both systems allow a thorough overview of employee activities and performance.

Another striking similarity between ABB and Haier is the role of middle managers. At ABB, frontline managers had evolved from implementers of top-down decisions to primary initiators of entrepreneurial action. In Haier, the managers of the ZZJYTs are considered to be entrepreneurs. They are responsible for business results as well as for the resources that they employ, and they have the ability to hire the best people in the company in a competitive fashion (different ZZJYTs bid for the most qualified personnel). The coaching and support roles of middle management are quite similar in both organizations. Their principal role is that of providing frontline employees with the resources they need rather than giving them orders.

The role of top management is also quite similar in both companies. At ABB, top managers developed a broad set of objectives and established stretch performance standards. In Haier, top management deals with refinements of the business model and definition of the corporate mission by setting high-level goals.

Overall, the role of managers, from front line to top management, is quite similar in the two organizations. The only big difference is that the amount of decentralization in Haier is much greater than in ABB. This is probably a consequence of the fact that, as CEO Zhang Ruimin often says, the Internet has made it possible to exchange a much larger amount of information than was possible in the past.

A Model of Internal Hybrid Governance

Bartlett and Ghoshal maintain that the M-form was created through a philosophy of devolution of assets and accountability from the corporate to the division level, whereas the ABB model was based on the assumption "that the organization needs to be developed and managed on a principle of *proliferation and subsequent aggregation* of small independent entrepreneurial units from the bottom up, rather than one of *division and devolution* of resources and responsibilities from the top."[29] We believe that Haier's model is very similar to the ABB model—perhaps only a few steps ahead. However, we also believe that if we look at the purpose behind their conception, these models share the same characteristic: trying to infuse market incentives into a hierarchical structure. By this perspective, the difference between the M-form, ABB, and Haier is only a matter of degree. The business models of Haier, ABB, Oticon, Morning Star, and Nash Confectionery can all be described as internal hybrids, that is, hybrid governance forms that seek to meld the virtues of both market incentives and traditional hierarchical control.[30] The difference between external hybrids and internal hybrids is a matter of ownership, or of possession of residual rights of control over certain assets. According to Oliver Hart, it is these control rights that determine the boundaries of the firm: a firm is defined as a collection of jointly owned assets.[31] We can thus go back to table 7.1 and adapt it to accommodate both external and internal hybrids (table7.2).

What we can see here is that the main difference in governance structures is a difference in ownership in the attributes

Table 7.2 Distinguishing Attributes of Market, External and Internal Hybrid, and Hierarchy Governance Structures

	Governance Structure			
Attributes	*Market*	*Market Hybrid*	*Internal Hybrid*	*Hierarchy*
Instruments				
Intensity of incentive	++	+	+	0
Administrative controls	0	+	+	++
Performance attributes				
Autonomous adaptation	++	+	+	0
Cooperative adaptation	0	+	+	++
Contract law	++	+	0	0

Note: ++ = strong; + = semistrong; 0 = weak.

Source: Adapted from O. E. Williamson, "Comparative Economic Organization," *Administrative Science Quarterly* 36 (1991), 281.

specified above. In market-governed arrangements and in external (market) hybrid organizations, the residual rights of control over the assets are separated between the companies that are involved in the relationship or participate in the partnership, alliance, or network; in internal hybrid organizations, since market incentives are brought inside the company, the rights of control over the assets are owned by only one company.

External hybrids can be arrayed in a continuum from pure market to quasi-hierarchy, according to the degrees of coordination and control (which are normally a function of power) that are attributed to a dominant firm. It should be possible to array internal hybrids in a continuum from pure hierarchy to quasi-market, according to the degrees of decentralization

Figure 7.2 The Mirror of External and Internal Governance Forms

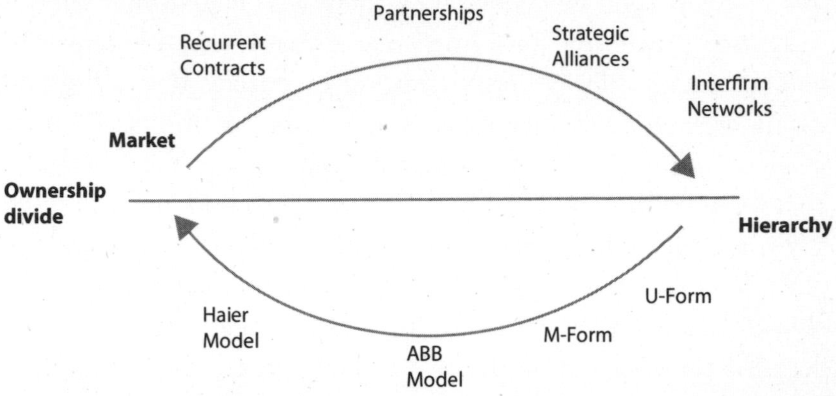

and devolution of power which mirror that of external hybrids (figure 7.2).

According to Todd Zenger, attempts to craft internal hybrids often violate patterns of complementarity among the elements of the organization: structure, the promotion system, the assignment of responsibilities, the incentive system, and the system of evaluation and measurement. Normally, managers "seek to remedy the deficiencies of hierarchy through common change initiatives that shift singular elements of traditional hierarchy toward the greater market control characteristics of team-based forms."[32] Zenger argues that when companies embark on decentralization through, for example, business process reengineering (BPR), which acts to change an entire end-to-end chain between the customer and the individuals in the firm who directly or indirectly serve the customer, they can then change these complementarities to the point that they trigger pressure to either adjust other elements or cause a reversion to traditional hierarchy. In sum, internal hybrids may be unstable and tend to be either reabsorbed by hierarchy or to develop into even more radical hybrids.

Whereas external hybrids, according to Williamson, are characterized by semistrong incentives and semistrong administrative controls (but we believe there may well be external hybrids with strong incentives and strong controls), internal hybrids can be characterized by either semistrong incentives or controls, or strong quasi-market incentives and strong administrative controls, depending on the degree of devolution.[33] If the M-form is characterized by a limited devolution of power and limited incentives, it is also characterized by weak, mainly ex post, controls. On the contrary, both the ABB and Haier organization models are characterized by powerful quasi-market incentives and detailed controls that, in the case of Haier, reach every employee on a daily basis (table 7.3).

Table 7.3 Distinguishing Attributes of Haier's Governance Structure

	Governance Structure			
Attributes	*Market*	*Market Hybrid*	*Haier Model*	*Hierarchy*
Instruments				
Intensity of incentive	++	+	++	0
Administrative controls	0	+	++	++
Performance attributes				
Autonomous adaptation	++	+	++	0
Cooperative adaptation	0	+	++	++
Contract law	++	+	0	0

Note: ++ = strong; + = semistrong; 0 = weak.

Source: Based on O. E. Williamson, "Comparative Economic Organization," *Administrative Science Quarterly* 36 (1991), 281.

In Haier's model, the intensity of incentives is high almost everywhere in the structure, especially for units directly facing the market. At the same time, information and presets make managerial review possible and reaction times fast, so that administrative controls can be guaranteed at all levels in order to align individual goals with the company's long-term objectives and avoid entropy. In addition, autonomous adaptation is encouraged at all levels of the structure, but cooperative adaptation is also encouraged as a way to exploit synergies among different ZZJYTs.

In sum, the degree of devolution from the norm in Haier's organization is so extreme that we can safely say that Haier's business model looks like a market within a hierarchy. It has many of the qualities of the market (intensity of incentives, autonomous adaptation, entrepreneurship) yet maintains the detailed controls and rules of a hierarchy. Performance appraisal is held every quarter, and employees up to senior managers and vice presidents can be promoted or demoted. This may look harsh for a hierarchy, perhaps because our view of a hierarchy is somehow softer, since we have been socialized toward a bias for market arrangements (in terms of efficiency) and we always assume that hierarchy implies some slack. But success and failure are exactly what happens in markets, and if a hierarchy has to mimic the market, promoting merit and punishing slack makes perfect sense.

The Evolution of Haier's Business Model

Having seen the effectiveness of Haier's business model, which is essentially a model of a market operating within the walls of a hierarchy, news of the possible evolution of market ZZJYTs into separate companies comes as a surprise (see chapter 5). Is Haier willing to break up the company into smaller independent units, which are not only strategically but also legally separated? And if this is true, isn't this a denial of the hierarchical model that has been described above? At first sight, it may seem so. Haier is thinking of transforming its market ZZJYTs into separate business units. These business units will be B2B companies and will have different shareholders of which Haier will not be part. There will be no direct ownership link between Haier and these companies.

On closer inspection, however, there are many other strong relationships between these newly created companies and the Haier Group. First, the majority shareholders of these companies will be Haier employees. This means that these people will be shareholders of a company selling Haier products and, at the same time, they will be Haier employees. The contract with Haier will be fixed and preset, meaning that since percentages on sales and services are agreed beforehand, the potential for conflict will be minimal. The shareholders of these companies remain Haier employees to the point that it is expected that their careers will take place within Haier. These employees will have the double role of employees of Haier and shareholders of a company that is operating for Haier. In addition, these companies will be limited in scope and dependent on Haier. They will be primarily a service company, since the title to the goods involved will not be transferred from Haier to them and Haier will invoice the customer directly. In fact, from a managerial point of view, the role of these companies is not very different from the role of the market ZZJYTs. But Haier believes that in giving their employees full empowerment and responsibility (making them shareholders of their own company), the level of market incentive becomes even greater. At the same time, the level of controls is increased because all of the operations of these companies are connected to Haier's ERP and Haier can verify everything.

Our interpretation is that Haier is moving forward in terms of power decentralization and people empowerment. And if it has to go outside its traditional boundaries as a firm to do it well, it will, but always while maintaining control. In a sense, we could say that if the actual business model looks like a market in a hierarchy, the possible future business model is a market and a hierarchy at the same time, or the overlap of a market form and a hierarchical one. In figure 7.3, we see that Haier can externalize some activities while maintaining control. The sovereignty of the B2B companies is limited by the career control that Haier maintains over its owners and employees, the tight licensing contract that they are required to sign, and the fact that actual sales and delivery are controlled by Haier, as are the relationships with end users.

Is this model more similar to a market or a hierarchy? From a managerial point of view, the question is meaningless, provided that the model grants the results expected. Even if we take a more theoretical standpoint, the answer to this question is not easy:

Figure 7.3 Market and Hierarchy in the Evolution of Haier's Business Model

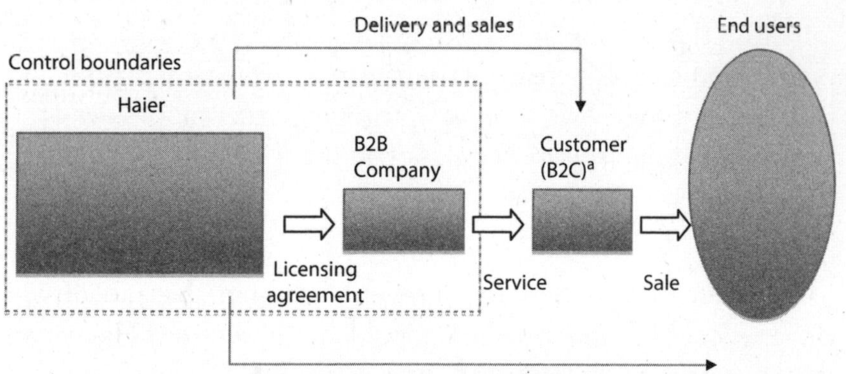

Control boundaries refer to Haier control, which extends to B2B companies. Haier sells and delivers products directly to points of sale which, in turn, sell to end users.

[a] B2C = business-to-consumer model.

- It is a hierarchy because the majority shareholders of the newly formed companies remain Haier employees, whose career expectations are still within the Haier Group. At the same time, it is a market because the relationship between the Haier Group and these companies is an arm's length market relationship, and the residual rights of control over the assets are separated among the companies.
- It is a hierarchy because Haier exerts strong control over these companies, through either the restriction that these companies must sell only Haier products (for which they receive a fixed, all-inclusive commission on sales) or the detailed information that the connection to Haier's ERP system provides.
- It is a market because the companies are free to sell value-added services to their customers, over which they have full control.
- It is a hierarchy because the shareholders of these independent companies are incentivized by career prospects within the Haier Group. If their activity is successful, they may become senior managers or vice presidents of the Haier Group. At the same time, since they are shareholders of these companies, they are also incentivized by the possibilities of increasing their income by increasing the profits of their own company, through either more sales of Haier products or more sales of added-value services to their customers.

We do not know, at the moment, whether this model will prove successful and will be adopted by the entire Haier organization. Haier is certainly trying to accomplish something that is unprecedented (at least in our experience): to create coexistence and cohabitation between two different governance structures, market and hierarchy, which, at least since Coase's 1937 article, have always been considered antithetical to each other.

We believe that the spirit behind this possible evolution of Haier's business model is exactly the same one that has crafted Haier's business model: that of empowering people by aligning their incentives with those of the company. Doing this requires carefully balancing incentives and controls. Whereas the market is characterized by strong incentives and weak controls and the hierarchy is characterized by strong controls and weak incentives, Haier's model is characterized, in its current release and its potential evolution, by the coexistence of very strong market incentives and very strong hierarchical controls. The difference between Haier's current model and its potential evolution is only a matter of degrees of incentives and controls. In this fashion, Haier's business model is an internal hybrid evolving into a new form of governance that combines market and hierarchy into a new and original form—adding governance structures rather than balancing them.

Haier Model and Agency Theory

Haier's business model appears to represent a possibly novel way to balance personal initiative and a company's need to control. We may say that Haier has invented a new governance form (which in our less formal conversations we have referred to as *Haier-archy*) that mixes the characters of the market with those of the hierarchy. A considerable contribution of Haier's business model can also be found with reference to agency theory.

Agency theory suggests that a firm can be viewed as a nexus of contracts (loosely defined) among resource holders, to the point where it can be misleading to draw a hard line between firms and markets. An agency relationship arises whenever one or more individuals, called principals, hire one or more other individuals, called agents, to perform some service and then delegate decision-making authority to the agents. Performance (or goal) and performance measures are defined by the principal, who then controls the agent's behavior and results.

When agency occurs, the agent may hide information from his principal, conduct activities that are in his interest rather than in those of the principal, or may simply act as a free rider, doing much less than what he is expected to do. These activities give rise to agency costs, which are expenses incurred in order to sustain an effective agency relationship (e.g., offering management performance bonuses to encourage managers to act in the shareholders' interests).

The organization implied in Haier's business model, specifically in the inverted triangle model, raises some questions about the agency problem. What is the relationship between principal and agent in the inverted triangle model? Who is the agent, and who is the principal?

According to Haier, there is no doubt that the principal should be the customer: "Customers cannot be wrong." Haier's priority is meeting the requirements of customers. This is the essence of the inverted triangle model. Yet what is the role of Haier's employees and managers in this model? With Haier's ZZJYTs, the first-tier ZZJYTs have the task of directly facing the market, understanding customers' needs, and providing them with the right products. They have the power to define their own goals, as far as these goals are coherent with market needs, and they are relatively independent in pursuing these goals. So there is no principal-agent relationship at this level, at least as we are used to seeing it. We know that the ZZJYTs' goals have to be approved by a committee, but there is a big difference between approving someone else's goal and autonomously deciding and imposing a goal.

Second-tier managers (middle managers) are responsible for supporting the first-tier ZZJYTs, providing them with the resources and the guidance they may need.

Third-tier managers are the business division managers or functional managers who are responsible for setting strategies for the whole group; they decide which market to enter and set the incentive processes for ZZJYTs and provide them with resources.

So by reading the Haier business model in a literal fashion, one could say that the market is the principal and that ZZJYTs are the agents, or that first-tier ZZJYTs, being closely connected with the market and interpreting customers' needs, are the principals, whereas second- and third-tier managers are the agents. Figure 7.4 illustrates the difference between the traditional principal-agent relationship and that in Haier's business model.

One of the characteristics of the agency model, which is peculiar to Haier's business model, is the fact that because employees have a large degree of initiative and are responsible for the goals that they set themselves, they can effectively monitor themselves. This addresses one of the main administrative costs in most organizations, that of monitoring employees.

A more sophisticated way of looking at how this model deals with the agency problem is that of considering the activity between principals and agents as continuous or dynamic contracting rather than once-and-for-all contracting.[34] In this fashion, a firm can choose between a traditional form of control using once-and-for-all contracts and a more dynamic nexus

Figure 7.4 The Traditional Principal-Agent Relationship and That in the Haier Business Model

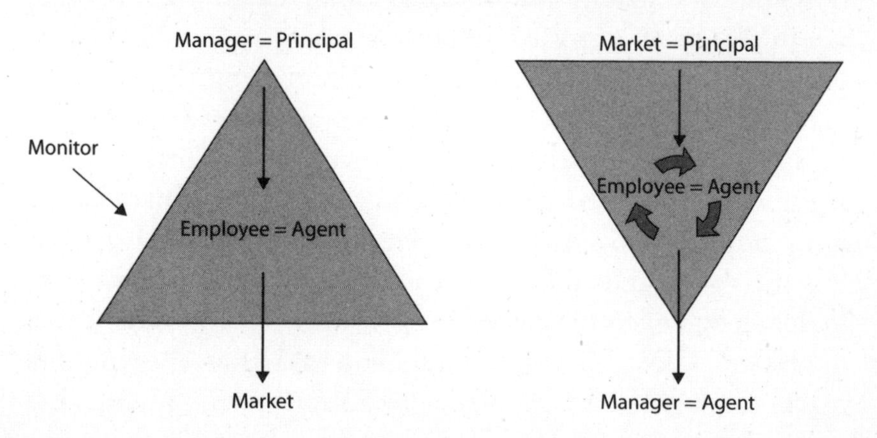

of contracts, where employees exercise initiative by contracting and recontracting with each other in pursuit of common objectives. Clearly while once-and-for-all contracts are consistent with top-down hierarchy, continuous or dynamic contracting requires a much more flexible organizational structure. In traditional hierarchies that use traditional forms of control, the relationship of effort to outcomes may be unclear because of the distance between the person and the business result. But in more dynamic and flexible organizations, where there is a nontrivial degree of decentralization, people are motivated to work harder when they see that their effort leads to the outcomes that they value.

Combining Incentives with Control

Over the past decade, organizational structures have been heavily affected by the development of the Internet. Social technologies now help organizations navigate their external environments and forge stronger links with customers and vendors. It stands to reason that integrating social technologies into the work flow and using them to optimize internal processes can provide additional competitive benefits.

By giving economic actors a vast amount of virtually costless information, the Internet has greatly reduced both transaction costs and administrative costs. However, contrary to what we might have expected from economic theory, firms have not rushed to externalize transactions by turning to more market forms of governance. On the contrary, they have chosen to maintain and even to continue developing their structures. If the market was the most efficient governance form, why did firms not rush to externalize transactions? And if hierarchy was the governance form of last resort, why did they choose to maintain and even to develop these governance forms more?

Haier's CEO, Zhang Ruimin, has said that the Internet made it possible to reduce administrative costs and thus overturn predictions of transaction costs. He did not even mention that the Internet has also reduced transaction costs. This is not an omission, or if it is, it is indicative that Haier's top managers consider the possibility of turning to market solutions (outside firm boundaries) only when the internal solution (which, by the way, is a market inside the firm's boundaries) does not prove efficient.

We observe industries moving toward concentration and large firms becoming bigger, while small firms are purchased or driven from the market. We believe that the main driver of this seemingly inescapable drift is the search for monopolistic power and superior resources. Firms become bigger and increase their structure because they are motivated by the possibility of increasing their power in the market and by securing strategic resources. This implies that the advantage of market power and superior resources wins out over the cost of running a suboptimal organization (a hierarchy). Indeed, it would appear as if economic theory has been too focused on efficiency and on the cost side of economic activity, losing sight of the potential profits that may be obtained from a superior market power or from superior resources.

We believe that the search for monopolistic rent and superior resources and knowledge is a better explanation for the boundaries of the firm than the supposed advantages of the market. However, if cost efficiency is not a sufficient explanation of the existence and the development of firms, it is effective in explaining the efficiency of market incentives versus internal organization (hierarchy).

Haier appears to have learned this lesson quite well. It has crafted a model that mixes market incentives in order to give initiatives to employees, with controls, to keep the organization tight and focused. The original feature of the model is that this blend of incentives and controls does not involve a small number of incentives and controls, but rather full market incentives together with full hierarchical controls. In fact, the model is crafted in a way that full market incentives are coupled with full hierarchical controls in a functional and innovative manner.

This coupling of incentives and controls is brought down to the basic unit of every organization: the individual. Incentives are applied at the individual level, as are the daily controls on business activity. This may sound familiar in a small service firm, but it is extraordinary in a manufacturing firm with over eighty thousand employees.

Finally, this powerful business model has been put to the service of customers. It has oriented the organizational culture to satisfying customers, reversing traditional business processes, which now move from consumers' needs and go up the supply chain, which has been reengineered for this purpose.

8

A TRUE DISRUPTER

How Embracing Change Creates Value

We believe that Haier's story and the lessons that can be learned from it address universal issues that businesspeople across industries and geographies face. Haier's quest to fully use the talent that it employs is neither unique nor new. It does, however, represent what may well be the ultimate advantage over low-price competition and commoditization in mature industries, and for that reason alone it should merit our attention. What makes Haier's experiences uniquely interesting, however, is the ambition that characterizes the way it has gone about addressing its challenges and reinventing its business model and the thoughtfulness with which it has implemented a complete rewiring of its corporate culture to support the new business model at least three times in as many decades. In fact, we suggest that Haier is in the process of creating an entirely new form of governance model, a bold venture for any firm. Nor should we overlook the success that Haier has enjoyed as a result of such boldness. That it is a company in an emerging market makes it even more remarkable and suggests that the lessons to be gained from this experience are not confined to a small segment of elite organizations in high-tech industries and resource-abundant locales.

To be sure, making generalizations from small samples is always risky, and when a single company is the example, they can be quite dangerous. On top of this, Haier's story is that of a Chinese company, embedded in the social, political, and industrial setting of that unique society. As a result, there is no denying that Haier's results have to a large extent been shaped by the idiosyncrasies of the Chinese economy, which in just thirty years has become the second largest economy in the world. It is worth considering that during this same period, many other Chinese companies did not succeed, or certainly did not succeed to the extent that Haier did. Perhaps even more telling is that Haier is one of three Chinese firms (Huawei and Lenovo are the others) that inevitably come up whenever globalization is mentioned.

We believe that there is something extraordinary in Haier's development that is well worth studying. We have chosen to concentrate on its changing business model and the cultural reinvention that has accompanied these changes as a way of illustrating Haier's managerial practices. We believe that these are both fundamental to Haier's success and therefore definitely worth investigating.

The Main Attributes of Haier's Story

Looking back at chapters 3 and 4, we can identify the desire to create value through serving customers better, be it through better-quality products, a more responsive organization, or ultimately creating zero distance with the customer as a principal theme that runs through everything that Haier does, along with an unceasing belief that it is through the unleashing of talent that these value-creating business model objectives are most likely to be accomplished. This combination of business model goals and a desire to create an organizational culture that liberates talent consistently runs through the entire Haier story, from Qingdao Refrigerator to today's global brand. We also think that the willingness to reinvent the business model and supporting corporate culture in an effort to respond to changing competitive conditions, without sacrificing the commitment to pursue talent fulfillment, has consistently guided Haier in its choices; this is not three decades worth of many stories, but rather a single story that has played out over thirty years.

The key to understanding and appreciating the dynamic relationship between the business model and corporate culture is found in the direct linkage established between the value generated for the customer, the company, and the employee through explicit measurement, recognition, and rewards. This linkage between the results (value) and the efforts is the force driving everything else within the company, enabled by the creation of sufficient organizational freedom to enable the employee to be able to fulfill this promise.

At Haier, the entire organizational culture has been turned upside down, depicted as an inverted triangle where the customer is at the top and everything else has been redesigned or restructured with one specific goal in mind: adding value to the customer. As Haier's business model has evolved, this goal was initially pursued by having the best quality in the industry, evolving eventually into the aspiration of having zero distance with the customer, which means being more aware of the customer's market needs in ways that go well beyond what traditional businesses can achieve—for example, by providing better service in an otherwise commoditized product market. The organizational unit through which these results are to be achieved at Haier is the ZZJYT: small, autonomous units of ten to twenty people, each with direct responsibility for a geographical area, a product, or a manufacturing process and seen as an entrepreneurial platform in an otherwise large, complex organization.

The philosophical belief that is held dear at Haier is that the creation of value for the customer is a precondition for the creation of value for the company. There can be no long-lasting value creation for the company if it does not provide value creation for the customer. The creation of value for the company is accomplished through a sophisticated incentive system to create value for employees: customer value generates corporate value,

Figure 8.1 Haier's Value Engine

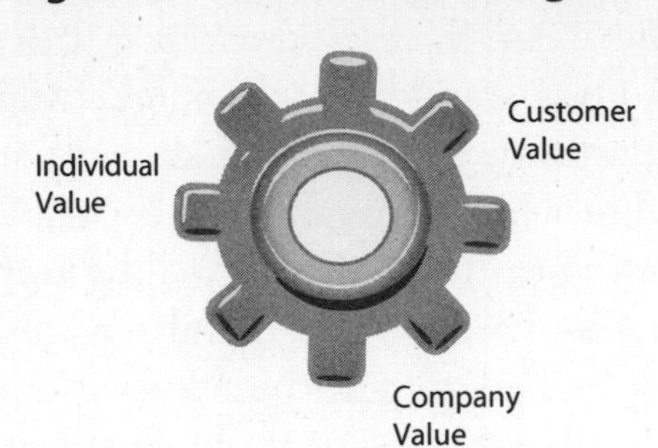

which in turn generates value for the employees. It is a virtuous circle, sustained by continuous innovation in creating newer business models, more sophisticated incentives for employees, and more sophisticated administration of these incentives (figure 8.1).

To succeed in its business model objective of achieving zero distance from the customer, it is critical that Haier employees act as if they are individual entrepreneurs. Only in this way can Haier be agile, responsive, and innovative in the pursuit of ever better customer service. As a result, Haier not only emphasizes entrepreneurial spirit as it recruits employees, but insists on placing them in an organizational culture where internal competition and risk taking are an accepted part of everyday corporate life, which Haier believes encourages them to act as entrepreneurs. Haier's business model relies on the entrepreneurial energies of its employees in many ways. In return, it addresses its employees as entrepreneurs and gives them both high responsibility and the freedom to set their own goals and determine how they will reach them.

In chapter 5, we suggested that the driving force behind Haier's ability to achieve its business model objectives operates as shown in figure 8.2.

This achievement of a corporate mind-set that both celebrates and practices entrepreneurship, competition, and achievement that we found in Haier is perhaps the most important

Figure 8.2 Haier's Cultural Engine

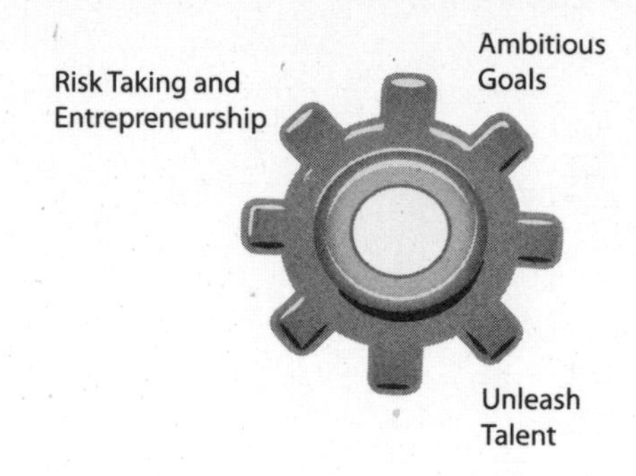

Figure 8.3 Haier's Cultural and Value Engine

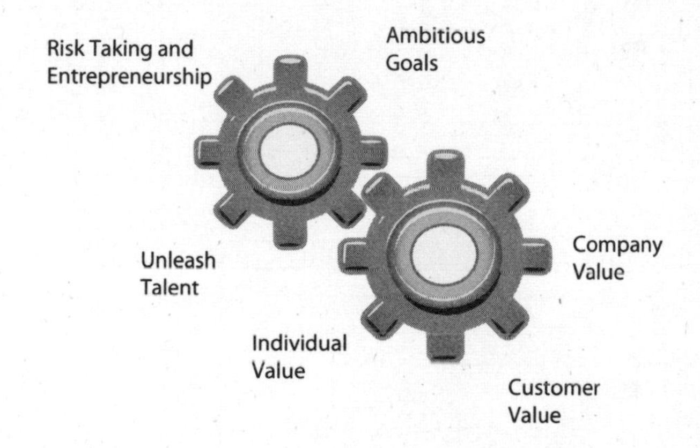

cultural component that enables its business model. It stimulates the production of value, which requires and stimulates the further development of the culture. We can say that the two virtuous circles work together and are mutually reinforcing (figure 8.3).

If the creation of value is the ultimate goal of a business model, then it is imperative that the choices that define the organizational culture support and reinforce the means by which the organization intends to create value. In Haier's case (figure 8.4), the relationship between the release of individual talent and

Figure 8.4 From Values to Value: Haier Business Model Unfolded

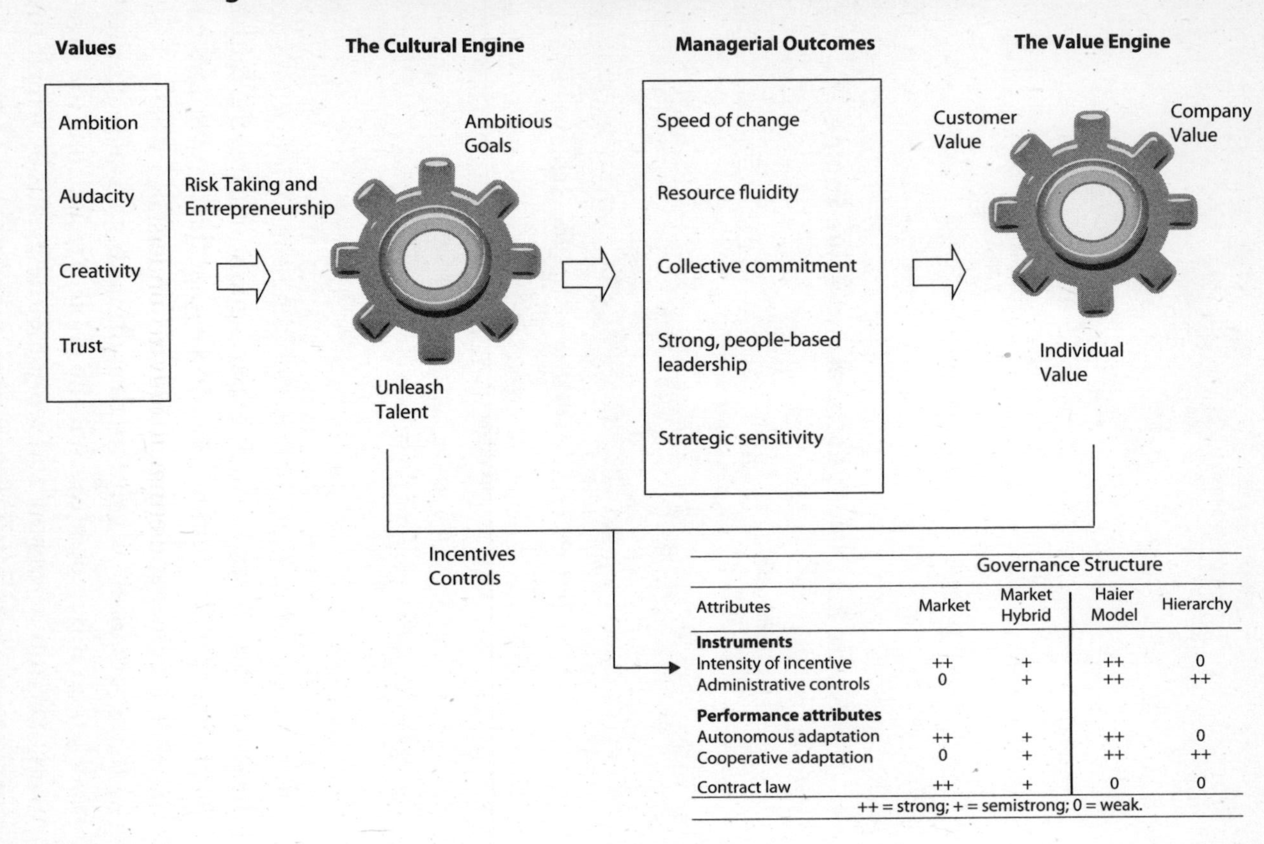

	Governance Structure			
Attributes	Market	Market Hybrid	Haier Model	Hierarchy
Instruments				
Intensity of incentive	++	+	++	0
Administrative controls	0	+	++	++
Performance attributes				
Autonomous adaptation	++	+	++	0
Cooperative adaptation	0	+	++	++
Contract law	++	+	0	0

++ = strong; + = semistrong; 0 = weak.

Table 8.1 Haier Group Revenue and Net Profit, 2008–2012

	Revenue (billions of U.S. dollars)	*Net Profit (billions of U.S. dollars)*
2012	27.4	1.45
2011	23.3	1.16
2010	20.8	0.92
2009	18.3	0.56
2008	17.1	0.32

Note: Haier Group's revenue is composed of the revenue of two listed companies: Qingdao Haier Refrigerator Co. on the Shanghai Stock Exchange and Haier-CCT Holdings Ltd. on the Hong Kong Stock Exchange

Source: Haier company information.

the creation of customer value is at the heart of the model. Not surprisingly, this relationship also shapes Haier's unusual governance structure, a blend of market incentives and administrative controls.

The results, shown in table 8.1, are testament to the success that Haier has enjoyed over the years. We believe that the results reveal that Haier's never-ending quest to reinvent both its business model and supporting corporate culture are not only ambitious managerial ambitions but also savvy responses to a dynamic, competitive marketplace.

What Can We Learn?

Remembering all of the caveats of generalizing from a single company, there remain some elements in Haier's business model that are well worth considering, if only to understand from a business strategy point of view how one of the world's most interesting companies is operating. We believe that there are at least six areas of learning from the Haier experience that are largely applicable to most organizations, no matter what industry they are in and no matter what their cultural context.

Haier Is Selling Talent, Not Refrigerators

More than anything else, the Haier story is about people. Has Haier made high-quality products? Has it out-innovated its competition? Has it ingrained itself more completely into customers' lives? The answer to each of these questions is a resounding yes, but that does not explain the Haier difference. Where Haier has excelled over other organizations in its competitive space is in choosing business model value propositions that rely almost completely on the talent of the people it has hired to accomplish all of these objectives.

To be fair, Haier is a much-desired employer within China's talent market, ranking thirteenth in 2011 and third in 2010 among the "fifty best employers" as ranked by Chinese college students, and so it has a preferred pool of applicants.[1] But what distinguishes Haier's efforts is what it does with that talent, and the secret to that is a multigenerational effort to create an organizational culture that not only speaks about entrepreneurship and the value of employed talent, but tries to create an environment where such attitudes are expected, practiced, appreciated, rewarded, and made the norm. As a result, Haier's great quality, its interesting innovation, and its market success are due less to the products that it sells than they are to the people who make those products and services possible.

Haier Relies on Trust and Merit to Release the Power and Energy of Talented Individuals

The red thread in Haier's thirty-year saga is a reliance on the relationship between talent and results to drive each of its successive business models. This has required a continuous reinvention of the organization's corporate culture in order to support the achievement of each new business model. In its present incarnation, the way that Haier works represents a series of linkages that begin by understanding the customer better than rivals do, by virtue of being closer to those customers' lives, and then judging performance results by regarding customer value created, eventually lead us back along Haier's inverted triangle into the very heart of the business model, where we find a consistent belief in the power of people, their talent, and their competence in responding to these customer needs. This is a company that believes in the power, energy, and innovativeness of the talent that it has assembled, and it has consistently worked to create a corporate culture worthy of these individuals. At Haier, there is a profound and continuing idea regarding the centrality of individual wants and contributions that extends to both customers and employees.

Individual rewards and compensation are also at the heart of Haier's business model. Haier employees are trusted to do whatever they can to win customers' loyalty, and be rewarded in return. Accordingly, Haier employees do not receive completely fixed compensation. Their total package is based to a large extent on the results that they bring in terms of creating value for customers and for Haier. The business model is structured such that the welfare of employees is deeply intertwined with that of the company. Clearly this is designed to create a mutual sense of commitment, with the mechanism of linking employees' salary to value created touching every employee in the company.

In fact, the climate of collective commitment is clear at Haier headquarters. People work hard because they have personal incentives for doing so, and these incentives are devised in such a way that they benefit the entire company. We have the impression that in too many modern complex organizations, managers continue to believe in Douglas McGregor's theory X, or the assumption that employees require close supervision and control if they are to perform to expected levels. This is especially true in mature industries touched by commoditization, where cost reduction is the preeminent concern of senior management.

Haier has adopted an extreme version of McGregor's alternative theory Y and believes that employees are inherently ambitious and self-motivated, enjoy their work, and possess the ability for creative problem solving, but that all too often their talents are underused. McGregor argued for managers to be open to a more positive view of workers and the possibilities that such a view would create. He held that developing a climate of trust with employees allows human resource development and superior performance. This is exactly what happens at Haier: we see a causal relationship between trust in people's ability and the full use of their talent and capabilities, which results in the creation of value for the customer, Haier, and the employee. In fact, *human resource development* is a phrase that is widely used at Haier and is always connected to the idea of value creation rather than to its more bureaucratic meaning. In such a corporate environment, not only do employees enjoy the freedom that they might typically appreciate in a marketplace for their talent but also, as in a market, their compensation and career progression are linked to their results.

A by-product of Haier's rewards policy is the transparency of career paths, which are reassessed every quarter, resulting in an organization where the best people—those who have consistently produced the best results—take the top positions.

As we saw in chapter 6, other companies—Oticon, ABB, Nash Confectionery, and Morning Star—have aspired to the same objectives as Haier and have approached the design of their corporate cultures in similar ways. But these companies are the exception rather than the norm and, except for ABB, they have not been as large or as ambitious as Haier has been.

Rather Than Pursuing Scalable Efficiency, Haier Is Experimenting with a Corporate Culture That Can Drive Scalable Learning

The industrial revolution was based on a school of industrial engineering that concentrated on improving operational efficiencies. This meant that less labor was required per unit of output, less time was consumed in moving parts through a factory, and less variance was experienced in all aspects of factory life. All of these were good things, but according to this school of practice, variance was abhorrent and something to be controlled. In fact, however, variance is a natural aspect of capricious customer demands, unexpected technological surprises, and unforeseen competitive initiatives, and we should try to work with it rather than against it. Machines do badly at learning in the face of such unpredictability, but smart people excel.

John Hagel recently wrote about the differences between scalable efficiency and scalable learning and concluded:

> The real problem we are confronting [in contemporary industrial societies] is a growing disconnect between the institutional architectures we have so carefully designed over the past century and the pressures that are mounting in our global economy. This disconnect goes to the very core of why we have institutions in the first place. Until we address that most basic question, entrepreneurial tinkering will likely have marginal impact.
>
> Ronald Coase won the Nobel Prize in economics for an essay on *The Nature of the Firm* he wrote in 1937 that provided a simple and compelling answer to the question of why we have corporations. He argued that we need corporations because they reduce transaction costs—the costs of coordinating and executing economic activity. Put in slightly different terms—the rationale for corporations resided in the quest for scalable efficiency.
>
> This was an amazingly accurate analysis of the rise of the modern corporation in the 20th century. . . . Driven by forecasts of demand, *push* programs required highly standardized and rigorously specified work activities that were closely monitored to ensure predictability. The modern, thick process manual was the end-product. The job of the individual was to fit into this tightly regimented work environment and perform predictably and efficiently.
>
> . . .

> [But] what about all those wonderful things that . . . will never likely be automated—imagination, creativity, genuine insight and emotional and moral intelligence? These attributes have no place in the *push* driven institutions we have built. They are ruthlessly rooted out wherever they rear their ugly heads.
>
> Smaller, entrepreneurial organizations of course buck this trend, but what happens as soon as they start to scale? They embrace *push* programs and rapidly join the ranks of the regimented.
>
> . . .
>
> Equally importantly, we're moving from a world of knowledge-stocks, where competitive advantage resides in proprietary knowledge of lasting value, to a world of knowledge-flows, where competitive advantage can only be attained by participating effectively in a larger and more diverse set of knowledge-flows. In a world that's changing more rapidly with growing uncertainty, knowledge-stocks depreciate in value at an accelerating rate.
>
> This suggests an alternative rationale for institutions. Rather than pursuing scalable efficiency, perhaps we need a new set of institutions that can drive scalable learning, helping participants to learn faster by working together. While simple to state and intuitively appealing, this requires profound changes to our institutional landscape.
>
> Rather than relying on rigid push programs, we need to increasingly develop scalable pull platforms where people can draw out people and resources where they are needed and when they are needed, not just to perform predefined tasks, but to engage in creative problem-solving as unanticipated challenges arise.[2]

We believe that Hagel is right: new organizations based on imagination, creativity, genuine insight, and emotional and moral intelligence are necessary for competitive success in today's global environments. We think that he is also correct when he says this is not easy to achieve. We further believe that this is exactly what

Zhang Ruimin is trying to do. He may not have articulated the dream in exactly the same words, and the experiments taking place today at Haier are not necessarily the correct solution, but we think that Zhang and Haier are on the right track. Whether it ultimately succeeds in Haier's case is still an open question, but there is little doubt in our minds that this is a worthy effort. Organizations such as Oticon, ABB, Nash Confectionery, and Morning Star have also tried to pioneer such initiatives, and there will undoubtedly be more in the future. What makes Haier so interesting is that it is taking place right now, on an unprecedented scale, and in an emerging economy.

A Process of Continuous Cultural Reinvention Can Become a Normal Way of Working

During one of our meetings in Qingdao, a Haier manager said, "At Haier, speed is more important that quality." Shocking as such a statement might be, the message behind it lies in a recent comment by Zhang Ruimin:

> A successful business management model should pursue continuous innovations, in which case there should be no concept of success in business competition. Because all successes, assuming that other people say you are successful, must be of the past, and today you must pursue higher goals than yesterday. The moment when a person stands on the championship podium, he is no longer a champion, but must strive for the next championship.[3]

Speed and continuous change are deeply intertwined at Haier. Innovation is considered to be a continuous activity, requiring constant trial and error. When the pace of this trial and error is rapid, there is a sense of a flow of constant, ongoing improvement. And, in fact at Haier people are always experimenting and providing feedback. Even administrative controls are devised in such a way that every employee can have daily feedback on his or her work.

Quality is not overlooked at Haier in the pursuit of innovation. The way to achieve quality, though, is not through linear, sequential planning, but by learning from a continuous, fast trial-and-error approach to stay in touch with the customer through ongoing testing. To make such a system work, fast information exchange is crucial and is why "speed is more important than quality." It means that rapid information exchange, even when information is incomplete or imperfect, is more important than delaying until there is reliable information. The learning process becomes more important than the intermediate results, because long-lasting results arise only from nurturing a useful process. Haier is a process-managed company. There is an abiding belief that processes can and should be continuously improved, and a large part of Haier's approach to business models is concerned exactly with this: improving processes continuously.

One overriding lesson comes through loud and clear: Haier is not afraid of change, not even continuous change, and it makes no apologies for reorganization. Unlike many other large organizations that go to extreme and imaginative lengths to avoid a large cultural change, Haier has embraced organizational reinvention throughout its history. This attitude of accepting change as the new norm may be one of Haier's biggest gifts to students of managerial practice. But bear in mind that Haier's changes have always been purposeful; it has always been directed at reinventing corporate culture to support new business models in responding to changes in Haier's external competitive environment.

Haier's Thirty-Year Saga of Change Has Consistently Built on Lessons Learned

In chapter 1, we looked at growth trajectories that moved from protect and extend toward the achievement of new competencies and new markets. We commented that the one path never to take is the quick leap into simultaneously new markets and new processes without relying on lessons learned from experience. In the pursuit of new growth, it is tempting to try to cut short the learning process and move quickly, but abandoning a firm's competencies or market knowledge can be costly. Toyota did this only once and paid for it in terms of brand-disparagement and a loss of customer loyalty.[4] What is striking about Haier's growth trajectory over the past three decades is that it has been one of accretion. The canvases for each new business model show that each reinvention is built on the previous one, and no matter how bold Haier's latest business model or cultural choices have appeared, they have always been built on prior experience that provided the knowledge and confidence necessary to make such seemingly daring leaps. There has never been disarray or disconnect in the evolution of Haier's household appliance business.

Strong, Self-Confident, Top-Down Leadership Is Essential for Successful Innovative Change

Sparking a managerial revolution is not for the faint-hearted, and to do it repeatedly in the pursuit of the dream of unleashing individual talent requires leadership courage. This is possible only when the leadership team is convinced of the underlying philosophy of releasing unexpressed talent and energy and only when it has the self-confidence to weather the storms that are inevitable with fostering big change. Haier is unleashing the energies and ideas of the talent that it has throughout its organization, down to the very bottom of its organizational pyramid (which is now the very top), but such bottom-up liberation is possible only with strong, self-confident top-down leaders. The fact that Haier has done this repeatedly over the past thirty years is as much a credit to the leadership team as it is to the employees who have made it work.

Applicability of the Lessons Learned

We believe that all managers, no matter what their industry or their market history, should study the lessons of Haier's past three decades. To dare to outperform is about dreaming bigger than the rest of the competitive pack, and to execute on these dreams means attention to detail that is vividly represented by the wealth of granular managerial choices that have characterized Haier's continuing reinvention of its corporate culture. At the start of chapter 6, we quoted a part of Gary Hamel's dream for future organizations; we share Hamel's dream as a worthy one, perhaps the ultimate challenge for our profession as managers or students of managers, and we think that Haier has a legitimate claim to have achieved as much in the pursuit of this dream as any other organization you might suggest.

Postscript

While We Were Writing . . .

Among the themes that have consistently run through this book are Haier's impressive pace of change, willingness to re-invent itself, and the capacity to surprise. As evidence of this, Haier launched yet another version of its business model as this book was going to press.

On December 26, 2012, Haier announced its fifth strategy stage—the networking strategy stage—which appears less than a year since the previous stage, described in earlier chapters, was launched. It was only in March 2012 that we traveled to Qingdao to learn how the ZZJYT model worked because it had been extended throughout Haier's entire structure. Now, less than one year later, the group is embarking on another major change, which is also going to encompass the whole organizational structure.

The new stage of Haier development comes from two beliefs, both of which have been seen before as part of Zhang's strategic vision. The first is the idea that "successful enterprises move with the times":[1] that an enterprise remains successful only if it changes as fast, and as appropriately, as the markets around it are changing. The second belief is that market power has been shifting along the value chain for some time now, from producing enterprises to the end users, who have more options, more requirements, and greater market influence than at any time in the past. In these times, enterprises need to be able to move faster in order to "keep up with the speed of end users in clicking the mouse."[2]

As a response to these changes, Haier has decided to transform itself around the service enterprise it created in the stage 4 development described in this book, into a platform enterprise that provides personalized, customized service in order to give end-using customers the best household appliance experiences available in the market. This new stage 5 version of Haier will no longer be an organization with boundaries but instead an open platform without any boundaries between value-chain partners or even nontraditional suppliers for that matter. In this open system, end users are buyers and cocreators of value. Haier envisions that R&D and even manufacturing will gradually expand outside of its present organizational boundaries. With this new platform, the reinvention of Haier will not be closed but open to the whole society. According to Zhang, future competition will be among platforms more than among rival companies and, in order to win, companies will need to be as open as possible in order to engage the best resources among all stakeholders. Haier wants to become an open platform in which more stakeholders can be invited to help create value.

As radical as this transformation appears, we see, once again, that Haier's innovation path is one of accretion, building on existing knowledge, rather than attempting to become something completely new. Haier's stage 5 transformations are based on the already existing idea of everyone sharing in value creation depending on their contribution (win-win model of individual-goal combination), as well as on the concept of zero distance between employees and end users. The difference with stage 5, compared with much of what has been described in this book, lies in the fact that the necessary speed to respond to personalization requires instant collaboration between departments or teams; therefore it is envisioned that it will be necessary to flatten the structure even further, reducing the number of tiers from three to two, and giving each ZZJYT the full power to behave exactly like a real company. In this new stage 5 organization, each ZZJYT becomes a node in a dynamic network in order to better synchronize and integrate the enterprise network with the network aspects of a complex, modern marketplace.

The evolution from the inverted triangle to the node-based network will make the internal structure even less hierarchical, with fewer grades and no boundaries. Every node of the network is a ZZJYT, which will be a full organization, with the power of decision making, value distribution, and personnel placement. Every node will also be an interface, connecting global end users directly to Haier's first-class resources so they can provide an effective complement to each other (this is the participation of end users in cocreating value).

ZZJYTs will now be classified into only two types: end user–type ZZJYTs and resource-type ZZJYTs. End user–type ZZJYTs will be oriented toward end users, to developing the market, to keeping zero distance with the end users' changing demands, and to responding to end-user demand in real time. Resource-type ZZJYTs will provide end user–type ZZJYTs with resources and help them to achieve the desired end-user value.

These two types of ZZJYT organization will be achieved through the merger of existing first- and second-tier ZZJYTs. Zhang believes that the second-tier ZZJYTs must be directly linked to market performance in a way that they are not presently. In Haier's stage 4, second-tier managers acted as resource providers but in stage 5 their functions will be merged together with those of the people directly facing the market, ensuring that they behave closer to the Haier adage that "your value is what your goal is." No longer will a Haier second-tier manager be able to say, "I can provide a design program and a product" as though it were an abstract promise. Zhang believed that this somewhat disconnected, multiactor conversation, which typified the stage 4 three-tier inverted triangle, had distorted and slowed down the fluidity of the conversations that were hoped for between the customer facing first-tier ZZJYTs and third-tier ZZJYTs, which set company strategy.

In stage 5, the organizational distance between Haier's internal actors and the customer will be dramatically reduced. There will now be end users on the Internet who want a product and can place an order in direct, real-time contact with former second-tier managers who will be part of the ZZJYT and must directly produce this end-user value. It will no longer be enough that these former second-tier experts are ready to help first-tier ZZJYTs to produce value; now they will actually be producing that value as part of the first-tier ZZJYT, and they will have to show tangible achievements in producing that value because their remuneration will be directly and completely tied to the end-user resources and the end-user value generated.

In an exchange of views with the Morning Star Company (USA), which shares a similar management philosophy with Haier, Zhang found that Morning Star relies on an interesting metaphor: "They said they are just like a spider web. The spider web has the capacity of self-repair. When a cobweb is broken, the spider will immediately weave it." The metaphor Zhang used to describe Haier was a radar net: "Haier is like radar net that can capture the invisible things [such as market trends or nascent customer desires] continuously."[3]

Extending this metaphor, it is Haier's hope that its organization will gradually morph into different nodes, doing away with the second-tier ZZJYTs, which presently remain at a distance from the customer. Zhang believes that as long as second-tier ZZJYTs exist, it will be impossible for Haier to evolve closer to the customer in the future.

With the second tier gone, Zhang believes that the third tier ZZJYTs will focus on the organizational culture, which, to some extent, may be an endless affair. Externally, the third-tier ZZJYTs will still be required to discover new market opportunities that are emerging as a result of increased societal reliance on the Internet. The third-tier ZZJYTs will work on these two issues.

This will not be an easy reinvention, not that any of them have been, especially because it will affect many thousands of Haier's people. Even Zhang Ruimin recognizes the stakes that are involved in a change of such magnitude: "There will be an earthquake if it is not properly handled."[4] Yet, all of this has been built on existing experiences and is consistent with the direction already described in this book. Haier is moving, again, one step further: it is becoming an organization even less hierarchical and even more embracing of market incentives. More than an organization, it increasingly looks like a regulated market, where the top management has the duty and the privilege to write the rules with which the internal market has to comply. Will it be successful? This is difficult to say, but while we were writing this book in 2012, Haier increased its overall market share by an additional 0.8 percent, enabling it to achieve a global market share in major home appliances of 8.6 percent, making Haier the number one global brand in home appliances for the fourth consecutive year, according to Euromonitor.[5]

Appendix

How ZZJYTs Work

This appendix provides additional details regarding how the ZZJYTs work with each other, how performance is assessed, and the expansion of Haier's business model into Internet activities and new brands.

The ZZJYT Contract Process

The second-tier ZZJYTs offer business process support to the first-tier ZZJYTs. They contractually preset all the resources that they are to supply for the first tier. They then physically prepare these resources so that when the first-tier ZZJYTs need them, they are ready for delivery for the next three years.

There is also a contractual relationship between the second- and the third-tier ZZJYTs, similar to the contractual relationship between the second and the first tier: third-tier functional units provide management services to the second tier, and the second tier pays for these services but then invoices the first tier. As a result and because they are the ultimate revenue generators, the first-tier ZZJYTs pay for all the resources, even those supplied to second tier.

One might think that contract proliferation could be an issue for Haier. In a sense, though, contracts merely formalize agreements that the different departments already have regarding supplies, prices, and terms.

Haier has used its experience with the three-door refrigerator unit to standardize the contracts process. Today contracts are circulated around the organization in order to establish and share standards. These contracts can be vertical—between the different tiers of the organization to provide resources and expertise—and horizontal, such as those among the first-tier market, module, and manufacturing ZZJYTs. Three-door refrigerators has a good horizontal and vertical combination of contracts, and Haier is trying to transfer this structure to other ZZJYTs.

An important feature of Haier's model is sharing best practices. Because of the large number of ZZJYTs and the volume of their transactions, it is relatively easy for Haier to learn from the experiences of the various ZZJYTs, once it starts looking for them. Many ZZJYTs' best practices and activities have been set out in brochures and circulated throughout the organization.

Strategy and ZZJYTs

To be sure that ZZJYTs move in the right direction, members of the strategy department participate in meetings for the three types of first-tier ZZJYT: market, module, and manufacturing.

If a ZZJYT strategy is not working, resources for it will be cut off. Mr. Ba, head of strategy for white goods, says, "The ZZJYT leader can dance as he likes, but he must dance on the platform. Strategy provides this platform."

Strategy platforms provide the boundaries within which the ZZJYTs can act. If they meet the goals of the Haier Group, they are free to do almost whatever they want. Moreover, boundaries are not imposed; rather, they are decided with each ZZJYT's leaders through preset agreements.

In the three-door refrigerator group, the platform works efficiently, but this has not been universally so in other ZZJYTs. The outcome probably depends on the ZZJYT itself. For example, the three-door refrigerator ZZJYT wanted daily market data on its products in every channel and every region, and team members successfully pressed the IT organization to produce software to provide this information. As a result of the success of this ZZJYT, the two-door refrigerator group and then ZZJYTs for washing machines and other products will start receiving this information too.

This is an example of how best practices are shared. The three-door ZZJYT members were skilled at asking the right questions and identifying people in other ZZJYTs who could solve their problems. This team is also very good at pressing other ZZJYTs to deliver what they are looking for, which is mostly a matter of attitude. Pu, the leader of the three-door ZZJYT, considers himself a real entrepreneur, which is why he is so demanding. Other ZZJYT leaders may feel as if they are employees and not care as much. Haier's hope is that through best practice sharing, these other ZZJYT leaders will see what they can accomplish.

Targets and Individual Compensation

In the three-door ZZJYT, as in all other ZZJYTs, performance targets are based on market appraisals. Market segmentation can identify the consumers and how many might be purchasing which products.

For three-door refrigerators, for example, if the potential internal market is 10 million units and Haier's overall market share is 30 percent, a market goal of 3 million pieces could be established for the ZZJYT. The actual estimate for three-door refrigerators in the Chinese market for 2012 was 15 million units, and Haier at the time enjoyed more than a 25 percent market share. This meant that Haier should sell one out of every four three-door refrigerators, or approximately 3.75 million units. A stretch target of achieving a 33 percent market share for the three-door refrigerator ZZJYT would mean selling approximately 5 million units. The target was fixed and adjusted yearly to meet market conditions.

Many ZZJYTs, however, have failed to reach their targets because they lack ambition, competence, or resources or some combination of these. It may well be that in the future, the highest-performing ZZJYTs will take over the lower-performing ones. In a sense, this process has begun, with the best ZZJYTs attracting and using the resources of other ZZJYTs, for example, contracting with them for talent.

Performance Evaluation

Once a ZZJYT has reached its target and earned its bonus, the question of dividing the bonus among team members needs to be addressed. As we saw in chapter 4, everything in Haier is preestablished. In the case of individual rewards, each team member has an agreement set out with the ZZJYT leader regarding bonuses, and this agreement is used to establish his or her overall compensation. These individual agreements are closely held information within the ZZJYT.

Individual performance is thus evaluated on the basis of two dimensions:

- Objective results
- Preset agreements

Evaluations are both quantitative and qualitative. An important part of a ZZJYT leader's job is determining the compensation of the team members, and this means addressing the qualitative part of performance evaluations.

Each team member's salary lies within an interval, assigned by the ZZJYT leader, according to the employee's experience, skills, and other attributes. While the ZZJYT's achievements are determined according to objective results, determining individual compensation is done according to both objective achievements and subjective evaluation by the leader of all the elements that cannot be translated into numbers. In making such determinations, the ZZJYT leader might consult with the HR and finance staff, but ultimately the decision is his or hers to make.

An illustration of how Haier might evaluate the performance of a ZZJYT member (module manager) who is responsible for a single modular part used by one or more ZZJYTs (e.g., a refrigerator door unit) would reflect on several performance aspects.

Quality performance would certainly be a key determinant, but the market might trade off quality against other product attributes. As a result, different parameters would be used for the evaluation—for example:

- How often is the module (the refrigerator door) used in other products (in addition to the three-door refrigerator)?
- By how much was the module's production cost reduced?
- How fast are changes to the module implemented?

The use of these different parameters allows ZZJYT management to form a good idea of the quality of the work of this particular module manager.

Goals and Compensation

Individual performance must then be linked to individual compensation. Haier's employees' salaries include three elements: a base salary, which is very low and represents the minimum salary according to provincial law in Shandong (the province that the municipality of Qingdao is in), a contract salary that is above the local minimum requirement and reflects the premium that Haier offers to employees who meet their performance targets, and a bonus earned by surpassing the target.

As an illustration, let's assume the following situation:

Target	*Compensation*
80 percent	Base
90 percent	Base plus 90 percent of the contract
100 percent	Base plus the contract
120 percent	Base plus the contract plus a bonus

An employee who meets the target (100 percent) receives a base salary (around 30 to 40 percent of the total compensation) and the contract salary, which includes a specified bonus,

A Sample Calculation

Let's assume that last year's target profit for an employee in a module ZZJYT was RMB 640,000, and the target for this year, based on market projections, is RMB 800,000. If the employee reaches this target, the leader of this module ZZJYT will pay him a target salary of RMB 3,000 (per month); if the employee reaches only last year's target, he will receive only the Qingdao-mandated base salary of RMB 1,200 (per month). If he can surpass the target and reach RMB 1,000,000, he will be paid his target salary plus a bonus that increases proportionally as the actual results go beyond the target. If the results are well beyond target, his salary can double. To this salary is added a compensation package that includes stock options and training. If his performance is intermediate between the target and last year's actual profit, the salary is determined proportionately so that the variable part of it is decided on the basis of the distance between the actual achievement, the target, and last year's achievement. For example, let's assume that he can achieve only 90 percent of his target. Here are the calculations to determine his salary:

Last year actual profit	0.64 M RMB
0.9 of target	0.72 M RMB
Target	0.8 M RMB
Target surpassed	1.0 M RMB

Qingdao base: RMB 1,200

Target salary: RMB 3,000

These are the calculations:

$$\text{Salary} = (0.72 - 0.64)/(0.8 - 0.64) \times (3{,}000 - 1{,}200) + 1{,}200$$

$$= 0.08/0.16 \times 1{,}800 + 1{,}200$$

$$= 0.5 \times 1{,}800 + 1{,}200$$

$$= 900 + 1{,}200 = 2{,}100$$

Haier's employment premium paid for achieving the target. An employee who surpasses the target receives the contract salary plus an extra bonus on the extra profit generated. Normally the bonus for reaching the target is around 1 percent of the profit generated. When extra profit is generated, this percentage increases in a more than linear fashion.

If an employee has performed well but the ZZJYT does not produce enough profit to pay a bonus, the group pays a bonus (smaller than it might be under normal conditions) out of a pool that it maintains for such situations. According to Pu, "You must have the money in your pocket in order to pay people salaries."

Bonus compensation can take three forms: cash, stock options, and training. The total compensation (in cash, excluding stock options) cannot be larger than twice the employee's contractual salary.

The lowest compensation in the event that last year's target is missed is based on Qingdao's mandatory minimum salary (around RMB 1,200 per month).

The Role of ZZJYT Leaders in Individual Evaluations

In most cases, annual targets are fixed for a year, but monthly and quarterly targets may be changed to account for sales variability. If at the end of the year, the ZZJYT exceeds its target and upgrades, all ZZJYT members receive a higher preset salary for the following year.[1]

Each month, the ZZJYTs pay team members according to the overall team and individual performance. Evaluation is conducted quarterly and yearly. One implication of this is that if in the first quarter, Pu, the leader of the three-door ZZJYT, has poor performance, he must compensate with good performance in the next quarter. If his performance does not improve, the company will introduce a competitor from outside the team and the ZZJYT team members can vote on which person should lead them into the future. ZZJYT leaders can never relax.

Given Haier's propensity for introducing checks and balances into most relationships, it should be noted that not only does the leader evaluate the ZZJYT members but the members also have the right to evaluate the leader. This evaluation takes the form of voting. In three-door refrigerators, a vote is held every quarter. The voting system has three objectives:

- Obtain feedback from ZZJYT members on their expectations regarding the leader
- Identify any leadership problems within the ZZJYT
- Improve the leader's performance

There is also a quarterly review of the entire evaluation process, performed by the Haier Group.

The Upgrading Process of ZZJYTs

In 2011, the three-door refrigerator ZZJYT was Haier's best-performing ZZJYT. Twenty-six of the white goods module ZZJYTs were performing above industry standards and only four below. This assessment is not based solely on how their products sell. Some Haier products are very popular in the marketplace and some less so. Instead, Haier believes that the success of a ZZJYT rests on the quality of its people. The achievement of the three-door refrigerator ZZJYT is seen as the result of continuous improvements in the right strategic direction.

In order to promote continuous improvement, Haier has introduced a tool that links team performance to compensation and has defined three levels of improvement:

1.0: *Improvements in relationships with other ZZJYTS:*
This suggests that ZZJYTs are not isolated within the

corporation but connect horizontally and vertically to other ZZJYTs.

2.0: *Achieving zero distance with the market and other ZZJYTs:* Here, the ZZJYT achieves zero distance (horizontally) with the market and vertically with second- and third-tier ZZJYTs. These are seen as dynamic connections: the first-tier ZZJYT dynamically adapts to its customers and the second- and third-tier ZZJYTs follow. It also means that the first-tier ZZJYT can mobilize all of the resources (physical and managerial) it needs in order to satisfy customers.

3.0: *Achieves the state of being a continuously optimized virtual company:* This is the stage where the ZZJYT has reached such a profound understanding of its customer that the entire system behaves in synchronized harmony and the ZZJYT is always in tune with its customer.

Figure A.1 is an improvement plan for ZZJYTs that also reflects market competitiveness. ZZJYTs operating at the desired level of performance must be competitive and outperform their competitors. The figure shows different stages of evolution of a ZZJYT from underperforming to best performing. On the vertical axes are the reasons for improvement; on the horizontal axes, the competitive outcomes are reported.

Most of the ZZJYTs at Haier are performing between levels 0 and 1.0. Only the three-door refrigerator ZZJYT is at the 2.0 level. According to Haier's HR managers, many ZZJYTs lack the ambition, the competence, and the resources to achieve their desired objectives, and they need profound upgrading or their members may be fired. If a ZZJYT improves from level 1.0 to 2.0, its targets and compensation are adjusted accordingly, leading to higher goals and higher compensation for ZZJYT members.

Figure A.1 Upgrade ZZJYT—the Two Dimensions, April 2012

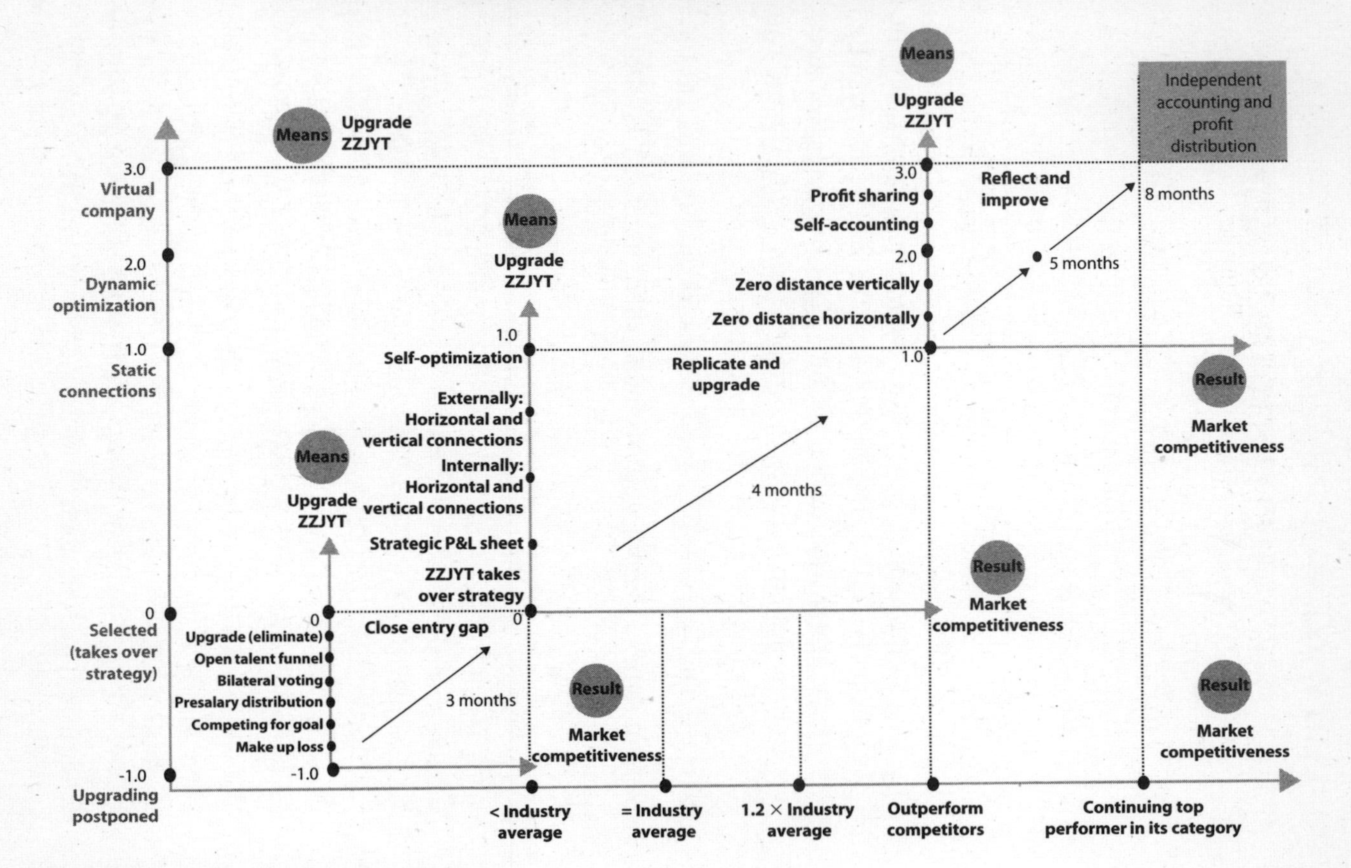

Source: Adapted from Haier documents.

Expansion of Haier's Business Model

Physical and Virtual Network

To the extent that Haier's reinvention of its corporate culture is successful, there will undoubtedly be significant implications for its value chain partners. One of the most promising outcomes is in the ability to respond to market variations with such agility that nearly complete knowledge of market fluctuations would be possible. If this were to occur, Haier would be able to realize full value from the situation only if it were also able to master just-in-time (JIT) manufacturing processes and zero inventory. This became a managerial challenge for the firm, led by Zhang Ruimin's stated intention to achieve both of these new goals.

For full impact, JIT requires the willing and active participation of upstream and downstream value chain partners. However, Haier had to confront the reality that JIT is not a widely practiced tool among Chinese manufacturers. Its response was to share complementary advantages in resources as a means of inducing value chain partnerships in the pursuit of JIT. Haier offers access to its global distribution network and the advantages of its high production volumes to encourage its suppliers to practice greater modularization of parts and standardization. Haier has also obtained technologies and designs from overseas value chain partners in return for providing its local expertise on the Chinese market.

The combination of ZZJYTs and JIT has allowed Haier to build a sound logistics network (physical network) based on the inverted triangle model. The network works through an end-to-end system that moves from the customer to the factory. It starts by forecasting sales and taking orders, which then pulls customized products and services, employing JIT production and JIT delivery. (See figure A.2.)

Developing a virtual network has been equally important for Haier. The virtual network is not only about e-commerce and

Figure A.2 Haier's Physical and Virtual Network

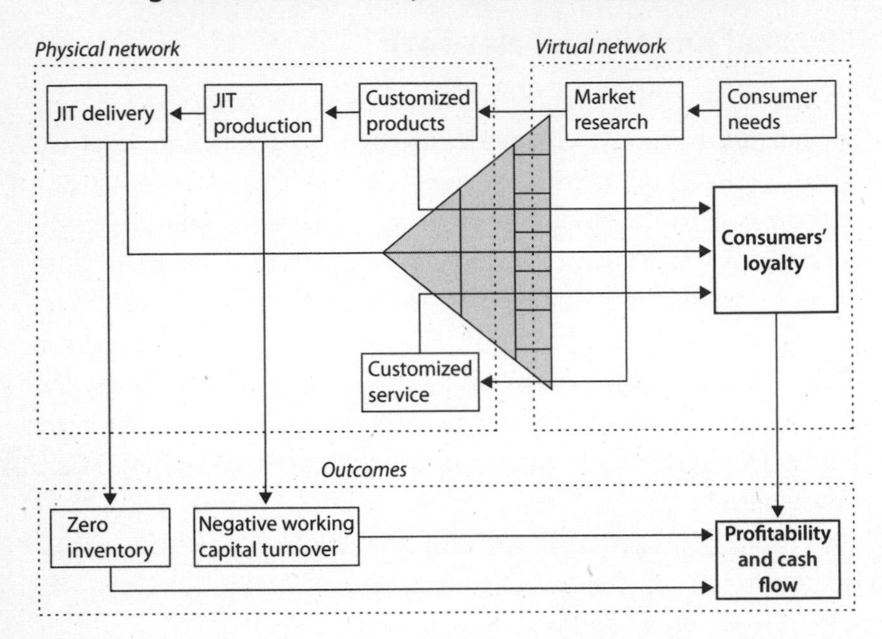

collecting consumers' feedback electronically, but also about providing customers with personalized home appliance solutions in order to gain their long-term loyalty. Haier's physical and virtual networks must be complementary if they are to maximize customers' satisfaction. Zhang has said, "We need to open community stores in urban areas and specialty stores in rural areas, and then go further to integrate these two together. You can quickly buy a product from our community or specialty stores in the virtual network, and if you don't feel so confident, you can go to our physical stores to check the product and get a more comprehensive understanding."

Transformation into a Service-Oriented Company

In June 2007, Zhang said that global white goods competition was no longer driven by technology innovation but by channels and service and that Haier's vision would change accordingly. By 2010 this had become fact: Haier announced its strategy of transforming itself from a manufacturing firm to a service-oriented one.

This was not an easy transformation. In fact, it was unusual for a Chinese company at this stage in China's development. China was, and to a large extent still is, considered the factory of the world, so it came as a surprise that one of its most important companies and one of its most important brands was making the transition from manufacturing to embrace services.

In fact, this was more of a rhetorical move than an actual one. Nevertheless Haier is changing from a product-oriented manufacturing company to a customer-driven service company. Even if this does not entail a diminution of manufacturing capacity, at least in the core businesses, it means a huge change in mind-set. It suggests that manufacturing is not as important for competitive advantage as it was in the past and that customer satisfaction has gained in importance. There is also the implication that manufacturing activities will be kept in-house only as far as they make it possible to allow delivering superior value to consumers. If and when this is no longer the case, Haier will likely turn to outsourced manufacturing.

Segmentation and Positioning

In the process of becoming a service-oriented, customer-centric company, Haier has launched two new brands: Casarte, which targets high-end, mainly urban consumers who are willing to buy the best products in the market; and Leader, a brand that targets mainly young users who think that the more traditional Haier brand is for families and older people, not them.

Both brands are advertised on the Web. In fact, Haier has begun to take advantage of the possibilities offered by the Internet to gather information from the consumers targeted by these new brands and interact with them. On Haier's websites, users can become designers of their products, and the Web relationship becomes a platform for discussing product features, product uses, and possible innovations with consumers.

Haier's new consumer segmentation allows this dialogue to be divided into different groups of users: Casarte, Haier, and Leader. Accordingly, Haier has four company websites:

- The traditional Haier website, www.haier.cn
- The website for e-commerce, www.ehaier.com
- Casarte website, www.casarte.cn
- Leader website, www.tongshuai.com

Consumers can find product information on the Web and then rely on physical stores to provide service, delivery, sales, and information. Rather than allowing the Internet sites to cannibalize the physical stores, Haier is trying to create meaningful integration between them, which avoids the potential conflict that is always possible between different retail channels. To be sure, products are still mainly sold through traditional channels, and websites are primarily for providing information. Thus, the websites are used more for communication, and retailers make the actual sales and delivery.

Sales of customized products personalized online by customers, who can choose product features and accessories, take place through www.ehaier.com, the only Haier website used for e-commerce. It sells only Haier products. In these sales, physical stores provide delivery and service and charge Haier a fee for their services.

Gooday Logistics

Zhang Ruimin has long believed that the Internet will change the world. When he originally articulated market chain theory, he thought that the Web would be an indispensable element for linking market performance directly to employees' pay. Later, when the ZZJYT model was introduced, Zhang conceived of complementary physical and virtual networks and wanted to use the virtual network for more than just e-commerce. As an early enthusiast of the Web and the possibilities that it could create, Zhang envisaged the virtual network as a tool for customers to personalize their choices and talk directly with Haier. Building on the success of social networks, Zhang also raised the idea of a Haier online community. In 2010, he launched the concept of two networks, the physical—showroom-based network—and the virtual—Internet portals—for Haier.

Haier's physical distribution network, Gooday Logistics, also has its own online shop, www.Goodaymart.com, which now sells mainly Haier-branded products. Haier is betting on Gooday's role as a physical distribution network service provider to boost sales in China's remote western regions and vast countryside, and to leverage existing Haier distribution competencies into new, non-Haier-customer market segments.

Haier appreciates that Gooday's geographical range and market share offer an opportunity to foreign home appliance and home electronic brands interested in the Chinese market. GE's and Hewlett-Packard's decision to use Gooday to distribute their own branded products with Haier suggests that relying on the Gooday network is a smart arrangement in terms of both cost and time for international brands that want to avoid building their own distribution network across China.

Notes

Chapter One

1. Jack Welch, quoted in *Inc.* (March 1995), www.qfinance.com/finance-and-business-quotes/change. Sam Palmisano, quoted in www.informationweek.com/global-cio/interviews/global-cio-sam-palmisano-reveals-secret/229216829.
2. Birger Steen, "Leading a Team of Russian Superprofessionals," in Pekka A. Viljakainen and Mark Mueller-Eberstein, *No Fear* (London: Marshall Cavendish, 2011), 215.
3. Peter Drucker, *Drucker on Asia: A Dialogue between Peter Drucker and Isao Nakauchi* (Oxford: Butterworth-Heinemann, 1997), 7.
4. Pekka A. Viljakainen and Mark Mueller-Eberstein, *No Fear*.
5. Dave Gray, "A Business within the Business," www.dachisgroup.com/2011/11/a-business-within-the-business.
6. Suzanne Berger, *How We Compete* (Cambridge, MA: MIT Press, 2005), 252, 255.
7. Bala Chakravarthy and Peter Lorange, *Profit or Growth?* (Upper Saddle River, NJ: Pearson, 2008).
8. Ibid.
9. Jim Collins and Jerry I. Porras, *Built to Last* (New York: HarperBusiness, 2004).

Chapter Two

1. The category of major home appliances consists of major and small home appliance sectors.
2. *Whirlpool Corporation* (Case 9–391–037, Harvard Business School, 1990).
3. Electrolux's website characterizes European design with terms such as *stylish* and *flexible*, with intuitive performance, emphasizing the incorporation of such designs into an integrated and attractive kitchen.
4. *Whirlpool Corporation* (Case 9–391–037, Harvard Business School, 1990).
5. "The Evolution of the Chinese Major Home Appliance Industry in the Last 30 Years, 2008," http://tech.hexun.com/2008–10–08/110993837.html.
6. Yasheng Huang, *Selling China: Foreign Direct Investment during the Reform Era* (Cambridge, UK: Cambridge University Press, 2002).
7. The refrigerator was one of the big three items, together with the television and washing machine, as dowry in the 1970s and 1980s.
8. Yasheng Huang, *Selling China: Foreign Direct Investment during the Reform Era*.
9. *Whirlpool Corporation* (Case 9–391–037, Harvard Business School, 1990).
10. William C. Taylor and Alan W. Webber, *Going Global* (New York: Viking Press, 1996), 10.
11. Ibid.
12. "Brand Shares (by Global Brand Name), Historic, Retail Volume, Percent Breakdown, World Consumer Appliance," *Euromonitor* (December 1, 2011).
13. http://baike.baidu.com/view/1624243.htm.
14. www.eeo.com.cn.
15. www.nfpeople.com. Unlike all the other white goods manufacturers, Siemens cut its wholesale dealers and implemented

a direct sales model. It also managed to require payment before product delivery.

16. According to some market research companies such as Zhongyikang, its air-conditioner share has been growing since 2009.
17. http://baike.baidu.com/view/276113.htm.
18. "About Littleswan," www.littleswan.com/english/about.
19. www.littleswan.com/UploadedImages/634499493911718750f.pdf.
20. Haier, *Annual Report* (2010).
21. Datamonitor, *Household Appliances in China* (June 2010).
22. GD Midea, *Annual Report* (2010).

Chapter Three

1. Alexander Osterwalder and Yves Pigneur, *Business Model Generation: A Handbook for Visionaries, Game Changers, and Challengers* (New York: Wiley, 2010).
2. http://31.toocle.com/detail—4647279.html and company interview.
3. http://en.wikipedia.org/wiki/Haier.
4. Jeannie Jinsheng Yi and Shawn Xian Ye, *The Haier Way: The Making of a Chinese Business Leader and a Global Brand* (Paramus, NJ: Homa & Seka Books, 2003).
5. Apologies to Jay Galbraith for our adaptation of the wording of his model and for our highly personalized description of each element.
6. Harvard Business School has written a series of cases on Haier's acquisition strategy. L. S. Paine, *The Haier Group* (A, B, C). (Boston: Harvard Business School, 2001). The case numbers are 9–398–101, 9–398–102, and 9–398–162.
7. The value chain concept was first described in Michael Porter's book *Competitive Advantage: Creating and Sustaining Superior Performance* (New York: Free Press, 1998).

8. These are perceived to be the early form of the contracting system in the ZZJYT model that we explain later.
9. Although this sounds quite similar to the ZZJYT model presented later, there is in fact a fundamental difference. As a division or department, the goal of a team is to maximize their own profit (linked directly to their pay), which translates into maximizing revenues and minimizing costs. In such a context, serving the market or serving clients becomes secondary. It could become a game of how to sign more contracts and reduce costs internally. A possible consequence could be that each division is "earning" money in the division, but this internal "profit" is not reflected externally in the market share of the company or the overall company performance. In fact, this is different from the ZZJYTs (inverted triangle model). In the ZZJYT market, the team's and team members' performance is directly linked to the market. Therefore, although teams and individuals in both models are performance driven, the model for a real market runs after it as the only purpose, while the latter makes sure that serving clients and market orientation become the co-product of reaching performance.
10. For more details on market chain, OEC, and SST, please see William A. Fischer, *Building Market Chains at Haier* (Case IMD-3-0939, IMD, 2000).
11. This is the ideal 100 percent quantitative evaluation method, which is not realistic because in organizational theory, it is impossible to evaluate all the work with the piece-rate principle. In the ZZJYT model, evaluation combines quantitative and qualitative assessments.
12. This means that the target of each employee should be matched with his or her capability, and this target should be linked to the market.
13. Zhang Ruimin's webcast with IMD president Dominique Turpin at IMD (December 11, 2012).
14. Zhang Ruimin's webcast with IMD president Dominique Turpin at IMD (December 11, 2012).

15. Umberto Lago, interview with Zhang Ruimin (June 8, 2010).
16. Jeannie Jinsheng Yi and Shawn Xian Ye, *The Haier Way: The Making of a Chinese Business Leader and a Global Brand*, 55.

Chapter Four

1. www.informationweek.com/global-cio/interviews/global-cio-sam-palmisano-reveals-secret/229216829.
2. Andy Boynton and Bill Fischer, *Virtuoso Teams* (London: FT/Prentice Hall, 2005).
3. Bill Fischer, "Made in China: Smarter Companies?" Forbes.com (May 27, 2011), www.forbes.com/sites/billfischer/2011/05/27/made-in-china-smarter-companies.
4. "The Cities," *China Normal*,www.chinanormal.com/cities.
5. Hu Yong, "Haier ZZJYT—A Social Invention," internal document provided by Haier.
6. Tom Peters, *The Professional Service Firm 50* (New York: Knopf, 1999); Gary P. Hamel, *The Future of Management* (Cambridge, MA: Harvard Business School Press, 2007).
7. Stage 2 of Haier's development did not see a new management mode so it is not illustrated in the table.
8. Zhang Ruimin's webcast with IMD president Dominique Turpin at IMD (December 11, 2012).
9. And also Haier renews its culture and organizational structure and management spontaneously in response to market change.
10. François Jullien, *Conférence sur l'efficacité* (Paris: Presses Universitaire de France, 2005).

Chapter Five

1. Marketers realized that in traditional refrigerators, freezers have limited space for large dishes and reported this information to the three-door refrigerator ZZJYT. This ZZJYT

started to work on the problem and eventually came up with a possible solution: it created two large layers at the bottom of the traditional two-door refrigerator that can accommodate large dishes. These kinds of improvements solve problems for end users and create demand.

2. Certain functions such as marketing and finance can work on several ZZJYTs at the same time. In other words, they work part-time for each ZZJYT.
3. Competitive levels are determined at the second-tier ZZJYT level, with the help of outside experts such as consultants.
4. Excerpt from "A Collision of Thoughts between Zhang Ruimin and Hu Yong," internal Haier document.

Chapter Six

1. Gary Hamel, *The Future of Management* (Cambridge, MA: Harvard Business School Press, 2007).
2. John Micklethwait and Adrian Wooldridge, *The Company* (New York: Modern Library, 2003), xx–xxi. Italics added for emphasis.
3. Alfred Chandler, *Scale and Scope* (Cambridge, MA: Harvard University Press, 1969), 593.
4. Ibid., 594.
5. Thomas J. Peters and Robert H. Waterman, *In Search of Excellence* (New York: HarperCollins, 1982).
6. Phil Rosenzweig, *The Halo Effect* (New York: The Free Press, 2007).
7. Michael E. Raynor, Mumtaz Ahmed, and Andrew D. Henderson, "Are 'Great Companies' Just Lucky?" *Harvard Business Review* (April 2009): 18–19.
8. Ibid.
9. Phil Rosenzweig, personal communication to Bill Fischer, made in class at IMD (2007).
10. Warren G. Bennis and Philip E. Slater, *The Temporary Society* (New York: Harper Colophon, 1968), 4.
11. Yves Doz and Mikko Kosonen, *Fast Strategy* (Englewood Cliffs, NJ: Prentice Hall, 2008).

12. Ibid.; Jurgen Appelo, *Management 3.0* (Boston: Addison-Wesley, 2011).
13. Bill Fischer, "Air-Cover: Innovation's Secret Ingredient," *Forbes.com* (August 29, 2011), www.forbes.com/sites/billfischer/2011/08/29/air-cover-innovations-secret-ingredient.
14. Lars Kolind, *The Second Cycle* (Upper Saddle River, NJ: Wharton School Publishing, 2006), 6; the "market share" comment is from Donald Sull, *Why Good Companies Go Bad and How Great Managers Remake Them* (Cambridge, MA: Harvard Business School Press, 2005), 126.
15. Kolind, *The Second Cycle*, 27.
16. Ibid.
17. Ibid.
18. The Morning Star example comes from Gary Hamel, "First, Let's Fire All the Managers," *Harvard Business Review* (December 2011): 48–60.
19. Gary Hamel, *What Happens Now?* (San Francisco: Jossey-Bass, 2012); Gary Hamel, "First, Let's Fire All the Managers."
20. Gary Hamel, "First, Let's Fire All the Managers."
21. Ibid., 58.
22. The corporations in the study were AT&T, Andersen Consulting, Corning, Intel, Nike, and 3M in the United States; ABB, Body Shop, Cartier, Electrolux, ISS, IKEA, Royal Dutch Shell, Richardson Sheffield, and Semco in Europe; and Canon, Kao Corporation, Komatsu, and Toyota in Japan.
23. Christopher A. Bartlett and Sumantra Ghoshal, "Beyond the M-form: Toward a Managerial Theory of the Firm," *Strategic Management Journal* 14 (Winter 1993): 23.
24. William Taylor, "The Logic of Global Business: An Interview with ABB's Percy Barnevik," *Harvard Business Review* (March–April 1991): 91–105.
25. Ibid.
26. Winfried Ruigrok, Leona Achtenhagen, Mathias Wagner, and Johannes Ruegg-Sturm, "ABB: Beyond the Global Matrix towards the Network Multidivisional Organisation,"

in Andrew M. Pettigrew and Evelyn Maria Fenton (eds.), *The Innovating Organisation* (Thousand Oaks, CA: Sage, 2000).

27. Tatiana Zalan and Vladimir Pucik, *Rebuilding ABB (A)* (IMD-3-1797, IMD, 2007).
28. Rebecca Chung, Andy Boynton, and Bill Fischer, *Nash Confectionery: Rethinking India* (Case IMD-3-2198, IMD, 2010).
29. Personal communication with Bill Fischer, Singapore (2009).
30. John Hagel III, John Seely Brown, and Lang Davison, *The Power of Pull: How Small Moves, Smartly Made, Can Set Big Things in Motion* (New York: Basic Books, 2010).
31. David Bollier, *When Push Comes to Pull* (New York: Aspen Institute, 2005).
32. Doz and Kosonen, *Fast Strategy*.
33. John McMillan, *Reinventing the Bazaar* (New York: Norton, 2002).
34. Ibid., x.

Chapter Seven

1. Ronald J. Coase, "The Nature of the Firm," *Economica New Series* 4 (1937): 386–405.
2. K. Arrow, *The Limits of Organizations* (New York: Norton, 1974).
3. O. E. Williamson, *Markets and Hierarchies: Analysis and Antitrust Implications* (New York: Free Press, 1975).
4. O. E. Williamson, *The Economic Institutions of Capitalism: Firms, Markets, Relational Contracting* (New York: Free Press, 1981), 1544.
5. O. E. Williamson, "Transaction Cost Economics and Organization Theory," in N. J. Smelser and R. Swedberg (eds.), *The Handbook of Economic Sociology* (Princeton, NJ: Princeton University Press, 1994), 91.
6. R. Coase, "The Nature of the Firm," in O. E. Williamson and S. G. Winter (eds.), *The Nature of the Firm* (New York: Oxford University Press, 1991), 23.

7. H. B. Thorelli, "Networks: Between Markets and Hierarchies," *Strategic Management Journal* 7 (1986): 37–51; J. C. Jarillo, "On Strategic Networks," *Strategic Management Journal* 9 (1988): 31–41; G. Lorenzoni and O. A. Ornati, "Constellations of Firms and New Ventures," *Journal of Business Venturing* 3 (1988): 41–57; O. E. Williamson, "Comparative Economic Organization: The Analysis of Discrete Structural Alternatives," *Administrative Science Quarterly* 36 (1991): 269–296; and especially H. Demsetz, "The Theory of the Firm Revisited," in Williamson and Winter, *The Nature of the Firm*, 159–178.
8. Interfirm networks are defined as a set of autonomous firms that are engaged in creating products or services based on implicit and open-ended contracts that are socially, not legally, binding.
9. For example, C. Perrow, "Small Firms Networks," in N. Nohria and R. G. Eccles (eds.), *Networks and Organizations* (Boston: Harvard University School Press, 1992).
10. Thorelli, "Networks"; Williamson, *The Economic Institutions of Capitalism*; K. Imai and H. Itami, "Interpenetration of Organization and Market: Japan's Firms and Markets in Comparison with the U.S.," *International Journal of Industrial Organization* 2 (1984): 285 310.
11. C. C. Jarillo, "On Strategic Networks," *Strategic Management Journal* 9 (1988): 34.
12. Williamson, "Comparative Economic Organization."
13. Ibid., 281. By asset specificity, Williamson means assets specific to a given relationship, with investments made to support a given transaction. These investments cannot be redeployed to another transaction without incurring significant costs and thus lock the parties into the relationship to a certain degree.
14. Among them, M. Granovetter, "Economic Action, Social Structure and Embeddedness," *American Journal of Sociology* 91 (1985): 481–510; W. Powell, "Neither Market nor Hierarchy: Network Forms of Organization," *Research in*

Organizational Behaviour 12 (1990): 125–131; W. Powell and L. Smith-Doerr, "Networks in Economic Life," in Smelser and Swedberg, *The Handbook of Economic Sociology*.

15. Hobbes argued for a social contract and rule by an absolute sovereign. He wrote that chaos or civil war, situations identified with a state of nature, and the famous motto *Bellum omnium contra omnes* (the war of all against all) could be averted only by strong central government.
16. Granovetter, "Economic Action, Social Structure and Embeddedness," 495, 489. See also C. Cordon and T. Vollmann, *The Power of Two* (London: Palgrave Macmillan, 2008), for a microlevel view of interpersonal relationships as a determinant of value-chain partnership success.
17. R. C. Mayer, J. H. Davis, and F. D. Schoorman, "An Integrative Model of Organizational Trust," *Academy of Management Review* 20 (1995): 712.
18. P. S. Ring and A. H. Van de Ven, "Structuring Cooperative Relationships between Organizations," *Strategic Management Journal* 13 (1992): 483–498.
19. For example, C. Perrow, "Small Firms Networks," in N. Nohria and R. G. Eccles, *Networks and Organizations* (Boston: Harvard Business School Press, 1994).
20. "The world's biggest firms keep on getting bigger. . . . In the past 15 years the assets of the top 50 American companies have risen from around 70% of American GDP to around 130%. All of the top ten American firms have been involved in at least one large merger or acquisition over the past 25 years." "Land of the Corporate Giants," *Economist* (November 3, 2012): 66.
21. Coase, "The Nature of the Firm: Origin."
22. Ibid., 25.
23. "Too big to fail" is an expression that has become sadly popular during the recent economic and financial crisis and has been used for a variety of companies in different

industries, from banks and insurance companies to automobile manufacturers.

24. A. D. Chandler Jr., *Strategy and Structure: Chapters in the History of the American Industrial Enterprise* (Cambridge, MA: MIT Press, 1962).
25. Ibid., 42.
26. C. A. Bartlett and S. Ghoshal, "Beyond the M-Form: Toward a Managerial Theory of the Firm," *Strategic Management Journal* 14 (1993): 23–43; the corporations in the study were AT&T, Andersen Consulting, Corning, Intel, Nike, and 3M in the United States; ABB, Body Shop, Cartier, Electrolux, ISS, IKEA, Royal Dutch Shell, Richardson Sheffield, and Semco in Europe; and Canon, Kao Corporation, Komatsu, and Toyota in Japan.
27. Ibid., 25.
28. Independent units are operating only in China at this time.
29. Bartlett and Ghoshal, "Beyond the M-Form: Toward a Managerial Theory of the Firm," 42.
30. T. Zenger, "Crafting Internal Hybrids: Complementarities, Common Change Initiatives, and the Team-based Organization," *International Journal of the Economics of Business* 9 (2002): 79–95.
31. Oliver Hart and John Moore, "Property Rights and the Nature of the Firm," *Journal of Political Economy* (1990): 1119–1158.
32. Zenger, "Crafting Internal Hybrids."
33. Williamson, "Comparative Economic Organization."
34. Marshall Meyers, of Wharton School, explained this concept in a presentation given to Haier management at UIBE Business School, Beijing (December 2010).

Chapter Eight

1. www.china.org.cn/top10/2011–07/12/content_22974949.htm.
2. John Hagel, "From the Race against the Machine to the Race with the Machine" (August 2012), http://edgeperspectives

.typepad.com/edge_perspectives/2012/08/from-race-against-the-machine-to-race-with-the-machine.

3. Zhang Ruimin, "How to Become a Company of the Times," speech at IMD, Lausanne, Switzerland (December 11, 2012).
4. Bill Fischer, "Where Toyota Went Wrong," *Forbes.com* (February 10, 2010).
5. Gary Hamel, *The Future of Management* (Cambridge, MA: Harvard Business School Press, 2007).

Postscript

1. Zhang Ruimin speech at IMD, Lausanne, Switzerland (December 11, 2012).
2. Ibid.
3. Zhang Ruimin interview with Hu Yong: "The Best Leader of an Enterprise Leader Is Its Enemy." An interview with Zhang Ruimin on the future of management. English version is unpublished. Chinese version can be found at http://huyong.blog.sohu.com/249606792.html.
4. Ibid.
5. Haier has gained a top position in terms of retail volume market share in refrigeration (14.8 percent), freezers (18.6 percent), home laundry (11.8 percent), and wine cooling (15.3 percent).

Appendix

1. For more details on the upgrading process of ZZJYTs, see figure A.1.

ACKNOWLEDGMENTS

This book has a complicated parentage and supporting cast of actors, each of whom was essential to the final product.

Haier Group, the subject of this book, has been exceptionally open and supportive, providing resources, internal documents, allowing participation in internal meetings, and organizing brainstorming at the very top level of the group. The managers we met who have contributed greatly to this book are too many to be listed here. However, we owe special thanks to Haier's CEO, Zhang Ruimin, and president, Yang Mianmian, for their constant support of this project and their openness in exchanging thoughts and ideas. Ji Guaingquiang has been the head of the project at Haier and an invaluable source of initiative and support. We also thank Pu Xiankai, head of the three-door refrigerator ZZJYT, Mrs. Tan, vice president of finance, and Mr. Peng of the Finance Department. This book would never have been completed without the ceaseless effort, support, and organization provided by Gao Wei (Leighton), who translated, checked, and proofed every chapter. Gao was the soul of this project, as much as any of the authors, and in the process, he has become a good friend of each of us. Several of us have known Zhang over the years, and his overall sponsorship of the project was a great advantage for us.

Whenever one writes a book focusing on a single organization, it is probably important to comment on the relationship between the writing team and the subject organization. We can honestly report that Haier never once tried to influence our interpretation of what we observed or how we chose to report it. In fact, its willingness to allow Fang Liu to work with the three-door refrigerator ZZJYT was without any attempt to influence her experience. For this, we are extremely grateful.

Our publisher, Jossey-Bass, has been an absolute joy to work with on this project, and our editor, Susan Williams, has greatly exceeded any hopes that we might have had regarding editorial support; she has been a great guide and friend throughout the entire project! In addition, Kathe Sweeney played a critical role in establishing our confidence in the project at a point when that support was essential. Bev Miller was a major factor in transforming the book from many disparate ideas into a coherent and readable product. For Susan Geraghty, who oversaw the entire production process, who was always available for help, and who ultimately orchestrated the final product, there is no limit to the appreciation, respect, and gratitude we owe her.

As individual authors, we each have a story that has led us to this book and individuals to thank as a result.

From Bill: There would never have been a China book without Richard Lee, Jordon Baruch, Bill Dill, and Dick Holton, who were instrumental in making the Dalian project possible in 1980 and provided the impetus for my making China a central part of my personal and professional life. Denis F. Simon has always been a teacher, partner, collaborator, good friend, and leading influence in everything I've ever done regarding China, and from the start. Our great beach buddy, China colleague, and distinguished scholar Gail Henderson at the University of North Carolina (UNC) Chapel Hill has helped me think in a more sophisticated manner about China in many different ways. Two of my former "leaders," Jack Evans at UNC and Peter Lorange at IMD, allowed me to pursue my China dreams despite the institutional contradictions that they had to overcome. Pedro Nueno and Liliana Petrella were responsible for inviting me to join the CEIBS team in Shanghai, which provided me with a once-in-a-lifetime opportunity to work in China with an amazing team of colleagues at the China Europe International Business School (CEIBS): CL Kendall, Dick Levin, Jay Klompmacher, Jack Kasarda, John Pringle, Bill Bigoness, and Carl Zeithaml, all at UNC; Jack Lewis and Dick Drobnick, both at the University of Southern California; Roy Bowen, with the Georgia Association of Manufacturers; Bob Dalton, Carnegie-Mellon; Blair Odo, Japan-America Institute of Management Science (JAIMS); Frank T. G. Webb, World Health Organization; George Yip, University of California at Los Angeles; and Warren Banauch and Jean Hauser, Duke, all helped make China part of my professional persona. And then there were the "real" old China hands, such as Sidney Rittenberg and Otto Schnepp, who led the way and always made being a part of the China studies family so much fun.

IMD has consistently supported my China interests, including generous financial and institutional support for this particular effort, thanks to our colleagues overseeing the research activities of the school: Cédric Vaucher, Marco Mancesti, and Persita Egeli. We are also grateful for the invaluable help of Lindsay McTeague and Michelle Perrinjaquet on the page proofs. Katrin Tzieropoulos has been a joy to work with, and it was only thanks to her steadfast protection of my calendar that the project was made possible. I've been fortunate to have been able to make China part of my IMD persona by being invited into the Operating Effectively in China program by IMD's current president, Dominique Turpin, and into the EMBA Program's China Discovery Expedition with Andy Boynton, John Welch, and Phil Rosenzweig. Jean-Pierre Lehmann, Winter Nie, Dan Denison, Katherine Xin, Cyril Bouquet, and Rebecca Chung have all shared my interest in and passion for China. Marianne Vandenbosch and Tomas Casas also merit a big thanks for our China experiences together. Phil Rosenzweig and Andy Boynton played a major role in my understanding of strategy and how organizations work. They have been good friends and mentors and I hope that this reflects well on what they have tried to teach me. My collaboration with all of these colleagues has been a professional high point and great fun!

The most important accomplishments of my life are all associated with my family: Marie Annette, Kim, Amy, Billy, Sergio, Leah, Nicolas, Isabella, Mia, William, and Graham. I hope that each of them will be blessed with the same organizational opportunities for learning and growth that I have been fortunate to have received. Finally, Umberto Lago's initiative in asking me to join him on this venture and his goodwill and sharp economic perspectives have been a great joy in this project. Umberto made this whole project possible and, despite his never having met me before, was as generous a colleague as one could ever hope for. I now regard him as a good friend and am proud to have been able to share in this project with him and with Fang Liu as well. It was a great benefit to learn from her experiences, which provided many insights into how Haier, and China, work, as well as many lessons. She was always available for work and the inevitable search for "one last detail," be it in English or Chinese, and was a key member of our team. It has in fact been a great team effort, and one that it was a pleasure to be a part of.

Umberto: My friend Ivan Tomasi created the connection with Haier that ultimately led to this book. I am grateful to him, the real initiator of the entire project.

The University of Bologna has always been a great place to work, and I am grateful to my colleagues for all the liberty that I enjoy in choosing the subjects that I want to study. I am also grateful for the long periods that I could take off from my office duties in order to stay in Qingdao for interviews.

Bill Fischer and Fang Liu have been fine travel companions in this journey, and I cherish the days spent in meeting rooms for hours and hours as we tried to make sense of the varied materials that we had collected and write up the interviews. Bill's experience and managerial knowledge and Fang's familiarity with China have been an invaluable blend for this project.

Finally, I thank my wife and family, who accepted the fact that I was undertaking a task that would occupy many days of vacation and almost every evening for a long period of time.

Fang: There would never have been such an eye-opening opportunity if my parents had not given me the freedom and courage to discover the world. I thank all my professors and classmates at HEC Lausanne who taught me how to think differently and critically and integrated me into a totally different culture with kindness and openness.

Willem Smit led me into research with his incredible curiosity and ideas and introduced me to Bill, another life changer of mine. A big thank-you to everyone at Haier and in three-door refrigerator ZZJYT who were supportive during my stay there. Without them, the book would not have been so rich. IMD has been supportive in every China project I have undertaken, and Cédric Vaucher and Marco Mancesti have given me the freedom to choose the research that I am interested in. Besides Bill Fischer, Dominique Turpin, Cyril Bouquet, Joachim Schwass, Pasha Mahmood, and Orly Levy's interest in China gave me the opportunity to extend my knowledge of China to many others.

Finally, it was a joy to work with Bill, who not only shared with me his experience and insights on China but was always available to offer his wisdom on life; and Umberto, who drove the project forward with a lot of passion and patience and has been a lovely travel companion. It has been an incredible learning experience and a joyful journey! I also thank Thierry, Martine, and Jean-Philippe for providing invaluable help and support throughout the whole project and making my life in Switzerland so much richer.

Research Methodology

The research methodology was structured as follows.

Umberto Lago conducted twenty-five semistructured interviews with senior managers, ZZJYT managers, and group vice presidents in five visits over one and half years at Haier's headquarters in Qingdao, Shandong Province, China. Most of the interviews lasted about two hours and were taped for later transcription and comparison with field notes.

The interview data were complemented by archival data, including financial statements and internal performance reports. These data offered opportunities to direct interview questions and facilitate further comments and clarifications during the course of the interviews. They also served to help corroborate the interview data.

Interview transcripts were submitted to the subject managers for checking and for bringing eventual factual inaccuracies to our attention. Inaccuracies were corrected accordingly.

In addition, Umberto Lago attended meetings with Zhang Ruimin and Yang Mianmian as well as with other managers; he was also present at internal ZZJYT meetings, as well as formal Haier conferences in Qingdao and Beijing.

Fang Liu worked for seven days within the three-door refrigerator ZZJYT in order to understand how a ZZJYT works in practice and what changes it implies for the team members in terms of responsibilities, incentives, reporting processes, performance evaluations, and relationships within the team, as well as with the other stakeholders. She observed the daily work of the team; interviewed every member on the ZZJYT; and attended team meetings where budgets were reviewed, projects were followed, and information sharing was facilitated. Without this work, chapter 5 would not have been possible.

The authors jointly analyzed this material using theoretical, empirical, and conceptual insights and frameworks from the academic domains of economics and the managerial arts in order to turn our raw material into the arguments that are the basis of the book.

The Authors

Bill Fischer first moved to China in 1980 as a member of the faculty of a joint U.S.-Chinese government initiative, based in Dalian, to prepare senior Chinese business and government leadership for the forthcoming economic reforms. He has worked in China every year since then and from 1997 through 1999 was executive president and dean of the China-Europe International Business School in Shanghai. Prior to that, he was the Dalton L. McMichael Sr. Professor of Business at the Kenan-Flagler Business School of the University of North Carolina at Chapel Hill, and he has been a professor at IMD in Lausanne, Switzerland, for nearly twenty years. He won the European Foundation for Management Development's China case writing competition each year between 2004 and 2007 and in 1999 received the Silver Magnolia award, Shanghai's highest award for foreigners contributing to the city's development. He is the coauthor with Andy Boynton of both *The Idea Hunter* (2012) and *Virtuoso Teams* (2005), and the coauthor with Jack Behrman of *Overseas R&D Activities of Transnational Companies* (1980). He is a contributor to Forbes.com, authoring the blog *The Ideas Business*. He tweets regularly on China and innovation at @bill_fischer.

Umberto Lago has been a university professor, private and public manager, entrepreneur, and consultant. His Ph.D. in strategic management is from the Imperial College of London (Management School), and he is currently an associate professor of management at Bologna University.

Umberto has studied subjects as diverse as marketing channels, corporate strategy, and football finance and has published books and papers in academic and managerial journals. He has served as a speaker on these subjects in national and international conferences, in doctoral programs, public debates, and book presentations. He has been a member of the faculty at Bocconi University in Milan and a consultant for Monitor Group. He is currently a consultant for private companies and public institutions. He is also the Italian member of the UEFA Club Financial Control Body, an independent body whose aim is to evaluate European professional football clubs' financial health and economic performance.

He was a visiting professor at UIBE Business School, Beijing, in 2010.

Fang Liu was born in Wenzhou, China, and lived in several major cities in China, including Shanghai and Guangzhou, before she moved to Switzerland to pursue a master's degree in management. She earned her bachelor's degree in management from Guangdong University of Foreign Studies in Guangzhou and her master's degree in management from the Faculty of Business and Economics of the University of Lausanne, or Hautes Etudes Commerciale (HEC) Lausanne. She then joined IMD as a research associate. Her research has focused on management innovation, marketing, and global business. She has written cases on the global challenges of industry leaders, both Western and Chinese, in industries such as sportswear, consumer goods, and home appliances and has published articles about social media marketing and international management.

Index

Page references followed by *fig* indicate an illustrated figure; followed by *t* indicate a table.

A

B

C

D

E

F

G

H

I

J

K

L

M

N

O

P

T

U

V